The Quills of the Porcupine

The Quills of the Porcupine

Asante Nationalism in an Emergent Ghana

Jean Marie Allman

THE UNIVERSITY OF WISCONSIN PRESS

The University of Wisconsin Press
114 North Murray Street
Madison, Wisconsin 53715

3 Henrietta Street
London WC2E 8LU, England

4 2 5 3 1

Printed in the United States of America

Library of Congress Cataloging-in-Publication Data

Allman, Jean Marie.
The quills of the porcupine: Asante nationalism in an
emergent Ghana / Jean Marie Allman.
278 p. cm.
Includes bibliographical references and index.
ISBN 0-299-13760-0 ISBN 0-299-13764-3 (pbk.)
1. Ashanti Region (Ghana)—History—Autonomy and independence
movements. 2. Ashanti (African people)—Politics and government.
3. Ghana—Politics and government—To 1957. 4. Nationalism—Ghana—
Ashanti Region—History—20th century. 5. Nationalism—Ghana—
History—20th century. I. Title.
DT512.9.A84A45 1993
966.7—dc20 92-45198

To my parents,
John and Peggy Allman

Contents

Preface

When first conceived, this was to be a study in historical continuity and national resilience, an attempt to extend the well-documented and oft-debated history of the Asante kingdom[1] into the twentieth century by focusing on the Asante National Liberation Movement (NLM) of the mid-1950s. Founded late in 1954, the NLM demanded Asante self-determination in the face of Kwame Nkrumah's blueprint for a unitary goverment in an independent Ghana. It not only posed a serious threat to the stability of Nkrumah's government in the last years before independence, but shattered the illusion, present since 1951, that the Gold Coast's transition to full self-rule would proceed with rapidity and order. Most scholars who have examined these turbulent years in Ghana's history have focused their attention on the party which was to lead Ghana to independence. As a result, the NLM has been cast into the murky shadows of scholarly inquiry and branded as a tribalist, regionalist, parochialist ghost of the past—a fleeting aberration in the Gold Coast-wide struggle against colonial rule. The aim of this study was to understand the National Liberation Movement on its own terms, as part and parcel of Asante history, not as a brief aberration in the national history of Ghana.

Most of the primary documentation upon which the study is based reflects this original concern. The oral testimonies of active NLM participants, their private papers, NLM leaflets and handbills, contemporary newspaper accounts, and the records of the Asanteman Council and the Kumase State Council formed the basic blocks of inquiry. British colonial records relevant to the crisis in Asante also were consulted at the Ghana National Archives, Rhodes House (Oxford), and the Public Record Office. While the recent declassification of postwar colonial archives now makes possible a thorough examination of British policy in the last years of colonial rule, leading some scholars to emphasize imperial policy as the "prime mover" in the post–World War II period, this study was not envisioned as an extension of colonial history nor as an analysis of the transfer of power.[2]

Although the story which follows remains one of tenacity and continuity, it is by no means the simple story of a nation united on an historic march to reclaim its right to self-determination. To grapple with Asante nationalism in the twentieth century—as manifested in the NLM—was to confront the historically rooted contradictions of that nationalism and the social and economic conflicts which have pervaded Asante history for at least a century before the NLM's inauguration. If "Asante nation" and "Asante nationalism" were neatly wrapped when work began in 1984, with the unpacking process came the ideological antinomies and the theoretical disjunctures. In sorting through these perplexities, the vast body of theoretical lilterature on the national question, as well as various historical works which examine nationalism historically were indispensable. But, in the end, I do not provide an exegesis of nationalism here nor take on the monumental task of comparing separatist movements. If the following account contributes empirically to these broader debates, all to the good, but the density of material on the NLM required a more circumscribed agenda whose focus remained Asante nationalism—its historicity, antinomies, and tenacity—in an emergent Ghana.

There are a number of people to whom I would like to express my appreciation for the support and assistance they have given me in the preparation and completion of this work: from those whose testimonies brought me first-hand into the Asante of the 1950s, to those who offered substantive and stylistic criticism, to those who cooked and child-minded when I needed just "one more minute" to finish a day's writing.

My deepest gratitude goes to those Asantes who shared so freely their memories and their history, and who gave my family a home away from home. The recollections of so many active participants in the struggles of the mid-fifties have brought life and color to this study. The private papers of Bafuor Osei Akoto and Osei Assibey-Mensah have allowed me an inside view of the National Liberation Movement to which few have been privy. Nana Osei Agyeman-Duah, my dear friend and research aide, deserves special thanks as the engineer who helped me put it all together, from scheduling interviews, to transportation, to interpretation. He and his wonderful extended family have helped in more ways than I could possibly list.

I owe a special debt of gratitude to Ivor Wilks who, over fifteen years ago, initiated me into the ways and byways of Asante history. As mentor, tutor, and friend, his unstinting criticism, his generous sharing of sources and reminiscences, and his unwavering support were largely responsible for this project's completion. He has taught me many things, most by the example he has set. In addition to Wilks, many individuals have contributed (some anonymously) to the arduous process of transforming this work from a dissertation into a book. Basil Davidson offered clear suggestions and solid words of encouragement at a critical juncture. Kwame Arhin, David Henige, Tom McCaskie, and Crawford Young generously shared their ideas and criticisms during various stages of the revision process. Larry Yarak helped me over the final hurdle with his careful reading and detailed commentary. Barbara Hanrahan of the University of Wisconsin Press stood by the project with patience and determination for over two years.

While the framework for the study is limited by time and space to three very critical years in Asante history, it has been enriched and broadened by a variety of scholars who shared so freely their time, their criticism, and their craftsmanship. In this regard, I would like to thank Ibrahim Abu-Lughod, Dennis Brutus, John Hunwick, John McLane, John Rowe, Frank Safford, and Sterling Stuckey. I must also extend a special thanks to Jeff Holden for his trans-Atlantic assistance with recently released documentation at the Public Record Office. Without his help, critical revisions to the manuscript would have been impossible.

Research for this study was greatly facilitated by the support and cooperation of a number of archivists and librarians. I would like to thank in particular Dan Britz and Hans Panofsky of the Melville J. Herskovits Memorial Library at Northwestern University, Roberta Acquah of the Ghana National Archives in Kumase, Mr. Asamoah at the Manhyia Record Office, and the supportive staffs at the Library of the School of Oriental and African Studies, the Institute of Commonwealth Studies, Rhodes House (Oxford), the Public Record Office, the British Library Newspaper Library, and the Ghana National Archives in Accra. My sincere appreciation is extended to the Institute of

African Studies at the University of Ghana at Legon for granting me research affiliate status and for paving the way for an enriching research experience.

As a graduate student at Northwestern University, I was supported in the early stages of this project by a number of grants: the Northwestern University Fellowship, the Foreign Language Area Studies Fellowship, and the Northwestern University Teaching Fellowship. Field research in Ghana and Great Britain was funded by the Fulbright-Hays Dissertation Year Fellowship in 1983–84. A 1988 grant from the American Council of Learned Societies facilitated a return trip to the Public Record Office to examine colonial correspondence declassified since 1984.

Some of the arguments and analysis, particularly concerning Asante's youngmen, have appeared in a different form in the *Journal of African History* 31:2 (1990). They appear here with the kind permission of the editors.

Finally, I would like to thank my own extended family, whose collective support made it possible for me to complete this project, and to single out my sons, Brendan and Donovan, for their patience and understanding, and my mate, David Roediger. Not only has he far exceeded the bounds of duty by becoming proofreader, copy editor, and confidante, but he has shown me by word and deed the importance of combining high scholarly standards with a firm commitment to human liberation.

Abbreviations

AYO	Anlo Youth Organization
CMB	Cocoa Marketing Board
CPC	Cocoa Purchasing Company
CO	Colonial Office
CPP	Convention People's Party
DO	Dominions Office
GAP	Ghana Action Party
GCP	Ghana Congress Party
GNP	Ghana Nationalist Party
MRO	Manhyia Record Office
MAP	Muslim Association Party
NAGK	National Archives of Ghana, Kumase
NLM	National Liberation Movement
NPP	Northern People's Party
PRO	Public Record Office
ROA	Regional Office, Asante
TC	Togoland Congress

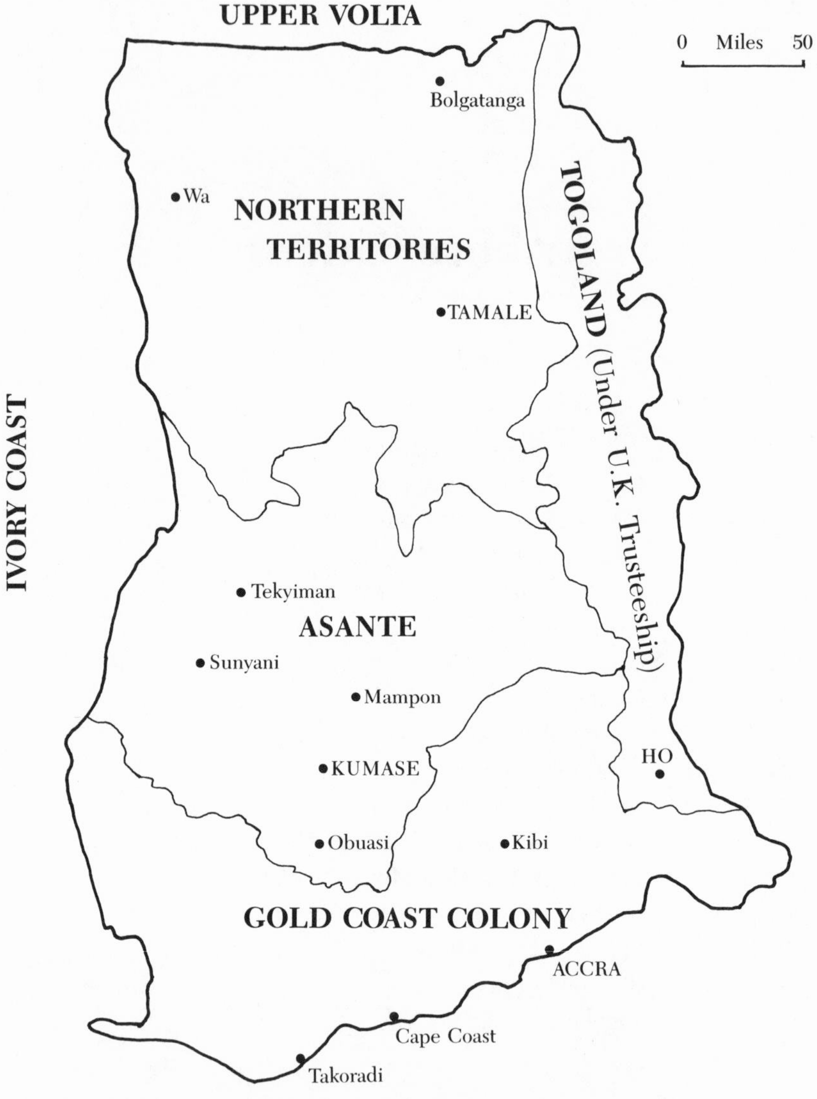

Administrative regions of Ghana before independence. Adapted from Gold Coast Survey Department, *Atlas of the Gold Coast*, Accra, 1949.

The Quills of the Porcupine

1

"Leaving the Dead Some Room to Dance"

Theories, Paradigms, and Problems in the History of Asante Nationalism

As a subject of academic inquiry, Asante in the 1950s stands in a curious scholarly limbo. Historians of the Asante kingdom have seldom ventured past the turn of the century, while social scientists, whose initial concern from the late 1950s was to explain why Asante posed such a problem to Ghana's nation-building enterprise, have long since abandoned the field. As one historian has remarked, an "intellectual 'dead-zone' in time" has separated "historical reconstruction from contemporary analysis."[1] One of the primary symptoms of this "dead zone" is the stark contrast between the ways in which the enigmatic construct of "Asante consciousness" is discussed by historians considering the sweep of Asante's past and by social scientists interested in Ghana's present.

That there has been some sort of sentiment we can label "Asante" or "Asanteness" most scholars would agree. But on the historicity of that sentiment and on whether it is best termed, at a given historical juncture, *ethnic, tribal, primordial,* or *national* consciousness, there is little concurrence. Historians of precolonial Asante, virtually without exception, freely utilize terms like *nation, nationalism,* and *national consciousness* in their discussion of the nineteenth-century *Asanteman.*[2] Social scientists concerned with the manifestation of those sentiments in the 1950s point to the "problems" of ethnicity, tribalism, or primordial attachments. This chapter is aimed at reviewing these paradigmatic disjunctures and exploring the possibilities for bridging the "dead zone" of intellectual inquiry.

The first scholarly discussions of Asante's National Liberation Movement appear in the works of social scientists in the 1950s and early 1960s who were more broadly concerned with modernization and nation-building.[3] Their primary focus was on the nationalist parties that spearheaded the drive for independence and were burdened with the historic responsibility for political integration of the new state. "Virtually overnight," writes Young, "nationalism moved from external interpellation to internalized paradigm."[4] In the Gold Coast context, the spotlight was thus on the Convention People's Party (CPP), and the opposition to Kwame Nkrumah's party was left in the shadows of inquiry.

The two notable exceptions to this dominant paradigm were the works of Thomas Hodgkin and Dennis Austin. When Hodgkin wrote his pioneering *Nationalism in Colonial Africa* in 1956, he refused to dismiss the "nationalist" aspirations of Asante supporters of the NLM and, in fact, defined as "nationalist" any organization "that explicitly asserts the rights, claims and aspirations of a given African society (from the level of language group to that of 'Pan-Africa') in opposition to European authority, whatever its institutional form and objectives."[5] Austin, writing eight years later, was not willing to apply such a fluid definition of nationalism to all of Nkrumah's opposition, but neither was he prepared to relegate that opposition to the sidelines of his inquiry. Indeed, into the 1990s, his magistral *Politics in Ghana* stands as one of the most detailed and thorough accounts of *both* Nkrumah's party and its varied and complex opposition from 1946 to 1960.[6]

However, Hodgkin's and Austin's work aside, most of the early examinations of the NLM internalized the nationalist paradigm of Ghana. Moreover, they were heavily influenced by the work of Clifford Geertz, who sought to explain movements like the NLM in terms of natural, primordial attachments. Geertz argued in 1963 that the new state would be "abnormally susceptible to serious disaffection" based on attachments rooted in blood ties, race, language, region, religion or custom. They seemed "to flow," according to Geertz, "more from a sense of natural—some would say spiritual—affinity than from social interaction." Yet these affinities could be countered, and the concerns of those primordial folk who feared the all-encompassing centralized state could be assuaged, so the argument went, if their discontent were channeled "into properly political rather than para-political forms of expression."[7]

This social scientific vision, evidenced in David Apter's pathbreaking work on the Gold Coast, reflected the general optimism in the late 1950s and early 1960s regarding independent Africa's future.[8] Social scientists believed, as John Lonsdale argues, that through political mobilization and "political imagination," parties like Nkrumah's CPP could "mould new national communities."[9] Indeed, from an early 1960s vantage point, their emphasis on political integration seemed to explain what had occurred in the first years of Ghana's independence. The National Liberation Movement, an Asante-based, extraparliamentary opposition, whose tactics ranged from mass political rallies to armed conflict on the streets of Kumase, gave way to a parliamentary, Ghana-wide opposition—the United Party. The varied and sometimes conflicting aspirations of Asantes seemed channeled into the safe confines of the national parliament. But by 1966 and the overthrow of Nkrumah by a military coup, it became clear that the confines of parliament were not so safe, and that "para-political" forms of expression were not so easily and so permanently thwarted. The "modernization" era in academic inquiry was rather short-lived, as John Lonsdale writes, lasting little longer than the "Black Star decade of Nkrumah's lease on power, 1957–1966."[10]

The next wave of scholars, again largely social scientists, remained transfixed by the political party and the state, but they approached the "problem" of sectional or "ethnic" attachments from an entirely different angle. What for Geertz and Apter were "primordial attachments" became the manipulated instruments of social competition for scholars like Fitch and Oppenheimer. Through a class analysis of Nkrumah's pre-independence opposition—a "Right Opposition," as their chapter titles proclaim—they explored the modern "tribalism" which served as a vehicle for articulating the class interests of "businessmen."[11] For Fitch and Oppenheimer, what was important was not the nature of these "tribal attachments," but the way large-scale cocoa farmers, powerful chiefs, and businessmen could manipulate them to gain the support of Asante workers and peasants in their broader class struggle against Nkrumah and his party. "It would have been politically impossible," they wrote, "to organize a popular movement whose announced objective was simply to enable absentee landlord chiefs of

Ashanti to regain from the CPP the profits that had originally come from the labor of the agricultural proletariat." Thus, "the NLM used traditional Ashanti symbols," they argued, "in order to gain support from the Ashanti peasants."[12]

So far as Asante history is concerned, Fitch and Oppenheimer did not offer a radical alternative to the works of the earlier "integrationists." While they took Asante "sentiment" out of the realm of the primordial, ahistorical world and placed it in the concrete world of economic and social relationships, there they abandoned it as the ideological instrument of Asante's ruling class. They implicitly dismissed the possibility that Asante "sentiment" could encompass the aspirations of Asante's subaltern classes or could represent, at the very least, a contested ideological terrain. They effectively denied the ability of subaltern groups to act on their own behalf. In short, they failed, as many of their predecessors did, to recognize the full, complex, and historic relationship between class and consciousness *within* Asante—a relationship which defies simple characterizations that would have chiefs and businessmen the Machiavellis of Asante's historical destiny and would leave the rest of the population the dupes and ultimate casualties of the broader economic struggle. This relationship, at once political and cultural, warrants full exploration.

The literature which appeared in the 1970s and 1980s offered important refinements to and revisions of the two dominant paradigms of the previous decades, the primordialist and the instrumentalist. It remained, however, largely ahistorical. What was of primary concern was "ethnicity's role at the moment of observation and its potential for the future," as Leroy Vail has recently remarked. Any history that might be "uncovered" was "mere 'background' to ethnicity's contemporary role."[13] Among those who sought to refine the integrationist paradigm via analyses of ethnicity were D. R. and A. C. Smock and P. Osei-Kwame. In a 1975 comparative study of Ghana and Lebanon, the Smocks were concerned with national accommodation by which "communal relations move along a continuum from continuous conflict to more frequent cooperation."[14] While their analysis focused on the period since Ghanaian independence in 1957, the Smocks looked briefly at the Asante NLM and saw it as an ethnic movement aimed at preserving traditional structures. Since independence, they argue, ethnicity has become "modernized" and has transcended these traditional allegiances. Thus, a "pan-Akan" identity has superseded the more narrow Asante traditional identity.[15] But for the Smocks, as for their predecessors, those identities remained ambiguously rooted in culture and ancestry, and unexplored in terms of their internal, historical dynamics. The ultimate good, national unity, was never questioned.

Osei-Kwame closely followed the Smocks in his investigative paradigm, although he viewed primordial ties as not incompatible with a broader, national allegiance.[16] In his conceptualization, national accommodation was a process by which "already existing intra-group cohesiveness extended to other ethnic groups." Thus, he argued, ethnicity does not preclude national identity, but in fact provides a basic building block for it.[17] In the Ghana context, Osei-Kwame's work stands as one of the first political integrationist analyses not to hold out "ethnicity" as a negative identity to be transcended. However, Osei-Kwame continued to share with the Smocks a basic "evolutionary view of human history," as Vail has called it, in which a better future means the "growth of national unity."[18] And in such a view, the Asante National Liberation Movement presented a peculiar problem for one who upheld ethnic identities as the building blocks of national unity. Osei-Kwame explained this theoretical aberration by arguing that some ethnic associations, like the NLM, are "dysfunctional."[19] Such a characterization may have described the NLM's disruptive impact on the nation-building enterprise, but it did not explain it. Again, the political and cultural link, the historical connections, remained elusive.

In many important ways, Richard Rathbone's work in the early 1970s revised the instrumentalist paradigm adopted by Fitch and Oppenheimer after Nkrumah's overthrow. Like Fitch and Oppenheimer, Rathbone sought to explain the political and economic forces behind the emergence of Asante "sentiment" in the 1950s. He did not cast that identity as natural, primordial, or inevitable. Unlike his predecessors, however, Rathbone did extensive research in Asante and recognized that the driving force behind the formation of the NLM was not the "big men" of Asante, but rather those very same men who had spearheaded the CPP drive into Asante in 1949–1951. Thus, Rathbone was prepared to view the "nationalism" of the NLM as at least comparable to the "nationalism" of the CPP in that both were ideologies aimed at legitimizing the specific aspirations of a catalytic class. Defining this class as a "new generation" of "aspirant businessmen," Rathbone argued that the "so-called" youngmen saw the NLM as "their only means of entering the gainful sectors of the economy" which had been "shut off" because of the "domination of the economic structure by the party in power"—the CPP.[20]

Rathbone made a significant analytical leap in singling out the youngmen as the catalysts of the political upheaval of the mid-1950s and in recognizing as "nationalist" the ideology they articulated. However, concerned with the wider, contemporary struggle between Asante's youngmen and the CPP during the transfer of power, Rathbone did not explore the historical dimension of his ground-breaking analysis. He saw the youngmen as essentially a post-World War II phenomenon. While useful in illuminating the immediate thrust behind the resurgence of Asante nationalism, this analysis could not account for the broad appeal of such nationalism among Asante's subaltern classes without falling back on an instrumentalist explanation whereby the chiefs and cocoa farmers of Fitch and Oppenheimer's account are replaced by the youngmen. Moreover, it could not explain the conflicts and contradictions inherent in Asante nationalism, for the events of 1954–57 did not simply represent the struggle of Asante's youngmen against the government of the CPP. Those events also reflected an historically rooted struggle *within* Asante (and within the NLM) between the aspiring youngmen and the established powers of Asante. It was the outcome of this long struggle, not the singular and immediate aspirations of the youngmen, which would determine the course of Asante's quest for autonomy.

However, for the purposes of this study, Rathbone's major insight regarding the central role of the youngmen in the 1950s provides an important vehicle for bridging the "intellectual dead-zone" so lamented by historians of nineteenth-century Asante. In order to make Rathbone's insight historical, thereby challenging his characterization of the youngmen as "aspirant businessmen," it becomes necessary to explore the story of Asante's youngmen and their extremely complex relationships with the ruling elements of Asante society. It becomes necessary to confront the political and social conflicts of the precolonial and early colonial eras and to consider the legacy of indirect rule, the increasing importance of cocoa to Asante's economy, the development of class or class fractions in Asante society, and the emergence of a self-conscious and vocal political intelligentsia. In short, it becomes necessary to envision Asante history in an ongoing trajectory.

It is crucial for the conceptualization of this study that historians of nineteenth-century Asante have sought to reconstruct that trajectory within a "national" paradigm.[21] Although none had challenged directly the dominant theoretical discourse which confines nineteenth-century nationalism to Europe,[22] their work places Asante squarely among the nation-builders of the last century.[23] Ivor Wilks discusses at some length the role of myth in legitimating the Asante political order from the late seventeenth through the eighteenth century and the historical process by which political ideology arose in the nineteenth century to replace those legitimating myths. "The notion that the political order was timeless and unchanging," he writes, "was being challenged by groups within the nation the interests of which could only be promoted through change—sometimes radical change." He points to the secularization of the monarchy, the bureaucratization of the government, and a number of legislative instruments, particularly in the sphere of individual liberties, as structural manifestations of this transformation.[24] In quite striking ways, Wilks's discussion parallels the analyses of "state" or "official" nationalisms in Europe propounded by such scholars as Benedict Anderson, Eric Hobsbawm, and Anthony Smith, who have been concerned with the forging of nation-states out of Europe's empires.[25] "I believe that in time," Wilks concludes, "we shall come to appreciate the extent to which the *Asanteman* was held together during the upheavals of the 19th century by cohorts of administrators working together to maintain the framework of civil society, articulating an ideology of nationhood that enabled a fundamental consensus to survive not only the bitter internecine struggles of the 1880s but also the traumatic loss of independence at the turn of the century."[26]

If Wilks provides evidence of the structural and ideological manifestations of Asante nationhood in the nineteenth century, Tom McCaskie's recent work has done much to contribute to our understanding of its symbolic representations, particularly with regard to Asante's Golden Stool, the paramount symbol of the *Asanteman*. McCaskie argues that the Golden Stool defined the "distinction between 'us' and 'them'—the notion of a unique 'Asanteness' that united the ancestors, the living and the unborn." Moreover, he argues, it embodied the "idea of a bounded and ordered culture (a legislated cultural space), the people or nation (*Asanteman*) presided over by the Asantehene as the juridically sanctioned custodian of the Golden Stool."[27] In a subsequent article, McCaskie follows the Golden Stool into the twentieth century, thereby crossing the "dead zone," and explores its continued importance in defining "Asanteness." He offers a fascinating interpretation of the 1921 episode in which the stool, having been hidden from the British, was unearthed by road workers and stripped of its gold ornamentation. The fact that the culprits looted the stool of its gold, but left the wooden stool itself intact, he argues, suggests that they "made a crucial distinction between their assault on the prerogatives of the nineteenth-century state (gold) and their continuing belief in the Golden Stool as the embodiment of the *sunsum* (soul, or spirit) of the *Asanteman,* of the spiritual component of a unique 'Asanteness.' "[28]

In significant ways, McCaskie's insights on Asante's precolonial and colonial past resonates with Anthony Smith's influential work on the role of *ethnie* in the formation of nations and in the articulation of national identity. Smith argues that in the ethnic "nation-to-state" trajectory, "nations were gradually or discontinuously formed on the basis of preexisting *ethnie* and ethnic ties, so that it became a question of 'transforming' ethnic into national ties and sentiments through processes of mobilization, territorialization and politicization."[29] If confronted with McCaskie's analysis, Smith would probably explain the Golden Stool's survival into the twentieth century in terms of the persistence of *ethnie* and the durability of its symbolic representations, even in the face of the disintegrating Asante nation-state. He would certainly not be surprised by the Golden Stool's central, symbolic role in the resurgence of Asante national sentiment in the 1950s. Indeed, it is Smith's notion of *ethnie* which facilitates his less Eurocentric definition of nationalism and thereby sets him apart from other Western scholars of the national question. "Once 'ethnicism' is conceded," he writes, "the way is clear to a more complex view of African nationalism and the concept of an African nation." African nationalism can thus operate on three different levels, according to Smith: "that of the ethnic community, the community of history and culture, which gives rise to 'ethnic nationalism'; that of the state, the heir of the colonial territory, a 'political community'. . . giving rise to 'territorial nationalism'; and finally that of the continent as a whole . . . giving rise to a 'Pan nationalism of all Africans.' "[30]

In echoing Hodgkin's definition of African nationalism nearly three decades later, Smith's work stands virtually alone in recent European scholarship on the national question. If there is much in Wilks's and McCaskie's work to suggest that Asante fits closely the dominant nationalist paradigms, the Western theorists of "nation" have largely excluded precolonial Africa (and some, colonial Africa) from their discussions. In short, Asante as "nation" falls through the proverbial cracks. For example, Eric Hobsbawm, like Ernest Gellner, views literacy and conversion to a "variant of a world religion" as key variables in the forging of nations. Thus, evidence of real (that is, parallel to the European experience) nationalism in Africa is limited to the "Christian Amhara" and the "Muslim Somali." In passing, Hobsbawm mentions "the only other sub-Saharan political phenomena that look like modern mass nationalism, namely the Biafra secession of 1967 and the South African National Congress [*sic*]." For Hobsbawm, even the independence movements of the post–World War II period fail to meet the nationalist litmus test because they merely "adopted a western ideology"—albeit one "excellently suited to the overthrow of foreign governments."[31]

Benedict Anderson, whose notion of an "imagined community" has so influenced subsequent scholarship on nationalism, provides a more encompassing, less Eurocentric definition of nationalism than Hobsbawm. "The nation," he argues, "proved an invention on which it was impossible to secure a patent. It became available for pirating by widely different, and sometimes unexpected, hands."[32] It is this process, according to Anderson, which explains the "nationalist" content of the anticolonial struggles in Africa. However, like Hobsbawm, Anderson links the nation's emergence to specific European prerequisites, in this case, the rise of "print capitalism, which made it possible for rapidly growing numbers of people to think about themselves, and to relate themselves to others, in profoundly new ways."[33] Thus, in Anderson's framework, the "very possibility of imagining" an Asante nation did not arise until well into the twentieth century.[34]

Despite the challenge, if not difficulty, of situating "Asante-as-nation" in the dominant paradigms of nationalist theory, completely discarding nation-based terminology is not the answer. Examining the emergence of "Asante sentiment" in the 1950s via the alternative paradigm of "ethnicity," as did Osei-Kwame or D. R. and A. C. Smock, obfuscates not only the important connections that need to be drawn between Asante's precolonial and late colonial past, but the social dynamics within Asante that gave form and substance to "Asanteness." Although ethnicity, as M. C. Young's bibliographic overview reveals, has been at the center of academic inquiry into African politics since the mid-1970s,[35] it remains primarily concerned with the contemporary "boundaries" that define ethnic groups, and not with the historical "stuff" that is enclosed.[36] As a mode of inquiry, ethnicity has come a long way since its "subversive" days as the bugbear of national accommodation,[37] but the questions it poses and the answers it offers are still generated within the framework of contemporary states. In other words, explanations for ethnicity's persistence and prospects for its solution are located outside the "ethnic group" itself. Ethnicity's internal, historical dynamics—rooted in political, cultural and class-based conflicts—are often obscured by the all-encompassing, ascriptive attributes of a mythical "collective ancestry" and "group affinity" which can only be explored through psychology.[38]

This is not to suggest that ethnicity should have no role in an analysis of the Asante NLM, but that it must be integrated into a "national" paradigm in much the same way that Smith has effectively incorporated the *ethnie* into his theoretical discussions of the nation. Such an articulation of paradigms is essential if both the politics of "nation" and the culture of "ethnicity" are to inform historical inquiry. "Modern nations," writes Smith, "are not a static target, to be attained once-for-all. They are processes, albeit long-term ones. These processes of mobilization and inclusion, territorialization, politicization and autarchy are never concluded and are always subject to redefinition in each generation. . . . They are long-term historical processes, continually re-enacted and reconstructed but within definite limits." At the center of those historical processes, according to Smith, is an "ethnic core" which is essential if a nation is to survive. "If they lack one," he writes, "they must 'reinvent' one. That means discovering a suitable and convincing past which can be reconstructed and re-presented to members and outsiders."[39]

If Smith's discussion provides a general theoretical framework for situating the specific problem of Asante nationalism in the 1950s, it does so only as a temporary, partial solution to a more pressing problem. The efforts of social scientists and historians of contemporary Africa to understand movements like the NLM have been encumbered by the limited development of a viable, creative political language, as Lonsdale has termed it, a language capable of "transmuting the parochial division of tribalism into the universals of human existence."[40] At present, there is no consensus. In recent works, Lonsdale has sought to recapture "tribe" from early anthropologists and contemporary politicians, instilling his conceptualization with historical dimension and with class and gender content and drawing strong parallels between "tribalism" and European nationalism. Both, he argues, "had to face moral problems which territorial African nationalist movements were able to evade."[41] Similarly, Leroy Vail's recent volume evidences a significant rethinking of ethnicity by highlighting the "role of class actors in creating and shaping ethnic ideologies" and by "moving the analysis of ethnicity beyond the more or less ahistorical stance of the currently dominant interpretations toward a more specifically historical interpretation."[42]

While this recent recasting of ethnicity and tribalism addresses many of the concerns I raised with regard to earlier "ethnic" and "tribal" analyses of the NLM, and while it is an important step toward constructing a viable discourse, it has not yet liberated those terms from specific, often negative, connotations. "Tribalism," as Gellner once observed, "never prospers, for when it does, everyone will respect it as a true nationalism, and no one will dare call it tribalism."[43] Indeed, the very use of these terms tends to suggest, as Smith argues, a "political or ideological preference, in this case for the preservation of the political *status quo,* based upon existing state boundaries." But is there such a real difference, he queries, "between the aims and aspirations of the BaKongo, Ashanti, Eritreans and Kurds, on the one hand, and the Congolese, Ghanaians, Ethiopians and Iraquis, on the other hand? We seem to be making value judgments about the relative status of various social and political groupings on the basis of their alleged 'viability' as potential 'nations.' "[44]

In approaching the Asante National Liberation Movement via theoretical paradigms based on "nation," I hope to avoid this political paradox. Doing so, of course, opens another set of political or ideological accusations: namely, of privileging Asante vis-à-vis Ghana, of being at heart an "Asante nationalist."[45] This is certainly not my intention, and I hope that readers will not mistake this study's historical parameters, its attempt to understand the NLM in light of Asante's precolonial and colonial past, for political allegiances.

Neither should the decision to cast the Asante NLM within a "nationalist" paradigm be viewed simply as a response to the limited development of alternative modes of discourse or as an attempt to avoid the "baggage" that inevitably comes with analyses based on "tribe" or "ethnicity." In the last decade, important, ground-breaking work has appeared in the theoretical literature on nation and nationalism, and more promises to be forthcoming as rapidly unfolding events in Eastern Europe and the former Soviet Union challenge existing paradigms, as the ethnic groups of yesterday become the nations of tomorrow. There is much insight to be gained from this literature, despite its too-often Eurocentric approach and the fact that it has seldom benefited from the input, empirical or otherwise, of Africanist scholars. While leading theorists have not reached a consensus on the "nation" and "nationalism," their works share a common vision of nation-as-process and of the multidimensionality of nationalism. For example, most agree with Gellner's contention that "it is nationalism that engenders nations, and not the other way around,"[46] and, with varying degrees of emphasis, all define *nation* via political, economic, *and* cultural criteria.[47] These remain important insights when examining the resurgence of Asante nationalism in the 1950s.

But the primary reason this study approaches the Asante NLM as a national question posed on the eve of Ghana's independence is that such an approach facilitates bridging the "dead-zone" of historical inquiry discussed above. It avoids the sort of theoretical and historiographical disjunctures whereby Asante's national precolonial past becomes a "tribal" or "ethnic" present. It promotes an historical understanding of the political and economic conflicts which have pervaded the *Asanteman* for over a century and, in a context in which class and nation are not easily separated, it allows us to appreciate that Asante nationalism was neither a momentary primordial response nor a "benighted form of false consciousness." Still less was it an ideology "disseminated in some uncontested way."[48] Asante nationalism was an important terrain of struggle. In short, by viewing Asante as historic nation, the persistence of Asante national sentiment becomes a manifestation of the internal dynamics of Asante society and not simply a by-product of external stimuli.

So defined, it is hoped that this study can contribute in some way to debates outside its immediate parameters. While it draws several important links between Asante's precolonial and late colonial past, it has only narrowed the historiographical gap, not closed it. Far more empirical work on Asante's colonial history needs to be undertaken, and such efforts may eventually force a rethinking of the very chronology of Asante history, the rigid division of Asante's past into "precolonial" and "colonial" periods. Certainly historians of Asante need to problematize "Asante-as-nation" and consider carefully its historicity across these seemingly impervious barriers. If this study raises questions about the specific chronology of Asante history, it may further contribute to ongoing, comparative efforts in African studies to construct a more viable political language for interpreting the historical complexities of nation and ethnicity. Such a language cannot help but spark a reconsideration of current Eurocentric paradigms, particularly as they periodize nationalism's development. Yet none of these broader considerations must overshadow the primary task at hand: the historical reconstruction of Asante's National Liberation Movement on the eve of Ghana's independence. Theoretical paradigms must not be allowed to obscure the drama of Asante's last years of colonial rule. In the end, as Lonsdale reminds us, historians must always "leave the dead some room to dance."[49]

2

Cocoa and *Kotoko*

The Origins of the National Liberation Movement

On the 19th of September, 1954, over 40,000 people gathered at the source of the sacred Subin River in Kumase, the capital of the historic Asante empire. Most were dressed in *kuntunkuni* (traditional funeral cloth) to underscore the gravity of the day's events. As noon approached, the crowd began to shout the age-old battle cry, "*Asante Kotoko, woyaa, woyaa yie!*" They continued in pulsing fervor until the official state drums called them to silence. At precisely twelve o'clock, a large flag was unfurled before the huge gathering. The flag's green symbolized the rich forests; its gold, the rich mineral deposits which lay beneath the earth; its black, the stools of Asante's cherished ancestors. In the center of the flag stood a large cocoa tree; beneath the tree were a cocoa pod and a porcupine—symbols that could be misinterpreted by none.[1] The cocoa pod represented the major source of wealth in Asante and the porcupine (*kotoko*) stood as the historic symbol of the Asante war machine. Like the needles of the porcupine, "*wokum apem a, apem be ba*"—"if you kill a thousand, a thousand more will come."[2]

In the heat of the afternoon sun, the crowd listened to a host of speakers. They came from every walk of life, from virtually every point on the political spectrum. They included Nana Bafuor Osei Akoto, senior linguist to the Asantehene; Kofi Buor, Chief Farmer in Asante and a former CPP stalwart; E. Y. Baffoe, former Director of the CPP government's Cocoa Purchasing Company; Cobbina Kessie, a longtime opponent of Nkrumah and member of the Ghana Congress Party; Bankole Awooner-Renner, a "prison graduate" from the CPP's days of Positive Action and current Chairman of the Muslim Association Party. The speakers seemed to have very little in common. Yet on that day in September they stood together on one platform at the source of the Subin River and inaugurated a new movement—the National Liberation Movement.

Bafuor Akoto, presented as the leader, read to the mammoth crowd the "Aims and Objects of the Liberation Movement":

1. To banish lawlessness, intimidation, disregard of age and authority, suppression of individual conscience and all traces of communism.
2. To establish respect for efficiency, integrity, and honest labour.
3. To honour, respect and be loyal to our traditional rulers and uphold the best in our cultures.
4. To secure due recognition of the economic, social and cultural background of the respective regions of the Gold Coast and work out a federal constitution to give them an effective say in the regional and Central Government of the country.
5. To encourage good neighbourliness among villages, towns and regions.
6. To safeguard the interests of farmers and workers, and ensure proper incentives for their labours.
7. To quicken the achievement of self government and help build a prosperous, healthy, tolerant, democratic and God-fearing Gold Coast Nation.
8. To foster friendly relations between the Gold Coast and the Commonwealth and other democratic nations.

ACTION: SAVE GOLD COAST FROM DICTATORSHIP[3]

After the "Aims and Objects" were read, the Movement's leaders announced their first course of action. A resolution, consisting of three points, was to be forwarded to the governor of the Gold Coast by the Asanteman Council. First, it demanded that the price of cocoa be increased from 72 to 150 shillings per load. Second, it asked that a federal constitution be drawn up for the Gold Coast. Lastly, it reported that the people and the Movement had taken a vote of no confidence in the government of Kwame Nkrumah and the Convention People's Party.[4] In many ways, the "Aims and Objects" and the Movement's first resolutions were in stark contrast to the crowd's activities on that inaugural day. Measured calls for safeguards were issued against a background of black and red mourning cloth, the beating of the *tumpan* drums, and the shouting of battle cries.

Nonetheless, from September 19 on, any predictions of a smooth and orderly transition to full self-government in the Gold Coast were cast into doubt. The 1954 general election was not to be the final election before the granting of independence. Over the next two and a half years, NLM leaders alternated demands for Asante autonomy within a federated Gold Coast with calls for Asante's complete secession. Violence plagued the major cities of the region as colonial officials watched their model colony teeter on the brink of civil war. Most Asante supporters of Nkrumah's CPP lived in exile in Accra. Indeed, Nkrumah, out of fear for his safety, did not cross the Pra River, the boundary between Asante and the Colony, until well after independence in 1957.

Given these far-reaching ramifications, it is obvious that the Movement's roots ran deeper than the demand for a higher cocoa price. But how much deeper? What follows is an examination of the Movement's origins: the people and events which ultimately "set ablaze the petrol dump of Asante nationalism."[5] The approach taken highlights the NLM's complex social roots in an effort to explain how chiefs, commoners, cocoa farmers, and intellectuals came together in a popular front under the banner of "cocoa and *kotoko*." It also underscores the NLM's disparate political roots, which fed on the failures of the CPP and the incompetence of precursor opposition movements. Finally, the chapter examines the adhesive which bound together the popular front—its historicity and its pragmatic limitations. Was it a form of tribalism or ethnic chauvinism which, by hearkening back to ancient days of glory, sought to protect Asantes from the new centralized state? Or was it a modern mass nationalism intent on challenging directly both the anticolonial nationalism of Nkrumah and the entire Anglo-CPP blueprint for an independent Ghana?

The Early Years of Opposition to the CPP

Prior to the 1954 general election, heralded as the last election before the granting of independence, political opposition to the CPP was disjointed and feeble. Nkrumah had captured the historic moment in 1951 when he and his fellow "prison graduates," following the campaign of Positive Action, competed in the general election, won a sweeping victory, and accepted positions within the government.[6] What opposition did exist prior to the 1951 election centered around those who had lost the moment, as makeshift alliances were formed between the old guard intelligentsia of the United Gold Coast Convention (UGCC) and the chiefs of the Joint Provisional Council and the

SAVE YOUR NATION
ALL YE SONS AND
DAUGHTERS
of the once powerful and respected
Ashanti Nation
who even at the command of a Governor and at the mouth
of Cannons did not surrender the GOLDEN STOOL OF
KING OSSEI TUTU
Your Nation is Politically invaded and economically
besieged.
Save Your Dear Nation from deceit, negligence, contempt
and fear of communism.
Your descendants are doomed if you do not Save your nation.
Transfer of Power with the Privy Controlled By the Dragon
will be a great danger
THE SPIRITS OF YOUR GREAT AND NOBLE
ANCESTORS CALL YOU TO ACTION.
MEET therefore in your thousands in your native Mourning
Attire at the source of the Sacred River Subin
at the Prince of Wales Park Kumasi On
Sunday September 19, 1954
from 8 a.m. to 4 p.m.
To discuss matters of National Importance and
INAUGURATE A POLITICAL PARTY.
SAVE YOUR NATION
THE GREAT ASHANTI NATION

NEW ERA PRESS, KUMASI OSEI ASSIBEY MENSAH

A leaflet for the September 19, 1954 rally

Asanteman Council.[7] Tiny groups proliferated, many of which were formed by future leaders of the NLM. Among others, there was the People's Democratic Party, founded by Cobbina Kessie and I. B. Asafu-Adjaye and the Gold Coast Labour Party, founded by John Tsiboe of the Asante *Pioneer*, S. H. K. Cleland of the Obuasi Mineworkers' Union, and Fred Loo of the Public Works Department Employees' Union. These groups, founded in Kumase, had their counterparts in Accra, as one party after another was formed in an attempt to recapture the political initiative from the CPP.[8] But the results of the 1951 election revealed that the CPP, winning thirty-four of the thirty-eight popularly contested seats, was in firm control. The political opposition emerged from the election the same way it had gone in: fragmented, weak, and ineffectual.

After the 1951 election, political opposition to the CPP was mobilized along more sectional lines. One obvious reason for this development was that it had proven impossible, as evidenced by the results of the 1951 election, to compete ideologically with the CPP as an alternative *Gold Coast-wide* nationalist party. The CPP had captured this arena and held sway over Gold Coast national discourse since the campaign for "Self-Government Now." No other group was capable of articulating that demand more dramatically or effectively. As Austin writes, "In challenging the CPP . . . they were on difficult ground, for it was not easy to see why the demand for 'Self-Government Now Under Nkrumah' should be less desirable than that of 'Self-Government in the shortest possible' time under Grant or Danquah."[9]

Certainly, the proliferation and tenacity of political groups mobilized along so-called sectional lines cannot simply be explained (away) by pointing to the CPP's hegemony over nationalist discourse after 1951. However, with much recent scholarship emphasizing the primordial and psychological dimensions of sectional or ethnic mobilization,[10] it is important not to lose sight of the precise *political* circumstances under which "sectional parties" emerged in the Gold Coast. Indeed, it may be useful to recall John Breuilly's observation that "once a political movement *within* the territory of the colonial state wishes to make claims to autonomy or independence it has to go beyond universalist anti-colonial arguments to arguments about distinct group identity within colonial society."[11]

The first to attempt to mobilize opposition around more immediate and localized issues were the Muslims who lived in the stranger, or *zongo,* sections of Ghana's southern urban centers, mainly Accra and Kumase. After a brief alliance with the CPP in the 1951 election, the Muslim Association broke with Nkrumah in August, 1953, and transformed itself into the Muslim Association Party (MAP). While this break was sparked by perceptions that Nkrumah had failed to provide Islamic education with the taxes levied in the Muslim community, it was reinforced by broader concerns regarding the civil rights of Muslims in the Gold Coast.[12] In 1953 and early 1954, the MAP decided to challenge the CPP at the polls in two major municipal elections. It met with a great deal more success than previous opposition groups, winning two of the seven seats contested in Accra and four of the seven contested in Kumase. Indeed, of the total votes cast in Kumase, the MAP drew over one-sixth.[13]

Whether future opposition forces looked to the MAP as a model for mobilization is unclear. Yet after the 1951 general election, the most effective and well-organized opposition to the CPP came from groups which mobilized on an ethnic, regional, or religious basis. The precedent set by the MAP was followed in 1954 with the formation of the Northern People's Party (NPP) and the Togoland Congress (TC).[14] All three of these groups would challenge Nkrumah's CPP at the polls in 1954—the supposed final election before independence. Although the CPP would win another resounding victory—capturing 72 of the 104 seats in the Legislative Assembly—the opposition, as a whole, would attract 44.6 percent of the total votes cast. Indeed, the Northern People's Party was able to capture 15 of the 18 seats allotted to the Northern Territories.[15]

While the mobilization tactics of this new opposition were sectional, it is important to emphasize that they drew on broader antagonisms plaguing Gold Coast society. Underpinning the cries of "Islam, Islam!," for example, were class and civil grievances for which there were no outlets in the mass nationalist CPP. As Bankole Awooner-Renner, the leader of the MAP, explained, "The Muslims formed about 60% of the police force, about 90% of the army and about 80% of the labour force of the country. They paid their levies and yet . . . they were treated like dirt on the ground."[16] In short, to equate organizational slogans with political motivations is to accept propaganda at face value. Central to any discussion of Nkrumah's opposition, and certainly of the NLM, must be an analysis of the grievances, antagonisms, and conflicts embedded in those often cryptic slogans. As Vail has recently argued in the context of southern Africa, it is not "adequate to approach ethnicity or 'tribalism', as if all examples were essentially the same. Concern with the content of the message will be of ever greater importance if we are to understand it."[17]

Murmurs of Discontent in Asante

The first indications that certain Asantes would follow the lead of their Gold Coast compatriots in the MAP, NPP, and TC surfaced during the debates over representational reform in 1953. The focus of this debate was the *Van Lare Report,* which provided for the allocation of seats to the Legislative Assembly, based on the population of the regions of the Gold Coast. It was a significant report because it was to determine representation in the 1954 Legislative Assembly, the body which would spearhead the Gold Coast's transition to full self-government.[18]

It had only been seven years since the Colony and Asante were united under one legislative body when the debate over representation erupted.[19] It was a debate which brought together Asantes from both the CPP and the opposition in a call for 30 rather than 21 seats for Asante in the Legislative Assembly. Van Lare's *Report* allocated electoral districts to the regions based on population (as reported in the *1948 Census*). Kumase was allotted 2 seats; the Asante Region, 19.[20] Thus, in a legislative body which was to contain 104 seats, roughly 20 percent of those seats would represent Asante. This allocation reflected a decline from Asante's 25 percent share of seats in the 1951 Assembly. As far as the Asante representatives to the Assembly were concerned, the report reflected a total insensitivity to the historic, economic, and political importance of Asante to the Gold Coast. Asante, they argued, should be entitled to no fewer than 30 seats.

During the debates over the *Report* in the Legislative Assembly, the anger of Asante representatives, CPP and opposition alike, was expressed in burning nationalist language—the language of loyal subjects of that supreme symbol of Asante national unity, the Golden Stool.[21] B. F. Kusi, who had resigned from the CPP a year earlier and would become a staunch supporter of the NLM a year later, spoke to the Assembly as follows: "If in 1900 we had the support of all sections of the country we could have fought the British Empire and driven the British away and it would have been unnecessary for us today to agitate for self-government. . . . All Ashantis express the sentiment that Ashanti is a nation. . . . Population alone does not make a country." Even staunch Asante members of the CPP declared their unflinching support for the demand for thirty seats. In what stands as a most prophetic statement, Atta Mensah declared, "It has been suggested somewhere that the intention of Ashanti in asking for these thirty seats is that should Government refuse to accede to our demand we would break away and form a federal government. Such false and malicious statements . . . are most unfortunate. It is not our intention whatsoever to wreck the smooth unity which Ashanti has contributed in a large measure to build."

Mr. W. E. Arthur, a CPP Colony representative, raised the ire of all Asante assemblymen when he suggested that Asantes should just be thankful that they were represented in the Assembly at all: "I want to remind my brothers from Ashanti that they were not taking part in the administration of this country in the early days and it was only as late as 1946 . . . that they were invited to take part in the Government . . . they must understand that Ashanti is a conquered territory." To this provocative statement, Nana Boakye Danquah, the Kumase Akyempemhene, replied, "The last speaker has said that the Ashantis were conquered and I would like him to prove to this House in what way or manner they were conquered. We were never conquered."[22]

At the core of the Asante assemblymen's appeals lay several important arguments. Not only were the major resources of the country located in Asante—its gold and timber—but half of its major export, cocoa, was produced there. As C. E. Osei, the Asanteman Council's representative argued, population cannot be the only criteria; "you must have money backing [a government]," and the Government must be prepared to "buy . . . [Asante's] good will."[23] But of all the arguments, the one which, as Austin writes, "lay at the heart of the Ashanti protest," was that "its rulers had once held sway over a great part of the Gold Coast."[24] Any delimitation of electoral boundaries had to take into account the historic, hegemonic might of the Asante kingdom.

Despite the Asante assemblymen's demands that history and the realities of the Gold Coast's economic structure should be the determining factors in electoral representation, Van Lare's recommendations were adopted by the Assembly. Asante was left with 20 percent representation in the independence-bound Assembly. Though tempers ran high during the debate over the *Report*, as preparations began for the 1954 general election, and independence loomed just around the corner, the bitterness appeared to subside. However, to the keen observer, it was clear that the debate had left an open wound on the emerging body politic. But for the moment, only murmurs of discontent could be heard from Asante.

While the first political rift between Asantes and the CPP government was acted out on the floor of the Legislative Assembly, the second rift occurred within the offices of the CPP itself. As the 1954 election approached, CPP candidates had to be chosen to stand for the twenty-one seats in Asante. In many cases, local constituencies disapproved of the candidates selected by Nkrumah and the CPP's central committee, and submitted their own candidates for registration. "Local interests," writes Austin, "were asserted in defiance of the authority of the central committee."[25] As the election drew near, some of the candidates accepted party directives and stepped down. However, many opted to stay on the ballot despite the party's pleas for strict discipline and unity. Nkrumah reacted strongly. As he later wrote, "I called these people 'rebels.' Firm action had to be taken. It was vital that the Party should not be allowed to become disorganised or to be weakened by the split that this would ultimately bring about."[26]

Less than two weeks before the election, there were eighty-one of these rebel candidates in the Gold Coast. The CPP responded by calling a mass rally in Kumase, at the Subin River Valley, to expel publicly each of the eighty-one rebels. That Kumase was chosen as the rally site indicates that the CPP was quite conscious of where fractures in party discipline were most likely to appear. On election day in Asante, June 15, nine days after the party expulsions, thirty-two rebels stood as candidates. The murmurs of discontent in Asante were growing stronger. At the Subin River Valley, these candidates had been expelled from the CPP, but the Subin River Valley had not seen the last of the Asante rebels.

Several scholars have offered explanations for this break in party discipline in Asante, analyses of why the rebel candidates refused to heed the CPP's promise that, although they were not chosen to stand in the 1954 election, "there is more beyond for all who will keep the faith and set the banner flying."[27] Austin argues that the rapid growth of the CPP and the necessity of centralizing power and authority in order to maintain party discipline often conflicted with strong local or communal ties.[28] At times, these communal ties won the day, as was the case with the rebel candidates, but the conflict was part of the process of a nation being born: the 1954 election, "in the long run was the . . . narrow gate through which the country would pass to independence. . . ."[29]

Other scholars, like Rathbone and Owusu, view this early split in the CPP as an inevitable result of the closed colonial economy. They provide examples of what both Young and Lonsdale have termed "instrumentalist" approaches to politics and the state.[30] For Owusu, "politics, or the power to decide how economic resources are to be distributed, who is to get what job, and the like, was seen initially by many as perhaps the only effective means, given colonialism, to the real national 'good', economic power." The CPP rebels, acting within the confines of a closed colonial economy, operated under the notion that "any political ideology which did not produce significant economic improvement was . . . irrelevant."[31] Political power meant economic power, and by denying these rebels a place on the CPP ballot, Nkrumah had basically undermined the very source of party adherence—the promise of economic reward.

Rathbone further develops this instrumentalist argument, though he emphasizes his "serious disquiet with the invocation by description of supposed class interests."[32] Focusing on what he terms "aspirant businessmen," Rathbone argues that it was upon this group that "the full restrictive weight of the closed colonial economy fell."[33] Much of the CPP's early support, he asserts, came from "aspirant businessmen" who had been closed out of the economy by the "established businessmen."[34] Once in power, however, there were limits on the CPP's ability to accommodate the interests of these "aspirants." According to Rathbone, "By 1953–54 the closed, colonial economy was as closed as it had been in the 1940s, as far as any new businessmen was concerned."[35] The result was a "new generation of aspirants"—the rebels—who would look for other means of gaining entrance to the economic and political kingdom.

Both of these analyses—Austin's "communal" approach and the "closed colonial economy" or "instrumentalist" arguments of Owusu and Rathbone—shed important light on the motivations and actions of the eighty-one rebels. They do not, however, explain the magnitude of events which were to occur only a few months later. Both the actions of the rebels and the representation debate evidenced more complex and deep-seated grievances—grievances not simply unraveled by one or the other of these two approaches. The events leading up to the inauguration of the NLM must be viewed through a lens which brings into sharp focus the "creative link between culture and politics,"[36] a lens equipped to explore both the historical dynamics of class interests in

Asante and the construction and articulation of Asante national sentiment. "The necessity to weave together the instrumentalist and the primordialist dimensions," as Young has argued, "is self-evident."[37]

The Last Straw

On August 10, 1954, K. A. Gbedemah, Nkrumah's minister of finance, introduced a bill into the Legislative Assembly, the Cocoa Duty and Development Funds (Amendment) Bill, aimed at fixing the price paid to farmers for cocoa at 72 shillings per 60-pound load. Gbedemah justified the freezing of the price by arguing that the government had come to the conclusion,

> firstly, that it is not in the general interest for the Gold Coast to be subjected to considerable or frequent fluctuations in the price paid locally for its cocoa; secondly, that having regard to all other circumstances which obtain in the Gold Coast today, the present price paid locally for cocoa is fair, reasonable and provides an incentive to increased production; thirdly, that it follows that it is in the general interest that the cocoa farmer should receive a good and steady income for a period of years . . . and fourthly and lastly, that the funds which may accrue to Government through the fiscal policy it is now establishing should be concentrated as far as possible on expanding the economy of the country as a whole with special emphasis on its agricultural sector.[38]

There were four days of heated debate over Gbedemah's bill. Opponents within the Assembly attacked the bill from a variety of angles: the farmer would receive less than two-thirds of what his cocoa was worth on the world market; he would be unable to support his family; a system of "peasant slavery" would be instituted; farmers would cease to sell their cocoa to the Cocoa Marketing Board and would begin to smuggle it across the borders to the Ivory Coast and Togoland, where they could receive a decent price.[39] Despite the vigorous arguments of the opponents, however, Gbedemah's bill easily passed the Assembly on August 13. The price was fixed at 72 shillings. The opposition to the fixed price on the floor of the Assembly was nothing compared to the opposition that would arise in Asante a few days after the passage of the bill. It was the last straw.

During the debate on the Cocoa Bill and immediately after its passage, farmers throughout the Gold Coast began to register their complaints with the various chapters of the United Ghana Farmers'

Council—the farmers' wing of the CPP.[40] Though not necessarily opposed to the spirit of the bill, they did expect a higher price for their produce. In Asante, cocoa farmers held a series of meetings in Kumase at the Asawase Community Center to discuss their course of action, and by mid-August they had formed the Council for Higher Cocoa Prices. The Council was headed by Kofi Buor, the Chief Farmer in Asante and, up until the passage of the Cocoa Bill, a staunch supporter of the CPP. The Council's first action was to cable the Queen of England and demand that the Cocoa Bill be repealed and a price of 150s. per load be offered to the farmers. Farmers in the Amansie-Mponua constituency went one step further by electing a committee to demand that their representative to the Legislative Assembly be withdrawn for supporting the new price.[41]

Less than two weeks after the passage of the bill, opposition in Asante to the price of cocoa mushroomed into opposition to the CPP, its blueprint for self-government, and its economic policies. As an editorial in the *Pioneer* remarked, "Great events . . . from little causes spring. Like an innocent match flame, the strange attitude of the all African CPP Government to the simple demand of farmers for a higher local price of cocoa has gone a long way to threaten to set ablaze the petrol dump of Ashanti nationalism."[42]

Politicization of the cocoa price came not from the farmers, however, but from the members of the Asante Youth Association (AYA)—the so-called youngmen of Asante. On August 25, the AYA met to discuss the cocoa price. A heated debate ensued between those who supported the CPP's development plan and those who did not. Among the opponents were men who had protested against Van Lare's *Report* and/or had "rebelled" during the 1954 election. The meeting ended in chaos. The books of the organization were seized by those who opposed the CPP's measures, and the Association was split in two—the anti-CPP faction calling itself the "All-Asante Youth Association."[43] As one of the orchestrators of the split, Osei Assibey-Mensah, recalled, "we chased them out of the hall! We then went and bought some Schnapps and poured libation, vowing no more support for the CPP. We would form our own party."[44]

Two days after the split, the All-AYA issued a statement which declared support for the farmers' demand for a higher cocoa price. It also called for the establishment of a federal system of government for the Gold Coast. The following day, August 27, a joint mass meeting was held at the Asawase Community Center by the farmers and the members of the All-AYA. The first link in a broad-based popular front was forged. Signing himself as the "Advocator for Farmers in Ashanti," E. Y. Baffoe composed one of the popular front's first leaflets—a leaflet which not only connected the cocoa price to broader political issues, but foreshadowed the direction and appeals of Asante opposition in the years to come.[45] Entitled, "Cocoa Price Agitation and the Position of Ashantis in Our Struggle for Self-Government," the leaflet beckoned,

> Yee Sons and Daughters of Ashanti,
> Great and Small, Old and Young,
> Arise, Our Share of the Good Fruit of our
> Labour for Self Government is Lost
> Because the Colony People having had Majority
> Key Positions of the Present Government are
> adopting means
> TO ENSLAVE ASHANTIS BY CHEATING US,
> IN DIVERSE WAYS.

First among these was the price of cocoa. "Ashantis," wrote Baffoe, "produce more cocoa than the colony. IS THERE ANY COCOA IN THE NORTHERN TERITORRIES [*sic*]? NO! Why should Government tax cocoa farmers to develop the country in which Ashanti's suffer most?" The leaflet concluded with this exhortation: "ASHANTIS! Save Your Nation and let others know that we are no FOOLS BUT WISE, kind and also we have the Worrior [*sic*] Spirit of Our Great Ancestors Within Us."[46] Cocoa and *Kotoko* would stand at the heart of the new movement.

The Forgers of the Popular Front: The Asante *Nkwankwaa*

But who were these youngmen who were attempting to weld the issue of cocoa to the spirit of *Asante Kotoko*? It is clear from the sources that they were the catalysts behind the solidification of opposition in Asante and were instrumental in developing its tactics and appeals. They were, as one cliché puts it, the "movers and the shakers"—but why? While most sources on the period, primary and secondary, point to the pivotal role of the youngmen, they differ dramatically in their definitions of this important, though enigmatic, social group—

youngmen being translated as "aspirant businessmen," "petite bourgeoisie," "commoners," or "verandah boys." Because the youngmen are generally a key component in studies of the rise of modern mass nationalism, most authors argue that the origins of the youngmen are to be located in the epoch of rapid economic and social change following World War II. With reference to Asante, most point to the founding of the Asante Youth Association in 1947 as the first concrete manifestation of "youth-ness." It is in this decade, so the argument goes, that the politicization of the common man became the order of the day.

Yet in Asante, the youngmen had been a potent and active political force since at least the mid-nineteenth century, when they were known as the *nkwankwaa,* a term which has been consistently rendered in English as "youngmen." The sense of the term was not that the *nkwankwaa* were literally young, but that they existed in often uneasy subordination to elder or chiefly authority.[47] As Wilks writes of the nineteenth-century *nkwankwaa,* they were men who "belonged to old and well-established families but whose personal expectations of succeeding to office or even of acquiring wealth were low."[48] Channels for political advancement were obstructed by the traditional requirements of office; channels for economic advancement were obstructed by both the state and its monopoly on trade and what could be termed the rising bourgeoisie, or *asikafo* (literally, men of gold, or rich men).[49] Perhaps best described as an emerging petite bourgeoisie with an economic base in trading and rubber production and economic interests directed at the establishment of free and unencumbered trade with the coast, the *nkwankwaa,* according to Wilks, probably acquired "their first experience of political action in the anti-war and anti-conscription movements" of the late 1860s and early 1870s.[50] It was in the 1880s, however, that the *nkwankwaa* made their first serious bid for political power in Asante. It was the Kumase *nkwankwaa* who, angered when Asantehene Mensa Bonsu raised taxes and imposed heavy fines for petty offenses, took a leading role in the movement which eventually overthrew the Asantehene in 1883.[51] Capable of mobilizing the support of the *ahiafo* (the poor, or underprivileged) and in alliance with the *asikafo,* whose economic standing was also threatened by Mensa Bonsu's austerity measures and his state trading system, the *nkwankwaa* were able to carry out a successful coup against the Asantehene; and since they were "unconvinced of the virtues of a monarchical system," they brought Kumase under a "republican form of government" or a "Council of commoners and chiefs," albeit for only a brief period.[52]

Though the *nkwankwaa* had made a serious bid for political power in the 1880s, their long-term goals differed markedly from those of the *asikafo* and *ahiafo*. In the last years of Asante sovereignty, the *nkwankwaa* were unable to forge a lasting political alliance capable of effecting a dramatic change in Asante politics.[53] By 1901, Asante was under the complete control of the British, and the *nkwankwaa* faced an entirely new political and economic landscape. In the first three and a half decades of this century, before the consolidation of indirect rule in Asante, the *nkwankwaa,* according to a 1924 colonial report, enjoyed "a feeling of independence and safety which gives vent to criticism of their elders, and a desire when dissatisfied to take the law into their own hands."[54] Their relationship with Asante's chiefs remained uneasy at best. Throughout the 1920s, the *nkwankwaa*'s involvement in destoolment cases against numerous *amanhene* alarmed government officials and traditional authorities alike.[55] With their social and economic position bolstered by the growth in trade and the spread of Western education, the *nkwankwaa* became more resentful of the powers exercised by the chiefs, namely their ability to levy taxes and impose communal labor requirements. In 1930, the *nkwankwaa* were particularly outraged by news that the Kumasehene, Nana Prempe I,[56] and his chiefs were considering a law which would require that a percentage of a deceased person's property be given to the Kumasehene and his chiefs. In a letter to the chief commissioner, they warned that it was a similar measure which led to the overthrow of Mensa Bonsu in 1883. After discussions with the chief commissioner, Nana Prempe I dropped the issue.[57]

That the *nkwankwaa* have origins dating back nearly a century before the founding of the NLM clearly has implications for our understanding of the events of 1954–57. Specifically, these precolonial origins allow for an historical (though admittedly tentative) class analysis of the youngmen—an analysis which repeatedly points to the *nkwankwaa's* reliance upon strategic alliances or popular fronts which they have forged with other groups in Asante society to further their own aims, be it an end to conscription, the abolition of communal labor, a lessening in taxes, or the opening up of free trade with the coast. The *nkwankwaa* have been artful initiators of these alliances, capable of winning the support of the *asikafo* and the *ahiafo*. Historically, they have also turned to the chiefs, or to certain elements within the ruling elite, to gain the support and legitimacy necessary to further their causes.

That the *nkwankwaa* have had to turn to others, particularly to the chiefs, points to their weakness as a class. It also goes some distance toward explaining their pivotal, dynamic role in the turbulence of Asante politics over the past century. The *nkwankwaa* have displayed an historic ability to take advantage of the fluid nature of Asante politics since the 1880s—galvanizing support in frequently opposing camps around common, though perhaps fleeting, issues, and playing power against power. They accomplished this in 1883, after winning the support of the powerful Kumase Akyempemhene Owusu Koko. In 1934, in alliance with most of the Asante chiefs, they staged an important, though unsuccessful, hold-up of cocoa in response to the low price then being paid for the crop by European merchants. In the following year, partly because of the growing challenge that the *nkwankwaa* posed to chiefly authority, the British government decided to centralize that authority by restoring the Asante Confederacy Council, with the Asantehene at its helm. Some of the youngmen of Kumase, perhaps in an effort to tear apart the recently restored confederacy, then collaborated with the Dadeasoabahene, Bantamahene, Akyempemhene, Adumhene, Nkonsonhene, and Akyeamehene, in a plot to remove the Asantehene, Prempe II, from the Golden Stool.[58] The conspiracy was quickly uncovered, but the fact that "irresponsible agitators" could win the support of such prominent chiefs required drastic action. Less than a year later, during 1936, the council took matters into its own hands: in response to the *nkwankwaa's* vocal opposition to the colonial government's reconstitution of the confederacy, their reluctance to perform various communal services, and their role in the destoolments of so many paramount chiefs, including the attempt to destool the Asantehene, the Asante Confederacy Council abolished the office of *Nkwankwaahene* (leader of the youngmen) and all *nkwankwaa* organizations.[59]

The position of *Nkwankwaahene* was not hereditary, nor did it confer membership in any council (whether local or divisional), but it did provide a recognized channel through which the youngmen could collectively criticize the government.[60] It was that channel the Confederacy Council sought to destroy. But the *nkwankwaa's* dissatisfaction could not be eradicated so easily. The Confederacy Council could not simply legislate away the historically entrenched *nkwankwaa*, who were intent on attaining political power commensurate with their newly acquired Western education, their growing economic power via the expanding cocoa economy, and their widening roles as the clerks, teachers, and accountants of the new colonial bureaucracy. Indeed, less than a decade later, Meyer Fortes would remark, "The suppression of the 'youngmen's' spokesmen has quite possibly been an important contributory factor in the present condition of instability and corruption in Asante politics."[61]

In many ways, the Asante Youth Association, founded in 1947, came to assume the role and functions of the "abolished" *nkwankwaa*, as its members shared common characteristics, as well as common grievances, with their counterparts of the late nineteenth and early twentieth centuries.[62] Most AYA members came from well-established families, but had no prospects of succeeding to traditional office. Their economic and social base remained petit bourgeois, but there had been many important changes over the last fifty years. No longer rooted primarily in petty trade and small-scale rubber production, the youngmen of the post–World War II period were an economically diverse lot. Most had attained some degree of education, which led them into such burgeoning occupations as journalism, teaching, accounting, and clerking.[63] Some were shopkeepers and small-scale traders, and some were involved in cocoa production, if only in a small way. Though many were related to chiefs, they had no realizable aspirations to chiefly office. They can also be distinguished from the old guard intelligentsia—the relatively sparse, though politically significant, group of Asante professionals like K. A. Busia and I. B. Asafu-Adjaye who had been trained to inherit the government upon the departure of the British, but who had been left out after the dynamic rise of the CPP. They were not the indigent *ahiafo*, nor were they the *asikafo*, whose wealth was based in a powerful combination of land ownership, large-scale cocoa and timber production, trading, transport, and construction.[64] They were, quite simply, the youngmen, the *nkwankwaa*, or, for lack of a less cumbersome class definition, Asante's petite bourgeoisie.

Although Wilks speaks of a "rising" petite bourgeoisie in the nineteenth century, the term is not unproblematic. It raises some of the very problems suggested in Kwame Arhin's admonition that "recent theoretical and conceptual disputations [are] . . . concerned not with what Africa has actually been or is, but the degree to which it has resembled and resembles Europe."[65] However, I would argue for the term's limited and careful use in constructing necessarily tentative discursive bridges to facilitate broader, comparative enquiry. Certainly African theorists, most notably Amilcar Cabral, have employed the term *petite bourgeoisie* rigorously and effectively.[66] Cabral considered the petite bourgeoisie the only class capable of manipulating "the apparatus of the state in the underdeveloped world," given the absence of a national bourgeoisie and a national proletariat. Interestingly, Cabral's description by comparison of the petite bourgeoisie in the capitalist world as capable only of allying itself "with one group or another" and not of "determining the historical orientation of the country" appears to fit more closely the historical experiences of Asante's *nkwankwaa*—a contrast perhaps explained by pointing to the differences in Portuguese and British colonialism, and best explored by building discursive bridges.[67] For the more manageable task at hand, however, it is sufficient to provide a short definition of *petite bourgeoisie* and leave the challenge of comparative history to future scholars. Young's descriptive definition, which follows an overview of the "troublesome diversities" plaguing usage of the term since the early 1980s, is valuable for our purposes: "The notion of a petty bourgeoisie is best reserved for small traders, artisans, teachers, soldiers, and the subaltern ranks of the public service."[68]

However, in the context of Asante history, the term *nkwankwaa* (youngmen) remains the most precise and the most useful both as a category of social identity and for historical analysis. It avoids reductionist Western paradigms and defies the sort of ahistorical, descriptive terminology that reifies notions like *verandah boys* or *aspirant businessmen*. These notions only capture in a limited, one-dimensional way the role of the youngmen in the building of the Gold Coast's mass nationalist movement. Certainly, this role was not inconsequential. What most distinguished the youngmen of the post–World War II era from the *nkwankwaa* of the previous decades were the organizational and propaganda skills they acquired by participating in (and in some cases, helping initiate) the anticolonial mass nationalist movement of the CPP. Many, including Kusi Ampofu, Osei Assibey-Mensah, and Sam Boateng, played central roles in the founding of the CPP in 1949. For them, Nkrumah's party was the organization of the "common man," the vanguard in the struggle against colonial rule *and* against the power and privilege of chiefly authority. Thus, the youngmen spearheaded the CPP drive into Asante and, in the process, mastered the arts of mass mobilization and propaganda. But even the youngmen's post–World War II political efforts were not without parallel or precedent. Richard Crook has argued convincingly that CPP mobilization and the forging of political alliances in Asante from 1944 through the riots of 1948 to the election of 1951 remained solidly rooted in "the elite network of agro-commercial interests so powerfully represented by the chieftancy."[69] Thus, in their pivotal role as the builders of the Gold Coast's first mass nationalist movement, Asante's youngmen did not transcend their past as artful initiators of alliances, nor break with their established tactics of playing power against power in Asante.

In 1954, though the political and economic landscape of Asante had changed dramatically, the goals of the Asante *nkwankwaa* were not so different from those of their predecessors. The youngmen continued to seek political power and, through it, economic power. However, instead of confronting the Asante state, the *nkwankwaa* were now confronting the CPP—a party which they had helped to found and build, a party through which they sought to reach the political kingdom and all else that would follow.[70] Their break with the CPP, though precipitated by the freezing of the cocoa price, was based primarily on a growing perception that the CPP was no longer providing a means of political and economic advancement; it was no longer offering the political kingdom to the majority of Asante's youngmen. The government's allocation of seats in the Legislative Assembly and the CPP's selection of candidates for the 1954 election were cited as *prima facie* evidence that the CPP did not and could not represent the youngmen of Asante. The freezing of the cocoa price and a development policy that was based on the expropriation of wealth from Asante cocoa farmers only served to reinforce the youngmen's growing alarm that the CPP was seeking to build its kingdom on the backs of Asantes *without* giving the youngmen of Asante a voice in that kingdom or allowing them to reap its rewards.

In justifying their split with the CPP, the youngmen presented a number of arguments over and above their dissatisfaction with Van Lare's *Report* and the 1954 nomination of candidates. Some had broken with the CPP long before the allocation of Assembly seats. Sam Boateng, an activist in the Trades Union Congress, recalled that his decision was based on a belief that the unions had been made into scapegoats after the Positive Action campaign. Many workers had been dismissed from their jobs for their political activities, he argued, but received no assistance from the party after the campaign. Boateng thus decried the increasing concentration of power in Nkrumah's hands: "After the 1951 elections, there was a general feeling that the CPP could not give us the kind of independence we actually required. It was generally felt that the way Nkrumah was handling affairs, we were heading toward dictatorship. The rule of law was being trampled on."[71] Others, like Kusi Ampofu, argued that the party had abandoned its original purposes:

> I was deep in the CPP. I was a National Executive member for four consecutive years. And I had to break away because so many things were going wrong. Things were not in accordance with the Constitution of the Party. . . . We found that the leadership of the CPP was deviating from the set program which had attracted us all to the Party in the first place. . . . We found that they were making a mess of the whole show [the struggle for independence]. We found that the leadership was thinking only of itself. Independence was no longer the main issue.[72]

AYA member Moses T. Agyeman-Anane, in a lengthy piece entitled, "National Charges Against Mr. Kwame Nkrumah," listed no less than thirty-two indictments against Nkrumah, ranging from the most broadly political to the most intensely personal. A representative sample of these charges follows:

> [Nkrumah] has failed to secure for the Gold Coast self-government within 48 hours as promised in 1950.
>
> His declaration of Positive Action in January 1950 brought hardship into many poor homes in the country.
>
> [He] has fraternised with imperialists as against his own demand.
>
> [He] has failed to provide houses for the common man.
>
> [He] has deceived the people of the country by telling them that anyone riding in a car is a stooge and an imperialist agent but he is himself now riding in an American Cardilac [sic] car costing about £2000.
>
> [He] has failed to marry in order to bear children to increase the population of the country [of which] he is Prime Minister contrary to custom.
>
> [He] has been practising nepotism.
>
> [He] has failed to provide feeder roads.
>
> By the passing into law of the Cocoa Duty and Development Funds Ord.,

his Government has deliberately stolen the farmers' money, as against the wishes of the farmers.

[He] has attempted to create himself a dictator of the country as against the political and social traditions of the country . . .

As a man with a degree of Bachelor of Divinity, he has indulged in the practise of heathenism as against the principles of Christianity.

He has failed to render an account for public money in respect of the CPC.[73]

The youngmen's list of stated grievances against Nkrumah and the CPP was seemingly endless. Yet, whether they had split with the CPP in 1950 specifically over the Positive Action campaign or held out until August, 1954, the youngmen shared one common and overriding grievance, as Owusu and Rathbone have demonstrated. Their political and economic aspirations were not being met by the increasingly centralized and bureaucratized party of Kwame Nkrumah. The problem now facing the youngmen of Asante, the full ramifications of which cannot be explored via instrumentalist paradigms, was how they were to galvanize mass support against the CPP.

The Cocoa Price: Weapon of Mobilization

The issue around which the youngmen would mobilize mass support to confront Nkrumah and the CPP was the cocoa price. They would take the farmers' demand for a higher price as their own, and then transform opposition to the price into full-scale Asante opposition to the CPP. There were several reasons why the youngmen seized upon the price of cocoa (rather than on Van Lare's *Report* or the nomination of candidates for the 1954 election, for example) in finalizing their break with Nkrumah and launching into a massive opposition campaign. On the most obvious level, some youngmen were small-scale cocoa farmers in their own right, or their families were dependent on cocoa for their livelihood. The frozen price of 72 shillings per load directly affected their economic livelihood. However, this limited, direct involvement does not explain the magnitude of the youngmen's response.

More importantly, the economic welfare of Asante, as a whole, was inextricably tied to cocoa. Approximately 51 percent of the cocoa exported from the Gold Coast in 1954–55 was produced in Asante at a time when the Gold Coast was the largest producer of cocoa in the world.[74] Cocoa accounted for over 80 percent of the total value of domestic exports. While it is impossible to retrieve precise statistics on the number of Asantes directly involved in the production of cocoa, the Labour Department's "Cocoa Labour Survey" for Asante, begun in 1951, can provide a rough estimation. The Labour Department maintained that approximately 20 percent (or 3,391) of Asante cocoa farmers participated in the study. Thus, their figures suggest there were approximately 17,000 Asantes who were cocoa farmers as a primary occupation or as a supplemental means of income.[75] Yet even this figure does not adequately reflect the number of people who, in one way or another, derived income from cocoa. In addition to those involved in the transport and marketing of cocoa, there were those who served as the laborers on cocoa farms. Included in this category were people who worked under an annual contract, those who were hired by the day, those who were hired to perform a specific task (for example, clear land) and those who worked on a share or commission basis.[76] The workers in this last category, generally referred to as *abusa* laborers, received one-third of the cocoa they produced. Clearly, their income was directly tied to the prevailing price of cocoa.

Unfortunately, there are no statistics on the percentage of cocoa laborers employed under each method of labor organization. However, in a ground-breaking study of the relations of production in Asante cocoa farming, Austin argues that by the 1930s in south Asante, the *abusa* sharecropping system was becoming increasingly prevalent as it replaced the wage contract system of previous decades. This was due both to the inability of farmers to attract wage labor in the face of low prices and land scarcity, and to the success of cocoa laborers in "sidetracking, and in a sense partly reversing, the trend towards greater separation of labour from control of the land: that is, towards a capitalist class structure."[77] If the trend toward *abusa* sharecropping observed by Austin in the 1930s and 1940s continued into the 1950s (and there is no evidence to indicate it did not), then an increasing number of farm laborers were directly and adversely affected by the freezing of the cocoa price in 1954. Moreover, the variations in pay recorded by the "Cocoa Labour Survey" for wage and contract laborers suggest that their income similarly fluctuated according to the price the farmer was able to receive.[78]

In short, the price of cocoa was an important issue for a substantial portion of Asante's population—from the farmers to the laborers, the transport workers, the marketers, the brokers, the traders, the shop-owners, and even the school children. As Assibey-Mensah recalled, "Since cocoa was our backbone, the Asanteman Council used cocoa money to send our intellectuals to study in Britain."[79] The freezing of the cocoa price was thus perceived as a direct attack on the social and intellectual fabric of Asante. But perhaps nothing better summarizes the centrality of cocoa to Asante (or better, Asantes' perception of cocoa as the economic backbone of their society) than a local highlife song made popular in the 1950s:

> If you want to send your children to school, it is cocoa,
> If you want to build your house, it is cocoa,
> If you want to marry, it is cocoa,
> If you want to buy cloth, it is cocoa,
> If you want to buy a lorry, it is cocoa,
> Whatever you want to do in this world,
> It is with cocoa money that you do it.[80]

Rich or poor, young or old, indigenous Asante or migrant laborer from the North—if you lived in Asante, you danced to this song.

Even before the freezing of the cocoa price, there was widespread disaffection with the government's cocoa policies. The CPP's failure to reform or abolish the colonial government-initiated Cocoa Marketing Board (CMB) and its establishment of the Cocoa Purchasing Company (CPC) provided the groundwork for confrontation. The CMB was perceived by the majority of Asante cocoa farmers as a way for the government to expropriate their surplus from cocoa production and thereby inhibit the accumulation of capital. The CPC was viewed as an extension of Nkrumah's party, as a company set up and controlled by the CPP with the primary aims of funding the party machinery and mobilizing party support by giving preferential credit treatment to pro-CPP farmers.

The CMB was established by the British government in 1947 ostensibly as a mechanism for stabilizing the producer price for cocoa and protecting the cocoa farmer from vast fluctuations in the world market. It operated under the theory that in years of high world prices the farmer would be paid slightly less than market value. The reserves built up by the Board during these boom years would allow the Board to pay the farmer a higher-than-world-market price during depressed years. As Tony Killick points out, though there was some ambiguity over how large these reserves should be allowed to grow, official arguments put forward in support of the creation of the Marketing Board made it quite clear that the Board was not intended to "accumulate any reserves over and above those necessary in order to maintain such [price] stability."[81] From 1947 to 1954, however, the reserves accumulated by the Board far surpassed those necessary to maintain price stability. Between 1947 and 1954, the payments made to cocoa farmers amounted to only 48.6 percent of the CMB's total proceeds.[82] As it moved closer to independence, the CPP viewed the reserves as a source for funding public development projects. As Björn Beckman asserts, the reserves would provide the foundation "for an extraordinary expansion of the public sector."[83]

Many Asante cocoa farmers not only considered it unjust that the government expected them to carry the financial burden of national development, but argued that the professed goal of the Board to "assist in the development by all possible means of the cocoa industry . . . for the benefit and prosperity of the producers" had been completely abandoned.[84] In a 1952 letter to the Chairman of the CMB, Nana Osei Kwabena, Asante Chief Farmer, wrote, "The Gold Coast Marketing Board was created for we farmers in the Gold Coast . . . [but] not even a farthing has been paid to a farmer. . . . Why is it that we who maintain the well-being of cocoa farms and derive money out of the cocoa farms for the formation of the Marketing Board are not paid, but you who look over the Board receive regular payments?"[85]

The farmer's dissatisfaction with the CMB and Nkrumah's development policies intensified with the creation, in 1952, of the Cocoa Purchasing Company, a subsidiary of the CMB. Originally set up as an alternative to the international purchasing firms, by 1953, it was allocated the task of alleviating the "chronic indebtedness" of the cocoa farmers. Between August, 1953, and September, 1954, £1,900,000 was released to the CPC, via the CMB, for the issuing of loans to farmers.[86] Yet farmers continued to argue that the CPC, like the CMB, was not operating in their interests, but in the interests of the CPP. Allegations against the company abounded: it was controlled by the CPP, it helped fund the CPP through a corrupt system by which loans were issued to fictitious persons, and it gave preferential treatment to politically loyal farmers by issuing loans only to United Ghana Farmers' Council members (the CPP's farmers' wing).[87] Krobo Edusei, the government Chief Whip, did nothing to undermine these allegations when he proclaimed before the Legislative Assembly, "The CPC is the product of the master brain, Dr. Kwame Nkrumah, and it is the atomic bomb of the Convention People's Party . . . the Prime Minister in his statement to the CPP told his party members that organisation decided everything and the CPC is part of the organisation of the Convention People's Party."[88]

Before the passage of the Cocoa Duty and Development Funds Bill, statements like Krobo Edusei's went largely unchallenged. There was no ready outlet for the farmers' discontent. However, the August, 1954 cocoa price, which was only 37 percent of the average prevailing world market price, served to focus and intensify the farmers' dissatisfaction with the Marketing Board.[89] The Board and the CPC were increasingly perceived as institutions operating not in the farmers' interests but against their interests. The frozen price was the impetus to action: Asante farmers were ready to confront the government over the price of cocoa, and they were ready to listen to what the youngmen had to say.

And the youngmen of the AYA were well prepared to take up the cause of the cocoa farmer, not only as an economic issue, but as a political and national—that is, Asante national—issue. The freezing of the cocoa price was the perfect catalyst for mobilizing an opposition to the CPP in Asante. Looking back, many of the early leaders of the NLM recalled that the cocoa price was merely the spark that lit the opposition. It was an issue that was given high profile in order to galvanize support, but it was not the NLM's *raison d'être*. As N. B. Abubekr remarked, "It wasn't a major issue. We thought to make capital of it because, at that time, we thought it was the only way we could win the support of the people to our side."[90] The August, 1954 price of cocoa would become the youngmen's weapon of mobilization.

The Problem of Legitimacy

The youngmen of Asante now had in the fixed cocoa price a weapon with which to mobilize support for a confrontation with Nkrumah and had been successful in forging the first link in their popular front by organizing the support of the farmers. However, they were still not in a position to wage an all-out campaign against the CPP. They lacked funding and, more important, they lacked cultural and political legitimacy in Asante. And this legitimacy rested with Asante's chiefs, the very soul of *Asante Kotoko*. But winning the support of the chiefs would prove much more difficult than mobilizing the farmers. Many of the chiefs, not without cause, viewed the youngmen of the AYA as traitors. Only a few months before the NLM's inauguration, many of the *nkwankwaa* were adamant supporters of the CPP and were directly associated with the party's oft-quoted policy of "making the chiefs run away and leave their sandals behind."

Yet the support of the chiefs was essential. As Sam Boateng remarked, "we were all youngmen and were politically insignificant. None of us could lead the Movement. . . . We needed finance, money to print leaflets, pamphlets, all these things."[91] Above and beyond finances, the support of the chiefs was an ideological necessity. As the pillars of Asante unity, the chiefs would bring with them the "spirits and ancestors of the entire Ashanti nation."[92] The struggle against Nkrumah would become the struggle of the Asante nation against "political slavery," "economic slavery," and "dictatorship."[93] As Austin writes, "those who saw the conflict that was arising between the farmers and the government as one affecting the rights and interests of Ashanti were also ready to see the chiefs as still the most potent symbol of Ashanti unity."[94] Just as the *nkwankwaa* of the 1880s had turned to Akyempemhene Owusu Koko in their bid to depose Mensa Bonsu, the youngmen of the 1950s turned to the paramount chiefs of Asante in an effort to legitimize, as well as finance, their struggle against the CPP.

Notwithstanding their mistrust of the youngmen, the chiefs could ill afford to turn away from any movement which held out the promise of effectively challenging Nkrumah and his attempts to curtail chiefly power. The majority of the *ahemfo* (chiefs) viewed Nkrumah as the enemy—the man who sought to abolish the sacred institution of chieftancy. As Austin writes, under British indirect rule, the chiefs "had been given considerable powers. . . . They had received generous subsidies from the central government, and acted with substantive law-making powers." The Confederacy Council "exercised its judicial powers through its courts," Andoh writes, "while its executive functions were exercised through offices and departments which it established within its secretariat."[95] However, after the passage of the 1952 State Councils Ordinance, the powers of the chiefs were drastically curtailed, to be assumed by the newly created local councils, two-thirds of whose members were elected.[96] "Government subsidies were still paid to the chiefs," notes Austin, "and . . . [they were recognized] as having authority in traditional matters, but the substance of their power, including the levying of the local rate, passed to the new urban and local councils."[97] In short, by 1954 the chiefs took seriously the CPP's threat of "making them run and leave their sandals behind." They saw themselves, *West Africa* reported, "with no means of expression in central or local government."[98]

The youngmen knew it would take time and much tactical maneuvering to gain the trust of the chiefs and win their broad support. They initiated their reconciliation efforts by including in their early leaflets and speeches a call for the preservation of chieftancy. They posited themselves as the defenders of the "sacred institution of chieftaincy." Though the official support of the chiefs of the Asanteman Council and the Kumase State Council was not forthcoming until mid-October, a *Pioneer* editorial of early September remarked, "the youth of Ashanti have made it supremely clear that they would NEVER see the sandals removed from the Ahemfie [palace] to the Arena, the Subin Valley, or even the National museum. They would rather them still kept in the Ahemfie so that the Chiefs could come out of their hide-outs to wear them again."[99]

While appeals for the preservation of chieftaincy went a long way toward winning the support of the chiefs, the youngmen's choice as leader for the new movement was decisive. As Sam Boateng remembered, "we went to people, so many big men . . . [but] most of the big men were afraid. They didn't want to indulge."[100] Finally, the youngmen succeeded in convincing Nana Bafuor Osei Akoto, a senior *okyeame* (linguist) to the Asantehene to serve as the movement's chairman.[101] In late August, recalled the General Secretary of the AYA, Kusi Ampofu,

> I went to Bafuor Akoto and I said that, with his position as the linguist to the Asantehene, he would be in the position to drag in the Asante *amanhene* to this issue. He could get their support. So, when I came over (there were three of us), he in fact, declined and said that he felt we had earlier disappointed the Asante nation on the thirty seats Asante had been fighting for in the Assembly and the allotment of constituencies. . . . [He] thought that the Asante Youth were just coming to deceive him. I had to go on my knees and try to convince him that we were not going to try and deceive anyone. He told me to stand up and touched my head and gave me £10 to start the movement. He said that everyone must come to an understanding.[102]

In Bafuor Akoto, the youngmen had found someone capable of building the bridges they themselves could not.

As one of the Asantehene's senior linguists and as the son of the former Kyidomhene of Kumase, Akoto was, as *West Africa* reported, "*persona grata* to Otumfuo himself as well as to most Ashanti Paramount and Divisional Chiefs." He provided the youngmen of the AYA with a direct line to the most important traditional rulers in Asante. Moreover, as a former apprentice engineer (for Swanzy Transport) and fitter (for Cadbury and Fry), Akoto's formative experiences were not so different from those of the youngmen. As *West Africa* remarked, "his place in the workshop had taught him to understand and share those [problems] of 'commoners.' " Finally, Bafuor Akoto was a major cocoa producer in his own right.[103] By winning his support, the youngmen had found a leader who virtually personified the popular front they were attempting to build. Akoto was capable of narrowing the gaps between young and old, chiefs and commoners, cocoa farmers and urban wage earners. Bolstered by his presence, it was not long before the youngmen made headway with Asante's chiefs.

Inaugural Rehearsal: The Unofficial Launching of the Asante Opposition

Less than a month after the passage of the Cocoa Bill, the newly-forged opposition in Asante was ready for its first public appearance. Thousands of leaflets, printed with the money Akoto had given the youngmen, were distributed throughout Asante, calling people—particularly the youngmen or commoners—to attend a September 5th rally:

ARISE! ARISE! ARISE!
All yea [*sic*] sons of Ashanti
There is Woe and Danger! Ashanti has become a Booty!
Ashanti is Invaded!
Arise and save your rich forests
of cocoa, timber, gold and diamond
This is the Trumpet call of all the voices of our Ancient
Warriors calling all Ashanti Youth to Swear oath of
allegiance to free themselves from Political and Economic
Slavery, Dictatorship and Discrimination
Go therefore in your thousands to the source of the Sacred
River Subin at the Ashanti Capital . . .
SAVE THE ASHANTI NATION FOR IT HAS HISTORY[104]

The site chosen for this initial gathering was clearly symbolic. Not only had it served as the CPP rally grounds for nearly five years, but it had been the site of the 1954 public expulsions of the CPP rebel candidates. Many of those rebels, their numbers reinforced, now returned to the Subin River to confront the CPP and to orchestrate its expulsion from Asante.

All reports indicate that this early rally was a success. The *Pioneer*, clearly sympathetic to the new opposition movement, reported, "Ashantis, predominately farmers of Kumase and its neighbouring villages swore an oath never to accept the Government's general policy toward Ashanti, and inaugurated a non-political Association of all Ashanti youth at a large meeting . . . [which] declared its aim as being in the main a united front against the CPP Government's ruling on the cocoa price."[105] But the issues raised at the rally reflected concerns much broader than the cocoa price. Speaker after speaker reiterated the argument that the CPP was both expropriating the wealth of the Asante region and desecrating its cultural and historical traditions.

Bafuor Akoto, the rally's keynote speaker, complained that the government had consistently slighted Asante in the issuing of government scholarships, as well as in the allocation of development schemes—despite the fact that "the revenue of the Government was obtained largely from the cocoa produced by Ashanti." And when Akoto mentioned that the government planned to name the new Kumase hospital after Nkrumah, "the people swore and sang traditional war songs that they would never allow this."[106] But the words which evoked the loudest cheers, those which foreshadowed the trajectory of the Movement's appeals within Asante, were the ones which proclaimed that "Ashanti people should separate themselves from the rest of the country" and that September 5 should be called "Ashanti Independence Day."[107] The gravity with which these words were spoken was underscored as the rally ended: libation was poured, a sheep was slaughtered, the drums rang out, and "war songs were chorused as the oath of unity was sworn."[108]

Though barely acknowledged by the colonial government seated in Christiansborg Castle or by CPP headquarters in Accra, the September 5 rally was nonetheless significant. Though the goals and the strategy of the Movement had not begun to crystallize, though no clear leadership was evident, and no platform defined, it was the first large rally in opposition to the CPP held in Asante. It reflected the potentially powerful, but as yet tenuous, links which were being forged between the youngmen, the cocoa farmers, and the chiefs, and it provided a glimpse of the passion that could be evoked when cocoa and *kotoko* shared the same platform. Though few raised an eyebrow in Accra, the rally did draw the attention of Ghana Congress Party (GCP) stalwarts, including members of Asante's old-guard intelligentsia. Between the September 5 rally and the official inauguration of the NLM, longtime politicos like Cobbina Kessie and John Tsiboe were quickly drawn into the Asante opposition. Meanwhile, the youngmen, invigorated by the success of the rally and their new-found strength, began to elicit the support of former CPP members like N. B. Abubekr and B. F. Kusi—two CPP members of the Legislative Assembly who had broken with the party in 1952. As Abubekr recalled, "We were invited to Kumase to see Bafuor Akoto. I had left the CPP then. . . . I was followed by B. F. Kusi. We were together friends in Parliament. So those people . . . who were planning to form the NLM thought they could make use of us . . . [we thought] Bafuor Akoto, being the Asantehene's linguist, . . . had very great influence—first, on the Asantehene, himself, and on the people of the country of Asante."[109]

Over the two weeks following the rally, as more people were drawn into the front, meetings were held nearly every day, many lasting throughout the night. It was at these meetings, held at the homes of both Bafuor Akoto and Cobbina Kessie, that the popular front was born, alliances forged, and old conflicts resolved, or better, swept aside. Indeed, the men who met—chiefs and youngmen, ex-CPP members and die-hard UGCC members, cocoa farmers and urban wage earners, *asikafo* and *nkwankwaa*—were not unlike those who had come together in Kumase, over seventy years before, to form the *kwasafohyiamu*, the Council of Commoners and Chiefs.

In short, the September 5 rally was the dress rehearsal for the NLM's inauguration and served as a springboard for the mobilization of a host of opposition forces in Asante. As J. K. Appiah reported with such eloquence, "When on a day in September this year a group of Ashanti youth gathered at the heart of Kumasi up the Subin River and swore by the Golden Stool and reinforced their Oath with the pouring of libation to the Great Gods of the Ashanti nation and the slaughtering of a lamb, an act of faith, of great national significance was undertaken. . . . And so Ashantis, backed by their chiefs and Elders, their sons and daughters, and taking guidance by the shadow of the Golden Stool are now determined to live and die a Nation."[110] Two weeks after the rally (and barely a month after the introduction of the Cocoa Bill into the Legislative Assembly), over 40,000 Asantes gathered at the source of the Subin River to inaugurate officially the National Liberation Movement.[111] In a very short time, what had begun as a few disgruntled remarks about the cocoa price had grown into a deafening chorus of denunciations aimed at Nkrumah and the CPP.

The Origins of the NLM Reconsidered

Shortly after World War II, in a study of British "native administration," Lord Hailey wrote:

> At one period Ashanti national sentiment undoubtedly looked forward to the evolution of the country into a separate political unit, in which the Confederacy Council would be the recognized organ of legislative and administrative authority. But the political integration of Ashanti with the Gold Coast Colony effected by the constitution of 1946 has for the time being diminished the general interest in this aspiration, nor does there in fact appear to be any substantial grounds for its revival. Ashanti has interests of its own . . . , but neither ethnic nor economic circumstances exist which would justify any scheme that involved complete political separation of Ashanti from the Gold Coast Colony.[112]

Justifiable or not, only a few short years after Hailey offered these observations, many were mounting the rally platform at the source of the Subin River to announce that there were indeed grounds for the separation of Asante from the Gold Coast. At the heart of this argument, an argument still requiring refinement and elaboration, lay Asante nationalism and the conviction that Asante, as an historic nation, had the right to self-determination.

Nationalism, as utilized here, encompasses the definition put forward by Ernest Gellner, and endorsed by Hobsbawm: it is a "political principle which holds that the political and the national unit should be congruent . . . a theory of political legitimacy which requires that ethnic boundaries should not cut across political ones."[113] However, it breaks with Gellner's definition in the primary role it assigns to culture and ethnicity and in maintaining, with Smith, that the " 'cultural forms' within which we operate are themselves powerful determinants of both our goals and the means we can employ to attain them."[114] Thus defined, nationalism was the all-embracing ideology of the National Liberation Movement from the very onset. The youngmen did not spearhead the formation of the NLM simply because, as one of their leaflets proclaimed, "Asante has history." Their reaction was not simply a primordial response thrown up in the face of a new, all-encompassing sovereign civil state.[115] Rather, the youngmen's invocations represented the very modern elaboration of an ideology aimed at justifying opposition to the CPP, legitimizing that opposition, and, finally and most important, mobilizing broad-based support among Asantes.

That Asante had, in fact, existed as an independent historic kingdom, though useful, was of secondary importance in constructing a unifying ideology, a "myth of tradition." As Hobsbawm has recognized, "The potential popular appeal of a state tradition for modern nationalism, whose object is to establish the nation as a territorial state, is obvious." But whatever the historic continuities, he has pointed out, "even a concept like 'France' [must] include a constructed or 'invented' component."[116] In the case of Asante, how those components were "invented," constructed, or "imagined," to borrow Anderson's terminology,[117] was largely shaped by Asante's political, economic, and cultural landscape. Thus, it is essential to look closely at the grounds which nurtured the revival of Asante national aspirations.

Asante in the 1950s provided fertile ground for the youngmen's nationalist message. It was a message which appealed to the large class of cocoa producers who were united in their opposition to the cocoa price and frustrated by a purchasing and marketing system aimed at expropriating the surpluses of cocoa production for public sector development. With the exception of a limited and somewhat superficial opposition to the cocoa price, however, the Asante farmers had proven themselves incapable of launching an all-out attack on the mechanisms of buying, marketing, and expropriation—the colonial-designed mechanisms which the CPP was intent on keeping in place. The *ahemfie* (chief's house) also sat on fertile ground. The chiefs saw their power further undermined by the centralization strategies of the CPP, the creation of local councils, and the refusal of the party to incorporate a second, Upper House into the independence-bound parliament. As Arhin writes, "they regarded Nkrumah and his party as parvenus, usurpers of power from the legitimate heirs to the British."[118] Yet the chiefs, like the cocoa farmers, had shown themselves incapable of confronting Nkrumah directly, fearing, perhaps, further assaults on their bases of authority.

Finally there stood Asante's old-guard intelligentsia, the doctors and lawyers who had been trained abroad, had worked with the British government to reform the political system after the 1948 riots and had always considered themselves to be the natural inheritors of the state apparatus after the orderly withdrawal of the British. By 1954, this old guard had been disinherited. In the guise of a host of small opposition parties, it had proven itself unable to challenge successfully the CPP in the elections of 1951 and 1954. The old guard had not only lost the political moment, but was incapable of mobilizing any significant, broad support to oppose the CPP. Its entire existence had been predicated on the notion that political power is handed to the most capable and deserving. Mass support was both cumbersome and irrelevant to the assumption of political office. As the noted African-American novelist, Richard Wright, concluded after interviewing J. B. Danquah, the personification of the old guard: "He was of the old school. One did not speak *for* the masses; one told them what to do."[119]

Only the *nkwankwaa,* with their long history of forging alliances and their recent experience, via the CPP, of mass mobilization techniques and propaganda, were in the position and had the tools necessary to fertilize and cultivate the grounds of opposition in Asante. They were political catalysts, just as they had been in 1883. They were the only class capable of articulating their *specific* aspirations for political and economic advancement—aspirations historically thwarted by the traditional Asante state, the structure of indirect rule, and now by the bureaucratization and centralization of the CPP—as Asante national aspirations. This ability stemmed largely from their self-definition which, as Hobsbawm argues with regard to the Irish lower middle class, "was not so much as a class, but as the body of the most zealous and loyal, as well as the most 'respectable' sons and daughters of the fatherland."[120] In short, the youngmen were the only class able to develop an all-embracing ideology—Asante nationalism—which could express the varied and often conflicting aspirations of Asantes in an emergent Ghana. Their "national imaginings," to draw from Smith, presented a "vision of ethnic fraternity of elites and masses through a historical drama in which a unified past is uncovered and re-presented . . . thereby to evoke deeper meanings of collective destiny and community in the face of . . . dangerous fragmentation."[121]

That the *nkwankwaa* were the only group capable of these "national imaginings" in 1954, however, does not explain why, given their specific economic and political aspirations, they did not opt to mobilize opposition to the CPP among the youngmen of the Colony or the North, thereby initiating a split within the ranks of the CPP itself. The answer lies in an understanding of the youngmen's role as a local or "vernacularizing nationalist intelligentsia" whose political formation was rooted in the day-to-day realities of Asante.[122] These youngmen were quite distinct from the other segments of the country's intelligentsia, whose political formation was greatly colored by broader Gold Coast and international experiences. The old guard intelligentsia were primarily schooled abroad and saw themselves as the inheritors of political power *because* of this training. Their successors, the leadership of the CPP, were no less shaped by international educational and political experiences, though their participation in such events as the Pan-African Congress of 1945 prepared them to lead a mass, rather than an elite, movement for independence. The political aspirations of both segments of this intelligentsia were fueled, formed and, to some degree, legitimized by their international experiences.

While Asante's youngmen were no less capable of formulating their own political aspirations and strategies, they were much more rooted in what Basil Davidson might term the "brute facts" of life in Asante.[123] Though most had received some degree of Western education in Ghana, few, if any, were "been-to's." They had acquired their political education in Asante, and when the price of cocoa offered itself as a weapon of mass mobilization, they turned to mobilize those with whom they had historically forged alliances, those who sat on "fertile ground." The price of cocoa was the perfect weapon. It was easily transformed into an Asante national issue, one affecting all the sons and daughters of the Golden Stool. And that supreme symbol of Asante unity, though it was not the "defining instrument of the accumulation and distribution of wealth" that it had been in the nineteenth century, remained, as McCaskie argues, a "cultural rallying point" capable of resurrecting " 'objective' religiosity."[124] So the youngmen of Asante stood on the platform at the Subin River and presented themselves as the new idealogues of Asante nationalism. And they fanned the fires of discontent by pointing to the failures and corruption of the reigning Gold Coast nationalist movement and the ineptitude of past opposition forces. They raised the issue of cocoa and resurrected *Asante Kotoko*.

But could this new popular front, spearheaded by the youngmen and inaugurated with such historic pageantry, fulfill the aspirations of all the disparate and conflicting groups seeking to wage their struggle through the resurrected *Asante Kotoko*? What concrete platform could the Movement put forward as an alternative to the CPP's? On the day of the inauguration, these questions and others had yet to be addressed; many had not been posed. Yet the "petrol dump of Asante nationalism had been set ablaze." The youngmen stood holding the match, and no one was quite sure how long the fire would burn, who was capable of directing its flames, or who, if anyone, had the power to put it out.

3

The Dump Ablaze

Murder, Mobilization, and Building a Popular Front

During the three weeks following the September 19 inauguration, the flames of the National Liberation Movement swept through Asante, reaching from the source, Kumase, to such major towns as Sunyani and Obuasi. Seemingly overnight, in village after village, the CPP flag came down, and the NLM flag was raised. The local newspaper, the *Ashanti Pioneer,* carried daily headlines documenting the sweeping spread: "Koforidua Farmers Support Federation," "Ex-Servicemen Support Liberation Move," "850 CPP Cards Given Up in Manso," "CPP Assemblyman Booed and Mobbed," "Krobo Edusei's Family Head Joins Liberation," "Villagers Boo CPP Gov't.," "Ashantis Now Awake From Slumber . . . "[1] Only three days after the inauguration, 5,000 enrollment forms had been issued. By the end of the month, the number had climbed to 9,000, and early in October, General Secretary Kusi Ampofu boasted that over 20,000 had enrolled in the Movement.[2] Local branches were inaugurated daily, both within Kumase and in outlying towns and villages.[3] The Movement leadership claimed that sixty such branches were operational by early October.[4]

The first weeks of building branches and raising flags elicited no official response from either the CPP or the colonial government in Accra. However, from the offices of political groups in opposition to the CPP and from the chiefly confines of Manhyia in Kumase, individuals watched with enthusiasm the rapid developments taking place on the streets and in the meeting halls of Asante. Many political parties, including the MAP, TC, GCP, and NPP, were contacted by the Movement leadership prior to the inauguration and informed of its "Aims and Objects." Many came forward in the days surrounding the inauguration to endorse officially what there was of a Movement platform: the demand for a higher cocoa price and the call for a federal government for the Gold Coast. The day before the inauguration, MAP leader Bankole Awooner-Renner spoke to a large crowd in Kumase, declaring that the new Movement had the full support of his party: "[T]he Kotokos had now arisen to join Islam to fight the common foe. We want to assure the Kotokos that whether it rains or snows, shines or otherwise, we shall stand firmly by your side. We give you that as our pledge."[5] The following day, the TC sent a telegram to Bafuor Akoto wishing him success and stating that the "present situation fully justifies and demands a move in order to re-establish and reconstitute Ashanti National integrity and save the Gold Coast from Kwame Nkrumah's Communist dictatorial Police State. The Congress support morally the Movement 100 percent."[6]

The most enthusiastic support, however, came from the ranks of the GCP. Many of its members, including B. D. Addai and N. B. Abubekr, assumed instrumental roles in the weeks of organizing and planning prior to the inauguration, though still officially in the GCP. On September 19, these men, as well as H. R. Annan (Regional Chairman of the GCP), and Nancy and John Tsiboe (publishers of the *Pioneer* and GCP stalwarts), were among the prominent citizens to attend the inaugural rally at the Subin Valley.[7] But support for the NLM was not limited to Asante members of the GCP. On the very day of the inauguration, with many of his supporters observing the festivities in Kumase, Nii Amaa Ollennu, leader of the GCP, addressed a large gathering in Manya Krobo, where he announced that he was "in sympathy with the events which led the Ashantis to demand a federal system of Government. . . . [T]he CPP Ministers were so full of conceit and their self importance . . . , like dictators, they completely disregarded any local sentiments."[8]

A week later, the GCP's most prominent member, Dr. K. A. Busia, veteran Gold Coast politician and head of the Department of Sociology at the University College of the Gold Coast, arrived in Kumase to deliver a speech, "What Is Federal Government?"[9] in which he sought to lend political and academic substance to the NLM's call for federation:

The case of the farmers was a genuine one. The originators of the idea of federation were not wrong to point at the economic question and link it with their desire to form a federal government. It was the way the Government was using the farmers' money which angered the people and they felt that if they had a federal form of government the Caesars who collected the taxes would listen to the voice of the taxpayers.

. . . Economic causes were the underlying causes of all federal constitutions, the idea being that the Central Government would not become so powerful as to override the federal or regional considerations of the other states forming the union.[10]

In the GCP, the NLM acquired an early ally prepared to offer veteran political know-how and a few doses of political theorizing.

While the first weeks brought the NLM a host of endorsements from a variety of opposition groups in the Gold Coast, they also witnessed the increased participation of chiefs, first on an individual level, then on an organized basis, in the day-to-day activities of the Movement. Many chiefs were no longer willing to observe the political activity taking place outside the *ahemfie* and began to press for a direct role in the Liberation Movement. Though chiefs in the Kumase State Council and the Asanteman Council did not endorse the Movement until mid-October, there were several indications both during and immediately following the inauguration that support was forthcoming. Several of Kumase's *asomfo* chiefs assumed prominent roles in the first days of the NLM.[11] Nana Antwi Buasiako, the Nkofehene,[12] worked closely with Bafuor Akoto from the very inception of the Movement. Described by Austin as a "young, energetic educated Kumasi sub-chief," Buasiako was elected the National Organizing Secretary of the NLM during the heated meetings prior to the inauguration and claims responsibility for both designing the NLM flag and popularizing the NLM's hand greeting—the right hand raised in a fist with all fingers clenched except the middle and index.[13] The Kronkohene, Nana Kwabena Amoo, made a public display of his support for the NLM when, at the inauguration, he announced he had purchased an £800 van for the Movement and donated £200 to assist in propaganda work.[14] These *ahemfo* (chiefs)—the first to assume activist roles in the NLM's struggle—were not Asante's most powerful chiefs. As *asomfo*, they were dependent on the Asantehene for their position; their stools were not hereditary. Nonetheless, they wielded considerable influence over the Asantehene and his divisional chiefs within Kumase.

They, like Akoto—a palace functionary, himself—would pave the way for the entrance of the "big" chiefs into the Movement's struggle.

The day following the inauguration, Bafuor Akoto officially announced the NLM to the chiefs of the Kumase State Council, declaring that the youngmen and the farmers had come together "to fight the farmers' cause, for the nation, and to restore the respect and dignity of chiefs and elders."[15] Not only had the youngmen risen to defend the oppressed cocoa farmer, Akoto argued, but now they were prepared to stand as the vanguard in the chief's struggle to maintain power and authority in the face of Nkrumah's centralized state. Although the chiefs were as yet unwilling or unable to give the Movement their official endorsement,[16] their response to Akoto's speech was positive. As the *Pioneer* reported, "The Gyasehene, Nana Kwasi Adu-Bofuor, welcomed the Movement. He said since every chief was more or less a farmer they should accept and support the movement. Mr. I. K. Agyeman, Senior Secretary, said there was not a single soul who was not a farmer. They should therefore thank God and support the Movement wholeheartedly and ask for God's blessing upon it. Mr. Agyeman's speech was greeted with deafening cheers and the Ashanti war cry by the crowd." The meeting ended with shouts of "Federation, Federation!" and all, "including the chiefs and elders raised their two fore fingers . . . in recognition of the Movement."[17] Only twenty-four hours after the inauguration, Kumase's divisional chiefs offered the NLM their enthusiastic recognition, if not their official endorsement.

Not until mid-October did the NLM make formal overtures to the Asanteman Council, the supreme body of the *Asanteman*. However, as early as September 23, there was every indication that the Council sensed the direction political winds were blowing in Asante and was prepared to take some limited action in support of the Movement. Acting upon an appeal made by the Asante Farmers' Union, the Asanteman Council forwarded a resolution to the government asking that it reconsider "its decision regarding the price of cocoa in view of its economic implications and the tension it has created in the whole country," that the Cocoa Ordinance of August be repealed, and that farmers be allowed "to nominate their own representatives [to the Cocoa Marketing Board]."[18] That the Council's first response to the NLM was a tempered one (compared to that of the Kumase State Council) may reflect "the historic polarity," as McCaskie argues, "between Kumase and non-Kumase office holders," a suspicion on the part of some *amanhene* that the Kumase chiefs would use the Movement to reassert authority over the outlying *aman*.[19] Nonetheless, the resolution did reveal a willingness on the part of the Council's majority to take up the economic demands of the Liberation Movement, if not, initially, its political demand for Asante self-determination.

Thus, in the three weeks following the inauguration of the NLM, the youngmen scored a series of important victories. Membership in the new Movement was growing dramatically. Local branches were springing up throughout the region, providing the foundation for a mass organizational structure. Words of encouragement and endorsements were streaming in from other opposition political groups, and many veterans of the earlier nationalist struggle—UGCC and CPP, alike—had cast in their lot with the NLM. Several chiefs had become actively involved in the leadership of the Movement, thus lending it a degree of traditional legitimacy previously lacking. Finally, there were concrete indications that the Kumase State Council and, to a lesser extent, the Asanteman Council were sympathetic to the new Movement. Everything appeared to be falling quite rapidly into place.

Yet appearances can be deceiving; the Movement still lacked direction. While the single issue of the cocoa price was straightforward, the Movement's broadening agenda, which now included Asante autonomy and the structure of postindependence government, was ill-defined. There was talk of federation, of a movement to save the entire Gold Coast from what was characterized as CPP dictatorship; there was talk of separation, of a movement to liberate the historic Asante kingdom. And while everyone denied that the NLM was a political party, membership cards were being issued, and NLM flags raised on the former flagstaffs of the CPP. Though supporters boasted of a strong Executive Committee, with the exception of a few titled positions, it remained a loosely knit group of youngmen, farmers, intellectuals, and chiefs—whoever happened to attend a particular meeting. Such inconsistencies and ambiguities are not surprising considering the newness of the Movement, its broad and diverse base of support, and its rapid rate of growth. Yet there was no indication in those early weeks that the leadership was capable of addressing the Movement's obvious weaknesses. There was no indication that the glue which bound together the popular front in the early days could withstand the strain of a sustained struggle against the CPP.

Three weeks after the inauguration, an event occurred in the

Asante New Town section of Kumase which propelled the leadership of the NLM, ready or not, onto the next stage of struggle. It forced the leadership to grapple with strategy, consistent and coherent propaganda, and the need for a firm organizational structure. It brought the chiefs of the Kumase State Council and the Asanteman Council out of their safe seclusion and into the Movement's storm. It drove thousands of new recruits into the Movement, challenging the fence-sitters to take a stand and thereby transforming the NLM into the leading opposition force in the Gold Coast. It forced Nkrumah and the CPP, as well as the colonial government, to sit up and take notice. And, finally, it forecast a political climate of bombings, murders, and street violence which would plague Asante for the next three years.

The Murder of E. Y. Baffoe

On October 9, 1954, Emmanuel Yaw Baffoe, propaganda secretary of the National Liberation Movement, was stabbed to death by the CPP's regional propaganda secretary, Twumasi-Ankrah. The two political activists had long been comrades, working together in the AYA and the CPP prior to the 1954 election. According to several accounts, on the day of the murder Twumasi-Ankrah appeared at the NLM central office in Kumase—an office which stood adjacent to the CPP's Asante headquarters.[20] Many reports suggest that he had been drinking that day. In what was apparently a fit of rage, Twumasi-Ankrah began to tear apart the NLM office, overturning tables and smashing a typewriter. He then went outside to dismantle the NLM's flagpole. The Movement's office staff immediately went to locate E. Y. Baffoe to inform him of the actions of his close friend. Baffoe immediately went in search of Twumasi-Ankrah and finally located him at the Asante New Town house of Yaw Asamoah, a staunch CPP supporter. It is not clear what transpired inside Asamoah's house when Baffoe confronted Twumasi-Ankrah. A few moments later, the crowd which had gathered outside heard Baffoe shout, "Twumasi is killing me!"[21] When the police arrived, they found Baffoe lying on the ground, near death, and Twumasi-Ankrah standing nearby with a dagger in his hand. The police immediately placed Twumasi-Ankrah under arrest, but were unable to get Baffoe to the hospital in time. He died en route.[22]

With the murder of Baffoe, the NLM, and the Gold Coast generally, lost a dynamic political activist. Born in the Nkoranza District in

1925, Baffoe had a brief but impressive career as an organizer and propagandist. As early as 1945, he was dismissed from Adisadel College for helping to organize a student strike. Later he became the CFAO Employees' Union Secretary and was imprisoned for seven months following the Positive Action campaign for inciting workers to strike. After 1951, he became the CPP's regional propaganda secretary and was appointed a member of the Cocoa Marketing Board and Director of the Cocoa Purchasing Company. However, Baffoe's active membership in the CPP ended in 1954 when the party refused to endorse his candidacy for the Legislative Assembly. Baffoe opted to run as a rebel independent for the seat in Wenkyi East and was promptly expelled from the CPP and removed from his positions with the CMB and the CPC.[23] A sense of frustration with the CPP and certain of its policies probably precipitated Baffoe's complete break with the party. Nkrumah's direct appointing of candidates for the election and the CPP's controversial, if not spurious, relationship with the CPC—the inner workings of which Baffoe knew well—must have played some role in compelling him to work as actively against Nkrumah's party as he had for it. He was one of the first to organize the farmers against the frozen cocoa price and served as one of the Movement's founders and most eloquent spokespersons.

Though the events surrounding Baffoe's murder remain clouded and though Twumasi-Ankrah's motives for taking the life of one of his closest friends will probably never be known, the NLM leadership was prepared to view Baffoe's murder as a direct assault on the Movement, as an indisputable case of political assassination. As a former member of the CMB and as director of the CPC, Baffoe had direct access to potentially incriminating information concerning the CPP's relationship to the purchasing company. Many believed he was murdered for what he knew. Indeed, only three days before his murder, Baffoe gave a ninety-minute speech in Nkawie which detailed his charges of rampant corruption within the two cocoa bodies.[24] As a colonial government "Security Appreciation" reported, "Baffoe knew, and has listed, the Ashantis who have given and received money from the CPC—commonly regarded as gong money—and many suppose that he was killed by direct orders of the Prime Minister."[25] Moreover, the fact that Twumasi-Ankrah had recently been in Accra led many to suspect that Baffoe's murder was planned and directed from CPP headquarters. Among those sharing this concern were members of the colonial government's Local Intelligence Committee. In a secret and confidential letter to the Colonial Office, Deputy Governor Hadow reported that local intelligence had obtained evidence that Twumasi-Ankrah and Yaw Asamoah visited Accra the first week of October and met privately with Nkrumah, Botsio, and Baako at CPP headquarters the day before the murder.[26] In short, suspicions were aroused in every corner, and the NLM had its first political martyr.

As news of Baffoe's death swept through Kumase, spontaneous demonstrations erupted everywhere. Infuriated mobs marched through the city, forcing the police to post guards to protect many potential targets, including the homes of Krobo Edusei and Joseph Mainoo (assistant manager of the CPC) and the offices of the CPP and its newspaper, the *Sentinel*.[27] All CPP propaganda vans were taken off the streets out of fear that further rioting would be provoked. During the first forty-eight hours after the murder, the NLM leadership did nothing to calm the mobs roaming through Kumase. Rather, inspired by the popular movement taking place on the streets, they issued further calls to action. As one NLM leaflet beckoned,

Awake
All yea sons and daughters of
the Great Ashanti Nation built
with Blood by King Ossei
Tutu and Okomfo Anokye
The Spirit of our Great Queen Yaa Asantewa
Calls you to ACTION
The Quills of the Ashanti Porcupine are erect whilst we are being slained in cold blood.
There is woe, there is danger, there is BLOOD, BLOOD, BLOOD everywhere. We are doomed if we do not awake to fight, bribery and corruption, disrespect, hooliganism, mock-burials and threat of Dictatorship and Communism which are brewing in the country.
Alleged mass arrest of Liberation Leaders and state of emergency cannot deter us.
We are a Nation, a Selfgoverning Nation already. We are resolute and unless we perish there will never be a second exile of our Golden Stool.

We are not yet distant from the Mother of Parliaments.
Emmanuel Yaw Baffoe is dead but
his soul goes marching on to
FEDERATION.
No. 10 Downing Street is CLEAR
The doors of the Buckingham are OPEN
AWAKE! AWAKE!!
AWAKE!!![28]

On the morning of October 11, the tension continued to build. Cars were firebombed and CPP supporters assaulted. Even the offices of the *Daily Graphic* were invaded by a mob of angry demonstrators apparently on the grounds that the newspaper had published an "exceptionally small" photograph of the NLM's inaugural rally.[29] Baffoe's death served to unleash the frustrations of many; it was a powerful catalyst for mass mobilization and action. As a result of the nearly ungovernable state of Kumase and its surrounding villages, the government announced less than forty-eight hours after Baffoe's murder that it had suspended the issuing of permits for any processions or public meetings.

While the government's ban went some distance toward curbing the violence in Kumase, it did not extinguish the Movement's advancing flames.[30] The ramifications of Baffoe's murder were not so easily smothered. As one colonial security memorandum lamented, "Now there is a martyr! The dangers of the situation are increased."[31] In fact, the day the ban on public gatherings was issued, the NLM received the first in a series of boosts to its morale and its membership. Bafuor Akoto appeared before the Kumase State Council and requested that the chiefs give the NLM their official endorsement. After an enthusiastic discussion of the "Aims and Objects of the Movement," the Council voted to support openly the NLM and sealed their vow of support with the swearing of the Great Oath of Asante. After the oath, members voted to inform the Asanteman Council of the events which led to the death of Baffoe and request its full support of the Movement. Finally, the chiefs decided that "the sum of not more than £20,000 be drawn . . . from the Asantehene's New Palace Building Fund for the support of this National Movement."[32] According to one report, the chiefs said they had decided to support the NLM because, "it was not a political party but a National Movement which aimed at eradicating all manner of evil practices and cheating from the country."[33]

The Kumase State Council's description of the NLM as a "movement" and not a "political party" was significant. The Local Council and State Council Ordinances of 1951 and 1952 and the 1954 Constitution (which eliminated Asanteman Council representation in the Legislative Assembly) had curtailed the political activities of the chiefs. There was now a line between the customary realm and the national political arena.[34] For chiefs to dabble in national politics was considered an abuse of sacred power which would "undermine the whole fabric of democracy."[35] But Akoto was able to convince the chiefs that the NLM was a national movement, which, like the chiefs themselves, stood above party politics. Thus assured by Akoto's remarks and spurred to action by the murder of Baffoe, the Kumase chiefs finally decided to take an official stand. As a result of their public announcement of support, a local district officer reported, "the prestige and influence of the State Council is undoubtedly greater at the moment than it has been for a long time."[36]

The Executive Committee of the NLM, now listing among its members Bantamahene Nana Kwaku Gyawu II (acting president of the Kumase State Council), cabled Secretary of State A. T. Lennox-Boyd the day after the Council's endorsement and urged him to appoint a royal commission to investigate charges of bribery and corruption against the CPP government. It specifically asked that the Cocoa Purchasing Company be examined, as well as the causes leading to the death of E. Y. Baffoe. The cable concluded with this message: "The Gold Coast National Liberation Movement presently consisting of the chiefs and people of Ashanti has lost all confidence in the Gold Coast Government and its Prime Minister, Mr. Kwame Nkrumah."[37] Thus, the Kumase chiefs, only three days after Baffoe's murder, were brought straight into the Movement's vanguard, where their customary legitimacy put weight behind the first in a long series of appeals to the colonial government.[38]

Official support for the NLM among chiefs was not limited to Kumase alone. On October 18, the day after Baffoe's funeral, Dwabenhene Nana Yaw Sapong II issued a strong statement declaring himself "a strong supporter and strong advocate of Ashanti old and new federation."[39] Following closely on the Dwabenhene's statement, which made headlines in Asante, came the news that the Asanteman Council would meet in an emergency session to decide its position on the NLM. Before the meeting, the NLM deluged the Council with letters, memoranda, and telegrams requesting full support for the Movement. The official memorandum to the Council, in a broad appeal that spanned issues from cocoa to the threat of communism, stated:

> We learnt with gratification the decision you took over the cocoa issue at your last meeting. Our appeal to you now is to help in the campaign against the larger issue, namely the stamping out of dictatorship and communistic practices from the land which your predecessors have left in your care. For the preservation of our noble institutions, in the cause of democracy and good neighbourliness and in the name of countless of your disillusioned subjects and your grandson and our comrade who has laid down his life for this crusade, we appeal for your support.[40]

In a private letter, General Secretary Ampofu urged the chiefs to "help us combat the evil which tends to threaten our civic rights and liberties, destroy our tradition and culture and plung [*sic*] us into a state of perpetual slavery."[41] As representatives of a variety of groups, several youngmen sent telegrams to the Council denouncing the CPP and declaring their support for the NLM. The telegrams were meant to give the impression that a number of independent organizations in Asante had already declared their support for the Movement. However, with the exception of the telegram from Frank Tawiah, general secretary of the AYA, all of the telegrams were issued by front or auxiliary groups founded by NLM activists in early October.[42]

At the October 19 meeting, after the letters, memoranda, and wires were read aloud, the Council permitted its members to voice their individual opinions on the NLM. Some of the paramount chiefs, including the Mamponhene, declined to express an opinion until they could confer with their respective state councils. Others, however, offered passionate words in support of the NLM. As the *Pioneer* reported, "Essumejahene said the day was a great and historic [one] which would be long remembered in the annals of the nation. He had said before that a time would come when the people would realise that they were not going right and that time had now come. Ejisuhene was cheered when he rose to speak. He swore the Great Oath to support the Movement. He said the present Government had cheated them long enough."[43] Because several of the *amanhene* were not present at the meeting and because others needed time to confer with their councils, the Asantehene adjourned the Asanteman Council for two days.

At the subsequent meeting, the Asanteman Council voted overwhelmingly to give the National Liberation Movement its full support.[44] A nine-man committee immediately drafted a resolution, to be forwarded to the Queen, which affirmed the Council's support for the NLM and appealed for the setting up of a royal commission to examine the question of a federal form of government for the Gold Coast: "Our advocacy of a federal set-up is a long standing one and although it has been quickened by the demand of the Liberation Movement, it has not originally inspired it as is borne out by the several statements we have from time to time made to Government on Regional Administration. It must also be remembered that the traditional constitution of Ashanti is federal in nature."[45] Both the vote and the resolution were fully endorsed by Asantehene Nana Prempe II, who declared that support "must mean real efforts and sacrifices to make the Move succeed. Ashanti knows no retreat."[46] However, he carefully prefaced his endorsement by letting the youngmen know he was still wary of their motives and would be watching them closely. "Otumfuo solemnly recalled," wrote one observer,

> the vilification, abuses and insults levelled against him by the youth when the Self-Government wave started. They all know how these self-same youth accused him of having sold Lake Bosumtwi, for having ordered or taken bribe for the cutting out of the swollen shoot infected trees . . . how these self-same youth raised a hue and cry when he had wanted to visit the United Kingdom and the connivance of these self-same youth by the CPP leaders. . . .
>
> The youth formed the majority. They had brought about all the changes and today the self-same youth had brought about the National Liberation Movement. Why should he (Otumfuo) be forced to "come out with a statement"? That, he lamented, showed disrespect. It was an insult, disgrace and shame.[47]

The Asantehene's endorsement of the NLM constituted a major political victory for the youngmen, yet the charges he leveled against them revealed deep-seated suspicions, if not outright hostility. They stood as an early indication that long-standing conflicts could not be swept permanently away by appeals to the Golden Stool or by the resurrection of *Asante Kotoko*.

However, as October drew to a close, most conflicts remained buried. The murder of Baffoe and the subsequent endorsements by the Kumase State and Asanteman Councils led to dramatic growth in the Movement as Asantes responded to declarations that "The spirits of your great and noble ancestors call you to action."[48] While a *Pioneer* headline announced that "Baffoe's Death Steps Up Liberation's Support," the Movement's general secretary reported that the death of Baffoe had more than doubled the strength of the Movement, marking "a new era in the ever increasing agitation for a federal system of Government for the Gold Coast."[49]

The dramatic increase in membership was directly tied to the youngmen's ability to cast the struggle as an Asante national struggle which transcended party politics. It was no longer a question of whether one was pro-CPP or anti-CPP. It was a question of history and Asante national heritage: were you a true and loyal subject of the Golden Stool? As General Secretary Ampofu explained, "Baffoe's death had sown the true spirit of nationalism in and reminded Ashantis of their past glorious history to press for building their nation anew." He concluded, "Let them stab us, stone us and dynamite our houses and even reduce our numbers but they must realize that when Asante Kotoko is wiped out a thousand more will come to take their place."[50] NLM leaflets and newspaper editorials echoed Ampofu's sentiments: the nation was being attacked; it must now respond. B. K. Ofori, writing from Accra, reminded all that "our ancestors fought and spilled their dear blood to crystallise this Ashanti of which we are so proud. . . . It is for us, Ashanti nationalists today to protect and defend those precious things that our ancestors have handed down to us. It is for us to stand upright and save the Ashanti nation. . . . Baffoe's death should not be in vain. He has followed the footsteps of King Osei Tutu."[51] Before Baffoe's murder, the youngmen rallied support against the CPP around specific issues—the price of cocoa and a federal system of government. With the making of a political martyr, issues and grievances crystallized around Asante nationalism. And to the resurrected *Kotoko,* Asantes flocked by the thousands.

The NLM was now prepared to take the offensive—both on and off the streets. Shortly after Baffoe's murder, Sam Boateng, Frank Tawiah, and Kwaku Danso organized the NLM Action Groupers—a semiclandestine group of liberation soldiers.[52] Long before the advent of the NLM, Nkrumah had formed the CPP Action Troopers. Now the NLM created its own paramilitary wing to be the Movement's vanguard, offensively and defensively, in the political battles being waged in the streets of Asante.

According to Boateng's recollections, the purpose of the Groupers "was quite simple—defense, most importantly to protect our demonstrations from being attacked by the CPP."[53] While defense, as a result of the murder of Baffoe, may have been one of the aims of the new organization, offensive maneuvers were on the agenda. The Groupers rapidly became organizers of direct action against members of the CPP. In establishing the Action Groupers, the leadership hoped to gain control over the NLM rank-and-file by providing a structure for waging street battles. At the same time, it hoped to force CPP supporters into the closet or out of the region entirely, leaving Asante united under the banner of "cocoa and *kotoko*."

Membership in the Action Groupers was drawn from a variety of sources. While many were, as Boateng claimed, "the energetic youth among the NLM,"[54] others were recruited from the Zongo (stranger) community in Kumase. They were not Asante but rather Zabarima, Mamprussi, Frafra, or Hausa. While it is true that these recruits were paid for their services—either with money or with food and clothing as recompense—they were not simply soldiers of fortune hired to fight the NLM's battles. Most of the Zongo recruits to the Action Groupers were energetic supporters of the Muslim Association Party, and many had served in the Zongo Volunteers.[55] It was in the context of the Action Groupers that the close bond between the MAP and the NLM was cultivated and nurtured. Together, they hoped to eliminate the CPP presence in Asante.

If Baffoe's murder served as the pretext for organizing the NLM's paramilitary wing, it also gave the NLM the publicity and legitimacy necessary to call for the first successful meeting of all opposition political parties in the Gold Coast. Prior to 1954, the vast array of political opposition groups in the Gold Coast had struggled as much amongst themselves as they had against Nkrumah and the CPP. Baffoe's murder brought the NLM to prominence and, seizing the opportunity, the Movement invited all of the major opposition groups to a round-table conference on the prospects for federation in the Gold Coast. On October 24, leaders of the GCP, TC, GNP, and MAP met in Kumase and declared their unflinching support for the federation demand of the NLM and stated their desire to meet again in the not-too-distant future.[56]

It is difficult to overemphasize the ramifications of Baffoe's murder.

Twumasi-Ankrah had set the stage: the quills of *Asante Kotoko* now stood erect. With the making of the NLM's first political martyr, the struggle of the NLM became the struggle of the sons and daughters of the Golden Stool. The Kumase State Council and the Asanteman Council could not afford to remain silent when one of their own sons lay dead—the first casualty of the new struggle. It was now clear that much of that struggle would be waged on the streets of Asante, not in the halls of parliament, and that no opposition party would be able to act independently of the NLM. From a few disgruntled cries over the frozen cocoa price, the Movement had exploded into a full-blown Asante nationalist opposition prepared to avenge the death of its first political martyr.

The CPP and the Colonial Government React

While the NLM rode the wave of support generated by the murder of Baffoe, the government in Accra finally decided it was time to react. From mid-October until the end of the year, leaders of the CPP government and top colonial authorities worked hand-in-hand in an attempt to quietly douse the flames of opposition in Asante. After the murder of Baffoe, they realized that some action by the government, beyond the ban on public meetings, was required. Just what that action should be remained an open question. They did not want to react in any way that would lend credence to the allegations of the NLM or would imply that issues like the cocoa price or federal constitution were open to debate at this late date. At the same time, they did not want to add to what was already a nearly ungovernable situation in Kumase.

Nkrumah and the CPP were in the international spotlight as participants in the great experiment of internal self-rule. They could not afford to have their hegemony called into question at this late date. The colonial authorities in Accra, most notably Governor Charles Arden-Clarke, were equally committed to the present constitution and what had been the very orderly progress, since 1951, toward self-government under British tutelage. As a former regional officer in Asante lamented, Arden-Clarke's sole consideration seemed to be, "Are we getting on towards self-government, are we building up Nkrumah, is everything going all right in that direction?"[57] In a November dispatch to the secretary of state for the colonies, Arden-Clarke admitted that the government's "desire to concentrate power at the centre" and its "apprehension of 'tribalism' " may have inhibited it from "consulting regional and local interests in adequate measure." Yet he assured the secretary that he would "continue to work for the recognition of regional interests by the Government." He could not, however, support the idea of federation.[58] Thus, there was some consensus in Accra between colonial authorities and the CPP on how to respond to events in Asante. There must be reaction, but not overreaction, quiet, reasoned negotiation, but minimal compromise.

In line with the government's intent to react, but react discreetly, four CPP government ministers—Archibald Casely-Hayford, Edward Asafu-Adjaye, Kojo Botsio and K. A. Gbedemah—wrote to Bafuor Akoto in mid-October inviting him and other members of the NLM Executive Committee to a meeting in Accra to discuss the unrest in Asante. "The Ministers appealed to Bafuor Osei Akoto," reported the *Pioneer,* "that they as leaders of the Convention People's Party and 'citizens' of the Gold Coast would like to settle the dispute with them."[59] Perhaps by issuing the invitation as party members and "citizens" and by characterizing the crisis as a "dispute," the ministers hoped to avoid the impression that the situation in Kumase called for direct government intervention. But the NLM, at its highest peak of activity since the inauguration, responded from a position of strength. It had no intention of casually discussing the "dispute" on CPP terms, in the CPP stronghold of Accra. "You appear either to be under a misapprehension of the present situation in Ashanti," decried Akoto in his response to the invitation, "or to underestimate its seriousness. . . . What you term our 'grievances' involve fundamental and serious disapproval of the policies and activities of the present Government. To discuss such a situation on the level you suggest, namely discussion between you as private citizens and leaders of the Convention People's Party and me and a few members of the National Liberation Movement can serve no useful purpose. The situation has grown beyond such attempts."[60] The CPP ministers struck a brick wall with their discreet invitation, the full text of which, along with Akoto's response, made front page news in Asante under the headline, "No Please, Akoto Tells CPP Leaders."

When the word spread in mid-October that the Kumase State Council and the Asanteman Council were planning to endorse the NLM, Nkrumah attempted a personal appeal to the Asantehene. On October 20, he sent a private letter to Nana Prempe II asking if he intended to give the NLM his support and, if so, did he realize that this would severely tarnish both his reputation as Asantehene and that of the Golden Stool.[61] The Asantehene responded succinctly to Nkrumah's inquiry two days after he had officially endorsed the NLM: "I wish to re-affirm my old stand that as the occupant of the Golden Stool I am above party politics."[62] The Asantehene could be a political actor in the NLM without, in his view, crossing the sacred divide between chiefly statesmanship and party allegiances because the struggle was between *Asante Kotoko* and the "evil practices and cheating" of Nkrumah and the CPP.[63]

On October 24, the very day the NLM called together all of the leaders of the major opposition forces in the Gold Coast and received their unflinching support in the struggle for federation, Nkrumah decided that, private appeals having failed, it was time to address publicly the crisis in Asante and reaffirm his position as the head of government. Before a large rally at the Accra Arena, Nkrumah described the NLM as "another attempt by imperialists and reactionary agents to bring together some chiefs and disgruntled opposition politicians to undermine the popular elected government."[64] He announced that the price of cocoa would not be raised and asked where the cries for federation were when the present constitution, which had been lawfully ratified, was being debated. Finally, in a dramatic move, he reported that the date for the granting of full self-government had been decided.[65] This announcement was meant to underscore the government's position that it was too late to consider the demands of the NLM. Independence was within arm's reach.

But the NLM was not convinced that a date had been set or that it was too late to initiate drastic changes in the structure of government. Rather than extinguishing the spreading flames of the Movement, Nkrumah's remarks at the arena seemed only to add fuel to the fire. Local branches continued to be inaugurated throughout Asante, expanding the Movement's organizational network to such major towns as Kokofu, Kumawu, Bekwae, and Edweso, while violence plagued the streets of Kumase. A week after Nkrumah's speech, three Kumase houses were the targets of bombings: C. E. Osei's (member of the Legislative Assembly for Asante New Town), Mary Akuamoah's (the wife of Krobo Edusei) and Archie Casely-Hayford's, (Nkrumah's minister of the interior).[66] Though two NLM Action Groupers were charged in connection with the bombings, they were later released because of lack of evidence.[67]

Nearly every CPP response in these early days only served to strengthen the popular front and to elicit more determined calls for Asante autonomy. In late October, the twenty-one CPP members of the Legislative Assembly for Asante, in a hastened effort to reaffirm their positions as the parliamentary spokesmen for Asante, wired the secretary of state for the colonies to assure him that they were the true representatives of Asante and that Asante did not want federation. The Asanteman Council's demands should be ignored.[68] Within Asante, this well-publicized telegram was greeted with defiance. At the numerous inaugural rallies throughout the region, the crowd's chanting of the Asante battle cry—"*Ogyao! Ogyao!*"—punctuated the rousing speeches of leaders like Akoto when he declared, "I will sacrifice my blood if need be for the salvation of the Ashanti nation."[69] In *Pioneer* editorials, NLM members let it be known who, in their eyes, were the true representatives of Asante: "The Asantehene is our King and his Council is our Native Parliament. Whether any totalitarian Government recognizes him or not, we shall give them our loyalty and service. Mr. Nkrumah should realize that by . . . the attitude of his supporters to Ashanti, we regard his party to have declared war on us. I must warn him that Asantehene is the nation and any attempt to insult him is regarded as highly questionable."[70]

Inflammatory responses like this only multiplied when the CPP's Twumasi-Ankrah, now on trial for the murder of Baffoe, announced during a court session that the Asantehene should be on guard—"if not, there was going to be a time when he would find his head in the streets being kicked like a football."[71] The Kumase State Council responded by ordering the slaughter of twelve sheep to protest the statement and to purge the Asante nation of such evil will. The slaughter not only underscored the new paramountcy of the Council in the Movement's struggle, but served to bolster the unity and fury of the NLM as a whole. By mid-November, tension and violence were at a peak, and the ban on public rallies was still in effect for thirty-one Asante towns. Nkrumah's words rang hollow when he publicly denied the need for any enquiry into the situation in Asante.[72]

What might be called CPP "Plan A"—an attempt to quietly reason with the leadership of the Movement—had failed. "Plan B"—to publicly reaffirm control of the government and deny both the existence of a crisis in Asante and the legitimacy of any NLM claims—had also failed. Clearly, a new strategy had to be devised to cope with the virtually ungovernable situation in Asante. It was at this critical juncture that Governor Arden-Clarke assumed an active role. Perhaps alarmed that the more inflammatory speeches made by CPP spokesmen might lead to a further deterioration in relations with Asante, the governor (at Nkrumah's invitation) met with the prime minister and members of his Cabinet. As he later informed the secretary of state for the colonies, he "talked . . . on the need to govern by persuasion and consent, not by coercion and force."[73]

While Arden-Clarke agreed with Nkrumah and his Cabinet that the commission of enquiry demanded by the Asanteman Council was not justified, he believed that the government had to assume a negotiating stance. But before the stage could be set, the NLM and the Asanteman Council must be made to understand that colonial officials expected the opposition to negotiate directly with the CPP government. Toward this end, Arden-Clarke sent a dispatch to the secretary of state in which he recommended that the Colonial Office respond to the Asanteman Council's resolution by asserting it was not appropriate that a commission be established. He further recommended that the Asanteman Council be informed that

> the lines on which the Gold Coast has been proceeding towards independence are indicated in the Constitutions of 1950 and 1954 and the success with which the Gold Coast has operated these non-federal Constitutions has enabled Her Majesty's Government in the United Kingdom to agree that the Gold Coast has now reached the last stage before independence . . . if, after achieving independent status, the people of the Gold Coast consider that there is a case for adopting the federal expedient, it would, of course, be open to them to commit this question to a constituent assembly or other appropriate body.

It was essential, Arden-Clarke concluded, that the government, "and all political parties and movements . . . be able to resolve the present and any future differences that arise between them in a statesman-like manner."[74]

The Colonial Office having been briefed on an appropriate response to the Asanteman Council's resolution, the governor held an informal meeting on November 26 between colonial officials and CPP leaders. There he suggested that representatives of the Asanteman Council and the NLM be officially invited by the prime minister to a meeting in Accra. Nkrumah agreed and it was decided that four members of the NLM and four representatives of the Council would be asked to attend. The chief regional officer for Asante, A. J. Loveridge, added that before the meeting took place he would advise Akoto to "publish a satisfactory statement on the attitude of the National Liberation Movement toward violence."[75] As planned, the invitation to a round-table conference in Accra was issued by Nkrumah on December 4, with the meeting scheduled for the following week.[76] In the invitation, Nkrumah stressed that he envisioned the session as an opportunity both to explain his "intention regarding further constitutional and administrative development" and to remove "the present misunderstandings as to what should be the proper relationship between Regional interests and Central Government."[77] In a dispatch to the Colonial Office, Arden-Clarke expressed optimism that the meeting would "enable a public statement to be made which will show that the Government is ready to work out, in consultation with Regions, a proper relationship between them and the Government at the Centre."[78]

Perhaps because of the wave of appeals made directly to the secretary of state by both the CPP and the NLM, colonial officials, from Arden-Clarke in Accra to Loveridge in Kumase, were now prepared to assume more active roles in resolving the crisis. But a more active role did not necessarily mean a more visible role. This is perhaps best revealed in a private letter from the governor to his family:

> The Ashantis, who are nearly as difficult and unruly as the Scots once were, have suddenly decided that they don't like the present Government, want Home Rule for Ashanti, and are vociferously demanding a Federal Constitution. . . . The last thing I want to do is to intervene openly so soon after the new Constitution. . . . Open intervention on my part would amount to an admission of failure to work the new Constitution. This latest Constitution is more difficult to work than the last, as it involves government by remote control instead of, as before, telling the Cabinet what to do at their weekly meetings and then seeing that they did it.[79]

Arden-Clarke clearly felt a personal stake in the success or failure of the new constitution. Though he could not assume a direct role in the negotiations with the NLM without undermining the legitimacy of Nkrumah's government, he insisted on a prominent role behind the scenes. There could be no admission of failure.

Since 1951 and the assumption of power by Nkrumah and the CPP following Positive Action, Arden-Clarke was committed to a specific blueprint for the transition to independence. He made the decision then to work with Nkrumah, to uphold the CPP's legitimacy as the ruling party and, in time, to walk shoulder-to-shoulder with Nkrumah toward full self-government. It was his mission. His stake became personal and paternal. As early as April 1951, Arden-Clarke wrote the Colonial Office explaining his decision to release the remainder of the political prisoners taken after the Positive Action campaign on the grounds that their "continued imprisonment . . . is seriously weakening the position of the CPP leaders and especially of Nkrumah, himself . . . [whose government] is presently trying to be reasonable and moderate in its conduct of affairs." No obstacle must block Nkrumah and his ministers' "genuine effort to work the new constitution."[80]

In many meetings, Arden-Clarke betrayed his personal feelings of responsibility for the orderly progress made since Nkrumah had assumed office under his tutelage:

> The progress in responsible government achieved since the CPP assumed power should be measured not merely by positive developments but by the many pitfalls which had been avoided. The very acceptance of office by leaders who had won the election by their attacks on the Constitution was itself a great step forward. The continuance in office of these leaders for ten months, during which they had gained much valuable insight into the methods of sober, democratic government and some realization of the administrative difficulties which had constantly to be overcome . . . marked the beginning of responsible, popular government in the country.[81]

In Arden-Clarke's eyes, it was a "responsible government" for which he was, to a large degree, personally responsible.

Joe Appiah, former CPP stalwart who joined forces with the NLM early in 1955, recalled of Arden-Clarke in his *Autobiography* that "this man with a tough reputation for dealing with tough situations suddenly realized that events were moving too fast toward the inevitable end of colonialism . . . and his own period of service. So he decided to ride with the glorious tide and thereby enhance his own reputation by ending his career as governor-general rather than as an ordinary governor of a little colony . . . [he] shut his eyes to wrongs that in earlier days he would have visited with a vengeance all his own."[82] Appiah's assessment was shared by others. In the last years of colonial rule, some British officials would charge Arden-Clarke with losing all objectivity when it came to the CPP government. In a report to London, one Commonwealth Relations Office representative accused the governor of withholding from the Colonial Office potentially damning information about the CPP. "The days when Governors on the Guinea Coast lived in slave castles, and did not correspond with the Colonial Office for six months at a time, seem very close here."[83]

In his belief that Nkrumah and the CPP represented the only logical and legitimate heirs to the colonial government, Arden-Clarke was far from alone. Many colonial officials in Accra were in full agreement and had maintained since 1951 that everything must be done to secure the power of Britain's heirs. "We are in many ways fortunate," declared a British colonial official,

> in having Nkrumah in his present position. He is intelligent, cooperative, courteous and friendly to Europeans, willing to listen to advice and (I believe) sincere. . . . In all the circumstances I feel that the right course now is to do what is possible to strengthen and consolidate his position in the Gold Coast, and by doing this we should, incidentally, make it clear beyond doubt that to a very large extent the responsibility for the conduct of internal affairs in the territory is firmly on African shoulders.[84]

In short, from 1951 on, many British officials, above all Governor Arden-Clarke, came to believe that Nkrumah and the CPP were the only possible partners in the great experiment of internal self-rule and that they themselves had an immediate, if not always personal, stake in that experiment. The events occurring behind the scenes as the colonial government and the CPP prepared to set up negotiations with the NLM can only be understood in light of these sentiments: personal loyalties were established, and the blueprint for full self-government was complete.

There was much surreptitious maneuvering as the CPP leaders and several colonial officials in Accra prepared for their meeting with the NLM. While the officials were intent on keeping a low profile in the negotiations, they nonetheless wanted to control access to vital information. There was some information to which colonial officials did not want to give Nkrumah access. Yet they thought the prime minister should be able to make certain disclosures if the crisis were to be resolved. On December 1, the secretary of state informed the governor that, despite his resolve that a royal commission—as demanded by the Asanteman Council and the NLM—was out of the question, he was not convinced "that it is desirable to say that HMG cannot contemplate any major changes in the constitution." The following day, Deputy Governor Hadow, in a letter to Arden-Clarke, strongly urged that Nkrumah should "not at this stage see the despatch."[85] There is, in fact, no indication that Nkrumah was made privy to the information in the dispatch in December, if at all. Hadow and Arden-Clarke believed that if Nkrumah were made aware of the secretary's sentiments, much of the confidence they had built up over the last three years would be undermined. Nkrumah must take his seat at the round-table conference convinced of the full support of the colonial government.

While Nkrumah was denied certain information prior to the scheduled meeting with the NLM, he was also deluged with other information officials felt it necessary that he master. In a December 9 letter, Deputy-Governor Hadow informed the governor that Nkrumah had been extensively briefed for the proposed meeting.[86] A copy of the brief given to Nkrumah, probably by Hadow, offered a step-by-step guide to conducting the meeting with the NLM – a guide which closely reflected the opinions of the governor as set out in his November dispatch to the Colonial Office.[87] If the Movement appeared intent on talking federation, the prime minister was to quote the Phillipson *Report*.[88] If Nigeria were cited the prime minister was to argue that Nigeria is much larger than the Gold Coast and has greater cultural diversity. If, however, it became apparent that the Movement only wanted some sort of regional devolution of powers, the prime minister was to build from there. Strategies were also outlined for handling questions concerning the CPC, the CMB, the date for independence, and the price of cocoa. Nkrumah's December 21 memorandum to his Cabinet on the positions to be taken at the proposed meeting suggests that Nkrumah was prepared to adopt the negotiating stance advocated by Arden-Clarke. Indeed, in word and spirit, it echoed both Hadow's brief and Arden-Clarke's dispatch to the Colonial Office.[89]

Although the sentiments of Arden-Clarke and Hadow were fairly representative of British colonial opinion in Accra, those of colonial officers throughout the Gold Coast were by no means homogeneous when it came to the crisis in Asante or the CPP's proposed negotiations with the NLM. Perhaps because they felt no personal stakes in the great experiment toward self-government, many of the government agents in Asante, including the chief regional officer, were less optimistic about the outcome of the meeting, believing that Accra officials had no appreciation of the gravity of the situation. Indeed, A. J. Loveridge, Asante's chief regional officer in 1954, believed that his public disdain for Nkrumah and the CPP actually encouraged the formation of the NLM:

> It may be that the National Liberation Movement . . . had been formed because I was coming back as Chief Commissioner. It was well known, I think, that I was not prepared to stomach what I regarded as the inequities of Nkrumah, and I had just come from the North—there was the Northern People's Party in the North that had been formed during my time and I got associated with the thing. . . . So, Nationalist Movements were reckoned red meat to Loveridge so it may have been the Ashanti people started their National Liberation Movement on the grounds that I would support it.[90]

Although there is no evidence that Loveridge's return precipitated the formation of the NLM, there is no doubt that his appreciation of the crisis far surpassed that of his counterparts in Accra and that his sympathies lay squarely with the Movement.

On December 8, Loveridge wrote to Hadow that he believed the CPP's December 4 invitation to the round-table conference would be accepted by the NLM and the Asanteman Council. However, he strongly cautioned, "there are deep roots to the Movement, perhaps best summarized by the phrase, 'fear of dictatorship'—a fear for which the cocoa price is held out as justification. The political aspects of the movement *might* be overcome by politics but the deep roots cannot be got rid of by politics. All this leads me to the point that the meeting *must be successful* and it cannot unless it is undertaken as an administrative exercise and not a political exercise."[91] In addition to underscoring the depth of Asante national sentiment, Loveridge's admonition echoed the arguments of Akoto and the Asantehene that the struggle transcended party politics. Loveridge had witnessed the battles on the streets of Kumase and knew that the Kumase State Council had agreed to give a substantial amount of money to the NLM. As far as he was concerned, "the NLM will be negotiating from strength."[92] But as he later recalled, his words of warning fell on deaf ears: "Arden-Clarke paid no heed whatsoever to the difficulties of administration. His sole consideration was, 'Are we getting on towards self-government?' . . . and that there were misappropriations of money, accidents of one sort and another involving the loss of life—all this sort of thing which I considered was essential—was simply overlooked by Arden-Clarke."[93]

That there was a high degree of tension between colonial officials in Accra and in Asante over the nature and magnitude of the crisis, that there were extensive briefings of the CPP by Accra officials after the invitation was issued, and that essential information was selectively withheld muddied the first efforts toward negotiation between the government and the Asante opposition. Would Nkrumah stick closely to the brief supplied by Hadow? Did some in the CPP have their own agenda for dealing with the Asante leaders? Would the officials in Accra heed Loveridge's warnings? All had to await word from the NLM and the Asanteman Council and none, not even the man-on-the-scene, Loveridge, fully appreciated the position of strength the NLM had now assumed and from which it was about to deal.

As news of the invitation swept through Asante, the *Pioneer* published a host of letters and editorials advising that Nkrumah's invitation be rejected. B. K. Ofori, an Accra supporter of the Movement, argued that since the NLM and the Council had both passed resolutions of nonconfidence in the government of Nkrumah, it would be hypocritical to turn around and negotiate.[94] The Edwesohene publicly advised that the invitation be rejected, and General Secretary Ampofu, though admitting no decision had been reached on the invitation, remarked, "The invitation is ill-timed and belated. The Prime Minister has refused to admit there is tension in Ashanti. He has discredited the people to whom he has now extended the invitation as an 'irresponsible minority of disgruntled elements.' "[95] Though public sentiment appeared to be against meeting with Nkrumah, there was no official word from either the NLM or the Asanteman Council as late as the day for which the conference had been tentatively scheduled. Loveridge was successful in getting Akoto to issue a statement in which he denounced the use of violence,[96] but that was the extent of responses coming from the NLM camp. The Movement had dealt its first card—time. It would make the government wait as it contemplated its decision. From the perspective of the CPP and colonial officials in Accra, the crisis was a thorn that had to be removed as expeditiously as possible. But for the NLM, the crisis—the growing numbers of supporters, the violence and mob action on the streets—was a source of strength. The longer it could be maintained, the stronger and more formidable the Movement would become.

On December 14, the Asanteman Council and the NLM assembled in a joint meeting to discuss Nkrumah's invitation. However, they did not issue their official reply for three days. While the minutes of the meeting are not available, the substance of the reply suggests that it represented a compromise between those who felt the invitation should be rejected outright and those who believed negotiations should take place immediately. The reply began with criticisms of Nkrumah's description of the Movement as "engineered by 'a small irresponsible minority' " and decried his remarks that anyone advocating federation was " 'an enemy of the country.' " It continued, "these public declarations . . . reveal an attitude which in our view does not foster confidence or afford an atmosphere in which useful discussions can be expected from a meeting between our representatives and himself." But the Movement did not reject the invitation outright—a decision reflecting the necessity of compromise within the leadership, as well as the leadership's desire to foster an image of reasonability with the colonial authorities. It left the door to future negotiations ajar:

> Before sending representatives to such a meeting . . . we consider that assurances should first be given us . . .
>
> 1. That the Prime Minister renounces his previous indictment of the protagonists of a federal constitution . . . and assures us that he and his colleagues will enter upon the discussions with open minds.
>
> 2. That before the proposed meeting, the opportunity will be given us to study what the Prime Minister describes as his intentions regarding further constitutional and administrative developments.
>
> 3. That an assurance will be given that the discussions at the said meeting will take place without prejudice to our petition to Her Majesty the Queen for a Commission to enquire into the proposal for a federal constitution.[97]

Once again, the ball was squarely in the government's court.

In a private letter to the Asantehene on December 29,[98] and in the text of his New Year's address to the nation, Nkrumah responded to the Movement. He insisted that the invitation to a round-table conference was still open, but asserted that the NLM's demand for federation was ill-timed and impractical. With a more compromising tone, he suggested that "underlying the Ashanti demands is the desire for closer consultation by the Government with the Region in matters of regional interest" and stated that the government "recognized the value" in this. "If a satisfactory scheme can be worked out with the Regions concerned," he offered, the government was prepared "to submit to the Legislative Assembly . . . legislation providing for Regional Councils."[99]

It was a stalemate. Negotiations on the nature of negotiations continued between the CPP government and the NLM well into February, 1955. It was a battle of semantics in which neither group changed its fundamental position—the practicability or impracticability of federation—but both offered up new catch phrases to describe their goals. Each side wished to appear willing to negotiate: neither was willing to compromise. Not until early February did the NLM respond to Nkrumah's second invitation to meet. In a ten-page "Joint Statement" the NLM and the Asanteman Council declared: "We desire to reaffirm our demand for a federal form of government and we shall be prepared to meet the Government to consider what form of federal government would best suit a self-governing Gold Coast. We would also like to say at once that the setting-up of Regional Councils is unacceptable to us, and we are prepared only to discuss what form of federal government would be best suited to this country." The "Statement" explained that "Ashanti had, until 1901, been a separate political unit, independent of the British Government and of the Government of the Gold Coast Colony. From that year, when Ashanti was annexed, until 1946, Ashanti was administered separately from the Gold Coast." Quoting the Gold Coast colonial secretary in 1929, it continued, " 'It does not lie within the proper province of the Legislative Council of the Gold Coast Council to deal with questions of administration in Ashanti. The Constitution of Ashanti is as separate and distinct from that of the Gold Coast Colony as is, say, the Constitution of Sierra Leone.' " The "Statement" concluded with the demand for a Constituent Assembly.[100] Nkrumah's response, issued less than two weeks later, consisted of yet another invitation. The prime minister stated that "although the Government favour a unitary form of Government, it has not committed the country to any special pattern and that it would consider the different needs of the Regions." He then offered to discuss "the problems of federal/regional systems of Government."[101]

And so went the war of words: invitation, rejection, clarification, redefinition, then full circle again. The process seemed endless. Not only were the two parties completely at odds on the question of federation, their underlying interests in the process of negotiation were diametrically opposed. It was in the government's interest to solve the crisis as quickly as possible; thus, it pushed for negotiations faithfully, responding promptly to all NLM replies. In contrast, the NLM was playing for time. The more protracted the discussions on negotiation, the longer it had to reinforce its ranks, consolidate its leadership, and develop its strategy. If the CPP had been built on the notion of "Self-Government Now," the NLM was prepared to wage its battle on the grounds that there must be a federal self-government, or no government at all. It greeted the New Year with a slogan which signified the importance of time in the struggle: "No Federation, No Self-Government."

One Front, Many Struggles? The Dynamics of Mobilization in an Escalating Crisis

As the Movement entered 1955, it was in a position of remarkable strength within Asante and of considerable influence outside of Asante. It was a force with which to be reckoned, and heretofore the CPP government and the colonial officials had been most unsuccessful in reckoning with it. Outside of Asante, the NLM was sympathetically received by other opposition groups and had succeeded, in mid-November, in winning the endorsement of the powerful Okyenhene of Akyem Abuakwa, Nana Ofori Atta II.[102] Akota described the significance of the endorsement when he wrote, "I believe that the fire which was kindled . . . will burn and keep burning until it completely destroys Kwame Nkrumah, this Satan in the guise of man and all he stands for. I also believe that henceforth our two great nations will unite as never before to fight and to keep on fighting until there is nothing more to fight against."[103] By late January, the Movement had made great strides toward gaining support in the Northern Territories and in the Colony. While the Northern People's Party represented the poorest region in the Gold Coast, the one most easily short-changed under a federal system, it maintained that the North would suffer more under a unitary system with power concentrated in Accra. Holding forth the North's "Protectorate" status as sufficient reason for its future to be considered separately from that of the Colony or Asante, the NPP leadership began to consider federation a possible solution to the many problems facing the Northern Territories. Thus, on January 21, it assured the NLM of the "sympathy and cooperation of the NPP in the cause of the National Liberation Movement."[104] Meanwhile, gains were being made in the Colony. A letter to Akoto in late January from Kofi Amponsa Dadzie urged that concrete plans be made for the extension of the Movement into the South: "Things are getting to a stage which requires very serious plans be pursued immediately in the Colony. . . . [We] have embarked upon a move to bring all the Political Leaders in the Colony and Togoland together to form one solid block in support of the National Liberation Movement before inaugurating a branch at Cape Coast."[105] By the opening of 1955, the NLM had achieved influence outside of Asante that was evidenced not only in its negotiations with the government, but in relationships with other opposition groups and in its initial spread into the northern and southern regions of the Gold Coast.

Yet the real source of the NLM's strength and the dynamics which governed its development remained centered in Asante, in the Movement's broad, diverse base of support. No longer a movement simply of cocoa farmers or of "chiefs and disgruntled opposition politicians," it represented a popular front ranging from youngmen to cocoa farmers, from chiefs to politicians and intellectuals, from urban workers to *abusa* laborers, a popular front bound together by an Asante nationalism that seemed, at once, as old as the Golden Stool and as young as the *nkwankwaa* now prepared to defend it. And in this dichotomous (if not paradoxical) appearance, Asante nationalism was certainly not unique. "Nations need heroes and golden ages," writes Smith, " . . . the 'antiquity' of modern nations [lies in] their rootedness in a past that . . . expresses their uniqueness." Moreover, argues Hobsbawm, by presenting themselves as the "opposite of constructed," nations appear as "human communities so 'natural' as to require no definition other than self-assertion."[106] Thus, the diverse leadership of the NLM "imagined" an "Asante" whose enigmatic borders and blurred social divisions bound together a mass-based popular front. Herein lay the Movement's strength as it entered 1955.

This is not to argue that the leadership constituted a tightly-knit executive orchestrating, with Machiavellian precision, the actions of its rank-and-file. Indeed, in these first frenzied months, the NLM Executive was as much inspired by the actions of Asantes on the streets as those on the streets were propelled by the leadership. Direct actions, including assaults and bombings, continued unabated after the murder of Baffoe, despite the ban on gatherings and despite public appeals by both Nkrumah and Akoto for their followers to avoid violence and report any incidents to the police.

On January 5, the situation reached a critical point. A riot in the Kumase Zongo left two NLM members dead and several people wounded.[107] The following day, the home of the regional chairman of the CPP was dynamited.[108] On January 7, the governor decided to intervene and signed the Peace Preservation Ordinance, which forbade "the carrying of dangerous weapons including firearms, cutlasses, daggers . . . in any public place or in any vehicle . . . in certain towns."[109] In a January 8 dispatch to the Colonial Office, Arden-Clarke justified the ordinance by reporting that there had been eighteen minor incidents on January 1 and, on January 5 alone, one man had been severely beaten, two explosions had occurred, a riot in the market had left several injured, two dead, and thirty-five in police custody, and a shooting in the Zongo had left one injured.[110] The proclamation applied to nearly every major town in Asante,[111] but its effect in curbing the number of violent incidents was only marginal. In Obuasi, on one day alone in early February, the district magistrate heard thirty-six new cases involving CPP/NLM assaults.[112]

In mid-January, the assistant commissioner of police in Asante informed the Ministry of the Interior that the intent of NLM violence was "to drive the CPP out of Ashanti and *more importantly* to demonstrate by creating a 'crisis' that a change in constitution is necessary."[113] While the commissioner's observations were insightful, they probably gave the leadership more credit for orchestration than it deserved. During the late November closed meeting of the NLM leadership, many members lamented that the Movement's Action Group was operating outside the control of the Executive and argued that its activities had to be checked. A four-man committee was appointed to attempt "to control the movement and activities of the Action Group."[114] Despite efforts to gain an upper hand over events in the street, direct action in Asante continued by people both within and outside of the Action Groupers without leadership instigation and sometimes without leadership approval. Assaults, riots, and the refusal to pay local rates all occurred spontaneously on a grass-roots level.[115]

If the fluid relationship between the leadership and the NLM's rank-and-file and the spontaneous actions initiated by people in the streets facilitated the Movement's rapid growth in the first months, by January 1955, they had begun to put a considerable strain on the Executive. In order to develop a coherent platform and devise a strategy for negotiating with the British government and/or the CPP, the Executive needed first to gain more control not only over the Action Groupers, but over its vast rank-and-file, and then to confront pressing strategic and ideological questions. When and how should the Movement negotiate with the government? Should it spread not just its influence, but its actual organization, outside of Asante? What should be the nature of its relationship with the rest of the opposition in the Gold Coast? As questions of gaining control of the Movement and developing long-term policy were posed, the diverse leadership of the Movement could no longer, as one, ride the wave of popular support. Members began to vie for authority and attempt to tip the balance of power in their favor. Conflicts and contradictions no longer remained buried.

Although they did not officially endorse the Movement until October and were hesitant to assert publicly their authority within the Movement, the chiefs of Asante were in the best position to tip the balance within the Executive. Their unique position rested on a variety of factors. First, their very presence lent the NLM legitimacy as an historically rooted national movement. Secondly, the paramount chiefs could exert tremendous pressure and influence, thereby assuring the support, whether voluntary or coerced, of the majority of Asante's population. Finally, they provided a financial backbone. Not only did many chiefs contribute personally to the NLM, but as a group they believed they had a responsibility to ease the Movement's fiscal burdens. At a meeting of the Kumase State Council on December 6, the Akwamuhene made a motion, unanimously passed, that "a loan of £5,000 be raised from the funds of New Palace Building Committee" for the National Movement.[116] The chair of the NLM's Finance Committee was the Kronkohene, Nana Kwabena Amoo.[117] As the major source of NLM funds and as the controllers of access to those funds, the chiefs were in a singularly powerful position vis-à-vis other members of the leadership. One former NLM leader recalled that most of the Executive had little knowledge of the Movement's financial standing. Money matters were the province of a select few: "Our finances were never submitted to us. There were many irregularities . . . if [anyone] . . . needed money they went to Bafuor Akoto and he gave them the money. That was all. Our knowledge of our accounts was limited only to that. . . . We didn't know how much we had and we were not told what expenditures there were and all that."[118] When it came time to make major policy decisions—as it would in 1955—the Asante chiefs, as the Movement's source of legitimacy and funds, had the weight to tip the balance of power in whatever direction they saw fit.

Asante's youngmen, the *nkwankwaa,* as the forgers and propagandists of the popular front, were by no means willing to accept the equation that money meant power within the leadership. Taking advantage of the fluid and open nature of the leadership in its first months, the youngmen sought to make their permanent marks on the Movement by building an organizational structure. General Secretary Ampofu issued a variety of administrative reports aimed at creating a tightly knit organizational framework, an elected executive, a speakers' pool, and a responsible and accountable bureaucracy made up of officers who, in turn, would direct a variety of committees. As early as October, he developed long-term strategies for gaining the sympathy of the British government, for placing agents in London, and for organizing opposition support to challenge the CPP in local council elections.[119] What the youngmen lacked in the way of financial resources and legitimacy, they sought to make up for in organizational know-how, political savvy, and out-and-out zeal.

In January 1955, it was still unclear when conflicts within the popular front's leadership would first materialize, much less how they would be resolved. Would the chiefs, as their unique position dictated, assume control or would the youngmen, as those who catalyzed the Movement, be propelled into positions of power as the key policymaking figures? Perhaps the old guard intelligentsia—the former leaders of the UGCC, several of whom sat on the Asanteman Council—would make their move, or the farmers, whose protests against the cocoa price first inspired Asante's resistance. Perhaps it was possible, although the history in Asante of popular front alliances argued against it,[120] that the tenuous balance of power between chiefs, youngmen, farmers, old-guard intellectuals, and politicians could be maintained, resulting in a dramatic break with Asante's precolonial and colonial past. The future of the popular front leadership was by no means predestined. The balance of power, so easily maintained in the first months when leadership rode the nationalist wave of popular support generated by the death of Baffoe, was soon to be tried, tested, and challenged as it grappled with long-term issues of strategy, ideology, and organization.

But as the Movement entered 1955, little did anyone know—not even those most privy to political maneuvers and intrigue—that all of the actors had yet to enter the scene. Waiting in the wings were men capable of bridling the storm, of developing a long-term strategy for the Movement, and of deciding where its battles should be fought—whether on the street corners of Kumase or in the hallowed halls of government. In January, 1955, these men were top-ranking members of Nkrumah's Convention People's Party. But they were also noted and respected "sons of the Golden Stool," and by February the leadership of the National Liberation Movement—chiefs, youngmen, old guard politicians, and farmers alike—would welcome them on stage with open arms.

4

"Revolutionary Movement" or "Her Majesty's Loyal Opposition"

The Months of Crisis and Consolidation

Almost one year to the day after the first grumblings over the price of cocoa in Asante, a front-page article in the *London Times* remarked: "In the intervening months the tide of opposition has begun to rise from both regional and class fissions. . . . Undeniably the impetus and rallying point have been provided by the National Liberation Movement in Ashanti. . . . Properly guided these opposition groups could coalesce into Her Majesty's Loyal Opposition, mishandled, they could degenerate into a revolutionary movement."[1] While the *Times'* observations were clearly aimed at those sitting in the Colonial Office in London—those ultimately responsible for handling or "mishandling" the situation—it poses the central question faced by the leadership of the National Liberation Movement as it entered its first year of sustained struggle against the CPP. Would it draw together all of the opposition groups within the Gold Coast around the federalist demand and challenge the CPP through proper political channels: petitions, commissions, and ultimately Parliament? Or would it take Asante nationalism to its furthest extreme by demanding complete secession, using diplomacy if practicable, armed struggle if necessary? The question was not a simple one. Indeed, many might argue that it was not fully addressed until independence in 1957. Some might say that the question is still being posed.

In any case, this was the central issue the Executive had to confront in 1955. In grappling with it, the leadership would have to weigh a variety of factors: sentiment among its rank-and-file, the posture of the colonial authorities and the CPP in Accra, the responses of the Colonial Office in London, and the possibilities and limitations of working with other opposition groups in the country. More importantly, they would have to face the contradictions inherent among them—contradictions only heightened by the top-level desertions of several CPP stalwarts in February, 1955. If the last months of 1954 were the months of mobilization, February–September, 1955 were to be months of conflict and crisis as the popular-front leadership bared its divided soul and grappled with the very meaning of "national liberation."

"Their Loss Is Our Gain": CPP Defectors and the Constitutional Path

The first two weeks of February, 1955, saw three of the CPP's most prominent Asante members desert Nkrumah's fold and join ranks with the National Liberation Movement. These men were, without a doubt, among the "best and the brightest" of Asante's sons to join forces with the CPP. In one case, the association with Nkrumah had been an extremely long one, dating back to Nkrumah's years in London and the events surrounding the Pan-African Congress of 1945 and the establishment of the West African National Secretariat.[2] But in 1955, these three men deserted the CPP and returned to Asante, to the Golden Stool and the National Liberation Movement.

During the first week of February, Joe Appiah, Victor Owusu, and R. R. Amponsah made public their announcements that they had left the CPP and were prepared to join forces with the NLM.[3] All three sat on the Executive of the party. Amponsah, the first to make an announcement, was a longtime supporter of the CPP. He was educated at Achimota College and at Stoke-on-Trent Technical College. Until 1951 he served in Germany as the liaison officer in charge of CMB-funded students.[4] Victor Owusu, a member of the Agona royal family, was also educated in Britain and held a degree in law. He explained that he left the CPP and joined the NLM because he was "satisfied that it is a spontaneous national movement in which the chiefs only play a secondary role to that of the young men."[5]

But it was the resignation of Joe Appiah, above all, that wounded the pride of the CPP, while boosting the morale of the NLM.[6] Appiah, like Victor Owusu, was a British-educated barrister. He had spent nine years in Britain, where he was an active member of the West African Students Union, serving as its president from 1949 until his return to the Gold Coast in 1955. In July, 1954, he married Peggy Cripps, the daughter of Sir Stafford Cripps, Chancellor of the Exchequer in the first postwar British Labour government. Appiah first met Nkrumah in London in 1945, where they became close friends and comrades. They lived together, ate together, and worked together throughout Nkrumah's two-year stay in London.[7] From 1952 until 1954, Appiah served as Nkrumah's personal representative in London.[8] According to his own recollections, Appiah began seriously to question the policies of the CPP after receiving a nineteen-page letter from Kwesi Plange, a member of the CPP's Central Committee and a close, trusted comrade of Nkrumah. Plange was the youngest person ever to enter the Gold Coast Parliament and was the first CPP member to sit on the Legislative Council.[9] His letter detailed what Plange perceived as the "corruption, the lack of sincerity" that had come to afflict the party.[10]

According to Appiah, after he returned to the Gold Coast in November, 1954, he went straight to Kumase, against the advice of CPP leaders in Accra who warned that, as a staunch member of the CPP, he might be killed or injured.[11] There he met with his family in Adum and conferred with Bafuor Akoto. Accompanied by his father, the chief secretary of the Asanteman Council, he also went to greet the Asantehene. Appiah recalled:

> And so I had to go and greet the Asantehene and everybody, and they came and they told me about the corruption and they told me about the pegging of the cocoa and they told me about the perfidy . . . that was prevailing—all of these evils, most of which Plange, himself, had pointed to in his nineteen-page letter to me. So it was easy to understand their point of view, but I hoped Nkrumah would take my advice, bring the price of cocoa up, sack these people—the corrupt ones, and they were all known to the ordinary people of this land—as an appeasement for rapprochement.[12]

After he returned to Accra, Appiah confronted Nkrumah with the allegations Plange and others had made and demanded that "people like Krobo [Edusei] and a whole host of them be dismissed from the Party." He assured his comrades, he would later write, "that I would be prepared to continue to serve the Party only if it was dedicated to the path of honesty and reasonableness and judicious accommodation of other views."[13] At the conclusion of the meeting, Nkrumah promised to send Appiah a reply to his allegations within two weeks.

Appiah returned to Kumase and waited for Nkrumah to act. He waited through the whole of December and January, until it was obvious that he would have to make a decision, perhaps one of the most difficult of his entire political career. As the secretary of state for the colonies remarked after a meeting with Appiah before his departure to the Gold Coast, "He appeared to be torn between a belief that there was substance in Ashanti grievances taken up by [the] National Liberation Movement and loyalty to Nkrumah."[14] But after two months of waiting for Nkrumah to respond to the allegations, Appiah reached a decision. Finally, he recalled, "I said, 'To hell with it!' . . . I told Amponsah, I told Victor that this is what I was going to do." Amponsah and Owusu decided that, "they would come out with me."[15]

In a February 3 statement to the press, Appiah announced he had reached the conclusion that the CPP was "either unwilling or unable to appreciate the growing anxiety in the country and I feel that there is a fundamental dismissal of all criticism and a refusal to accept that mistakes have been made and dishonesties wittingly committed." He went on to criticize the freezing of the cocoa price, the government's refusal to investigate the Cocoa Purchasing Company, the "doctrine of 'jobs for the boys' irrespective of qualification or integrity," and the CPP's attacks on chieftancy and "any who dare to criticise the Government." He then announced that he had resigned from the CPP, "with personal sorrow at parting politically with good friends and comrades with whom I have worked for Ghana's freedom," and had applied for membership in the NLM. He was convinced, he concluded, that the Movement was "truly National and opens its doors to all who seek to serve their country."[16]

There is no reason to doubt Appiah, Amponsah, and Owusu's declarations that they abandoned the CPP because of its corruption. Certainly, many scholars explain the emergence of CPP opposition precisely on these grounds: "disillusionment over corruption and nepotism."[17] Yet clearly there were other factors, at once obvious and recondite, which aided them in their decision, which made them choose to attack the CPP from without rather than challenging the corruption from within the party. The most obvious of these factors was that a formidable opposition had emerged in Asante which appeared capable of successfully challenging the hegemony of the CPP. Indeed, one former member of the NLM Executive has suggested that when the three left the CPP, they believed that the party was already in the process of breaking up.[18] Secondly, Appiah, Owusu, and Amponsah were all Asantes and were by no means immune to the NLM's nationalist appeal.[19] As Lonsdale has written in a broader context, "Individuals they were, members of a class, perhaps, but also human beings tugged at every step by all the cultural symbols with which their elders had taken such pains to endow them."[20] Indeed, prior to becoming the chief secretary of the Asanteman Council, Appiah's father, J. W. K. Appiah was the private secretary to the Asantehene—a position he assumed upon Prempe I's return from exile in 1924.[21] Victor Owusu was a member of the Agona royal family; Amponsah was a member of the royal family of Mampon. Their links to the Golden Stool were strong.

A final factor that must have played a role in the decisions of these three men was that the leadership of the NLM was prepared to welcome them unconditionally. Appiah, in fact, had informed the secretary of state for the colonies in late November that "his people in Ashanti had asked him to assume leadership of the National Liberation Movement."[22] It was obvious that the Movement could make good use of the skills and clout of men like Appiah, Amponsah, and Owusu. All three were well-versed in the ways and by-ways of the CPP and in the politicking of Accra. Moreover, Appiah and Owusu, as lawyers, were capable of representing the scores of NLM members facing assault and rioting charges throughout the region. (Indeed, by late February they were traveling about the region representing NLM defendants without compensation.) The NLM Executive realized that the defections of these three men would serve as a further incentive for mobilization. As Propaganda Secretary Buasiako recalled, "When they decided to leave, people thought, 'Oh, he [Nkrumah] must be very bad, very bad, if his close friends and colleagues who hold important positions would leave him.' And when they left, they brought so many people with them—people who followed their example."[23] In short, the leaders of the NLM agreed that the Movement could only benefit from accepting into its ranks the three "wayward" sons, and they in turn believed that their agenda, whatever it might be, was best served by joining forces with the Movement.

And so, with little suspicion and without much internal debate, the leaders of the NLM welcomed Appiah, Owusu, and Amponsah and made them part and parcel of the NLM's Executive.[24] "Like in every organization or society," recalled K. A. M. Gyimah,

> you take certain people to use. You use certain people against others. Now here was somebody [Appiah] who was Nkrumah's representative in London. Amponsah also was in Germany as a representative of the CPP in charge of education and everything. Now, these people resigned from the CPP. They resigned from top positions within the CPP. So, automatically, you have to give them a place here. And we accepted them because we felt, and we still feel, that they came with a genuine heart. And to compensate that, what they were given was what they deserved.[25]

There was never any question about offering Appiah, Owusu, and Amponsah executive roles within the Movement. They had come from leadership positions within the CPP, and they must assume leadership positions within the NLM. Their visibility could only serve to bolster the image of the NLM and sully that of the CPP. "They were popular among the people," recalled General Secretary Kusi Ampofu. "When they found out that they had come, it boosted us tremendously in the eyes of the people."[26]

But the ramifications of accepting Appiah, Owusu, and Amponsah into leadership roles within the Movement went far beyond the immediate effects of an enhanced public image and free legal services. The three men were brought into the Executive of the Movement precisely when the NLM was forced to grapple with the larger questions of strategy, goals, and the very meaning of "national liberation." These men were representatives of the new intelligentsia—the group which spearheaded the CPP's rise to power and assumed governing responsibility under British tutelage after 1951.[27] They were now to become a distinct force in reckoning with the fundamental conflicts and contradictions within the NLM. Forming a distinct bloc within the already diverse Executive, they profoundly shaped the NLM's approach to the larger questions and accelerated the pace at which the popular front faced its internal contradictions.

The CPP's paper in Asante, the *Sentinel*, reported that the addition of Appiah, Owusu, and Amponsah to the Executive had caused a "row over NLM leadership."[28] Although the article was clearly self-serving—an attempt to sow some seeds of discord—and was steadfastly denied by the NLM Executive, it had struck a true chord.[29] The presence of the three had an immediate impact on the tenuous balance of power within the Executive and forced its first major internal conflict. The focus of the conflict was R. R. Amponsah and the debate was over the specific executive position he would hold in the NLM.

Before Amponsah made public his announcement to leave the CPP and join the NLM, he wired the Movement to explain his intentions and to express his wish "to apply for the post of General Secretary of the NLM," adding he would be "grateful if my application . . . [is] favourably considered."[30] That Kusi Ampofu had held that position since the inception of the NLM (and had made no announcement of his intent to resign) was not mentioned in the wire. Amponsah's ambitions forced the Executive into its first internal battle. According to his own recollections, Ampofu was approached by several NLM members, including Amponsah's fellow CPP-deserter, Victor Owusu, and asked to step down. He was told that Owusu and Joe Appiah "were professional men. They had their livelihoods. But Amponsah is not a professional man." If Amponsah was to assume a leadership role in the Movement, it had to be a compensated role.[31]

At first Ampofu agreed to step down and serve under Amponsah as the assistant general secretary. But many within the Executive refused to accept his resignation, arguing that, " 'A man who is formerly a CPP can't come in and right away hold an appointment which is the most important appointment in the Movement.' "[32] This issue provoked the first major alignment of forces within the Executive. According to Ampofu, the Kronkohene went over the Executive, straight to the Asantehene, to plead Amponsah's case. "Otumfuo [the Asantehene] said he would go before the Executive," recalled Ampofu,

> and order them to make Amponsah the General Secretary. So, one day, at a meeting, a messenger came from the Asantehene saying that we should move the meeting to the Asantehene's house. It was there that he made it clear to us that Amponsah had expressed a desire to come and work for the NLM. But he has no job. . . . So, he's pleading with us to allow Amponsah to come and take over as General Secretary. . . . The Kronkohene told him [the Asantehene] that he had seen me and that I had agreed! So that is how Amponsah came in as the General Secretary.[33]

The delicate balance of power within the Executive shifted. The Asantehene, in alliance with the ex-CPP stalwarts (the new intelligentsia) and one of his key palace officials (the Kronkohene) pulled rank on the dissenters within the Executive. Amponsah was now the general secretary, making four times as much per month as Ampofu did and having a Movement vehicle at his disposal.[34]

Those outside the Executive were unaware of the political maneuverings which resulted in the change of personnel. While the CPP's *Sentinel* was busy announcing Ampofu's intent to resign from the Movement and rejoin forces with the CPP, the Executive was busy presenting a united front to the public. Ampofu even wrote a letter to the *Pioneer* in which he denied any intent to resign and avowed that having "great respect for intellectual greatness and experience, . . . I did this according to plan and in the best interest of the Movement."[35] However, such public protestations aside, the replacement of Ampofu at the Asantehene's insistence split the Executive wide open.

Though he never admitted it publicly Ampofu resented Amponsah's appointment as general secretary. Ampofu had vast experience in such positions, having held the general secretariat of the AYA before assuming the post within the NLM. Moreover, he quickly discovered that as assistant general secretary his duties were the same, albeit without the commensurate compensation. "In fact," he recalled, "I was doing the same thing . . . Amponsah agreed that he didn't know anything, so it was all left to me."[36] And disenchantment with the appointment of Amponsah was not limited to Ampofu. "Some of us," recalled N. B. Abubekr, "I mean, personally I was not in favor [of it] . . . I told Bafuor Akoto so . . . that that action they had taken was wrong. . . . But it didn't make any difference."[37]

With the appointment of Amponsah, against the wishes of many, a new power alignment emerged within the NLM's Executive—an alignment that would withstand the challenges of the succeeding months. On the face of it, the Executive appeared unaltered, but its power relations had been fundamentally transformed. Appiah, Owusu, and especially Amponsah were the catalysts for this transformation, but its success hinged on the support of the Asantehene, in alliance with several of his most trusted palace officials—the Kronkohene (Nana Kwabena Amoo), the Nkofehene (Nana Antwi Buasiako) and Okyeame Bafuor Osei Akoto. The balance of power tipped in favor of the Kumase chiefs and the new intelligentsia—the wayward sons of the Golden Stool. It was still too early to tell how this new alignment of forces would affect the old guard intelligentsia—men like I. B. Asafu-Adjaye and Cobbina Kessie. However, the fact that they held seats on the Asanteman Council as educated commoners offers some indication of the direction in which they would eventually throw their support. As for the cocoa farmers, their interests were represented within the NLM by Kofi Buor and B. D. Addai. The Asantehene personally appointed Buor Chief Farmer of Asante. B. D. Addai, like Asafu-Adjaye and Kessie, was a member of the Asanteman Council.

If it was as yet unclear (though predictable) where the representatives of the cocoa farmers and the old guard politicos would stand in relation to the new power alignment, the position of the youngmen was readily apparent. The replacement of Ampofu, one of their own, with Amponsah and the concomitant alignment of powers within the Executive was deemed a direct assault on the youngmen's authority with the Movement. To one former Executive member, it was quite simple: "Those who were paying the money for the organization were the people who were actually dictating."[38] The youngmen had only energy and zeal to match against the money and power backing the new intelligentsia. Shortly after Amponsah was made general secretary, Victor Owusu became a member of the Asanteman Council—the first representative of the new intelligentsia to sit on the highest customary body in the Asante Region. As the chiefs and the former CPP cadre consolidated their ranks, it must have appeared to many youngmen that the NLM's headquarters had been removed, *de facto* if not *de jure*, from Asante New Town to Manhyia.

By the close of February, 1955, responsibility for the formulation of NLM strategy and goals rested squarely with the three former CPP members, in alliance with the Asantehene and his palace officials. The questions that the original leadership had failed to confront by the opening of 1955 were now to be addressed by this power bloc. Amponsah, as the general secretary, was the first to confront the ambiguity in Movement structure and goals. Less than three weeks after he left the CPP, he issued his "Proposals for Reorganization" to the Executive of the NLM. "It is clear that the first phase of the struggle," he began, "—selling the idea of Federation in Ashanti—has been successfully completed. Consolidation and follow-up actions are to form the basis of the next phase."[39] In outlining the "next phase," Amponsah made it clear that he and the new power bloc were prepared to revamp the NLM's structure and completely recast its strategy.

The "Proposals" addressed a number of issues: the structure of the Movement, the formulation of policy, and the extension of the Movement outside Asante's regional boundaries. Amponsah first recommended that a committee be appointed to "draw up the policy and to prepare a draft Constitution." Another committee was to be responsible for organizing "the whole of Ashanti as a unit." He further considered it of great importance that the Movement's activities be extended to "centres outside of Ashanti." "There should be co-ordination of efforts," he proposed, "with our Northern Friends. . . . We might consider taking the initiative and assisting the initial organization of certain parts of the Colony, e.g., Akim Abuakwa, Akwapim and Sefwi areas, as well as some Togoland Centres. Consultations with certain personalities will be necessary."[40] All of the committees proposed by Amponsah were to be accountable to a reconstituted "National Executive" which would consist of representatives from all of the constituencies in the Gold Coast. Amponsah concluded his "Proposals" with the following warning: "There should be a sense of urgency about it since there is a possibility of a General Election at anytime."[41]

Amponsah's "Proposals" represented a radical departure from the ambiguity and openness that previously characterized the NLM. Amponsah clearly conceived of the Movement as a political party, one that had to be prepared to draw up an alternative draft constitution. Further, as a party, the NLM had to serve as the vanguard of other opposition political groups in the Gold Coast and spread not only its influence but its structure throughout the country. Finally, his "Proposals" were based upon the twin assumptions that there would be another general election in the Gold Coast prior to independence and that the NLM would, as a political party, vie for power in such an election. These were all assumptions that may have been held by *some* members of the Executive during its first chaotic months. However, they had never before been articulated. There was cocoa; there was anti-CPP sentiment; there was a movement fired by Asante nationalism, by the symbol of *Asante Kotoko*; and there were strong calls for Asante self-determination backed by vague demands for federation or secession. But now, with Amponsah's "Proposals," a definition for the Movement and a concrete strategy were placed before the leadership. The "Proposals," offering an alternative to the ambiguity of previous months, pointed the NLM in a new direction: constitutionalism. It was a direction Appiah's February statement originally forecast. "The porcupine—symbol of Ashanti's military might—" he reminded his audience, "uses its quills only in self-defense and its strength is the knowledge others have of their sharpness. . . . We must act through constitutional and legitimate channels. . . . Let us show the world that we are diplomats and statesmen not ranters and rioters."[42]

Shortly after Appiah, Amponsah, and Owusu joined forces with the NLM, Nkrumah issued yet another invitation to the leadership of the NLM and to representatives of the Asanteman Council to discuss "the problems of federal/regional systems of Government" at a meeting in Accra.[43] Heretofore, the NLM leadership's main strategy in communications with Nkrumah was to drag out the discussions on the nature of negotiations in order to stall for time. Time gave the leadership an opportunity to consolidate its ranks and debate questions of strategy and goals. With the additions of Appiah, Owusu, and Amponsah to the Executive, however, playing for time was no longer strategically crucial. On March 17, at an emergency meeting of the Asanteman Council and the NLM, it was agreed that the invitation should be rejected and that the demand for a Constituent Assembly be made.[44] That Governor Arden-Clarke had announced several weeks earlier that there would be no Constituent Assembly before self-government indicated that the Executive, led by the former CPP men, was not prepared to tailor its new constitutionalist strategy to the dictates of the colonial governor.

Throughout late February and March, the leadership of the Movement, in line with Amponsah's "Proposals," focused on the possibility of expanding the Movement's political base outside Asante. Not only did the ex-CPP leaders initiate this expansion, they facilitated it. Unlike most of the youngmen, they were well-known outside of Asante. They were national [Gold Coast] figures. Rallies were held in Cape Coast, and rumors began to circulate that the NLM would soon open a branch office in Accra, the stronghold of the CPP. In addition, attempts were made to enlist the support of Gold Coast nationals residing in the Ivory Coast.[45] Though the rallies held outside of Asante did not constitute the NLM's first attempts to gain support outside of the region, they did represent the beginnings of a concerted effort to extend the structure of the Movement country-wide. The prominent ex-CPP leaders spearheaded this effort, but they were not alone. Gold Coast opposition leaders of the Ghana Congress Party, notably K. A. Busia and J. B. Danquah, began to assist in the effort to transform the NLM into a Gold Coast-wide political opposition by addressing NLM rallies outside of Asante.

It may seem incongruous to argue that the newly aligned NLM

leadership was developing a strategy of constitutionalism, given their unequivocal refusal to meet with Nkrumah and government officials in Accra. They appeared intent on circumventing the existing constitution. Yet a clear, if embryonic, strategy was in the making, and its essence was quite simple. If the NLM could consolidate its strength within Asante and spread into the other regions (allying or merging with existing opposition parties), it would have the strength and legitimacy to call upon Great Britain to intervene in the constitutional crisis. There was no reason to negotiate with Nkrumah or with Governor Arden-Clarke because the constitutional path should be paved directly to London. And this is what distinguished the strategy of the post-February leadership from that of its predecessors: its refusal to negotiate with the government in Accra was part of a carefully engineered plan.

As early as April, there were indications that the leadership's new strategy might bear early fruit. On April 5, in another attempt to break the deadlock, Nkrumah motioned in the Assembly for a Select Committee to be chosen to examine the question of a federal system of government and a second chamber for the Gold Coast.[46] But before the members of the Assembly had a chance to vote on the motion, the seventeen opposition members, led by S. D. Dombo of the NPP, walked out.[47] This demonstration came as no surprise. Opposition newspapers condemned the formation of the Committee before Nkrumah made his announcement public, the *Pioneer* carrying an NLM statement that it was "nothing but a trap," seeking to "introduce what would in effect be the Government's own agent and thus parade the facade of democracy."[48]

The week following Nkrumah's announcement, a large conference was held at Tamale. It included representatives from the NLM, the NPP, the MAP, the TC, the GCP, the GAP (Ghana Action Party) and the AYO (Anlo Youth Organization). The conference resulted in a united voice of opposition to Nkrumah's Select Committee. The opposition asked all people of the Gold Coast to boycott the committee, condemning it as a "fraudulent strategy of the CPP Government."[49] In early May, the NLM and Asanteman Council issued their own "Joint Statement" on the committee, announcing that, because the government "is not genuinely interested in those matters which we have raised and for which it has set up the select Committee . . . we would not . . . be a party to this stratagem calculated to create the false impression that the Government is adopting constitutional and democratic methods to solve the present impasse."[50] Two weeks later, the Northern Territories Council added its name to the list of organizations boycotting the committee, resolving that "no useful purpose would be served by either sending a member to give evidence before your Committee or by submitting [a] memorandum to it.[51] Thus, Nkrumah's newest attempt to deal with the crisis in Asante was doomed to failure before it even commenced its enquiries. That no opposition member, much less any member of the NLM, would sit on the committee insured that no anti-CPP groups would submit their views. The committee's findings would have no legitimacy. Nkrumah, perhaps as a goodwill gesture to encourage support for his committee, raised the price of cocoa to 80 shillings per load in early May, but it was perceived as a feeble gesture. Opposition to the CPP, particularly in Asante, no longer rested on the price of cocoa.

Meticulously and surely, the new power bloc within the Movement—spearheaded by Amponsah, Appiah, and Owusu—was successfully mapping out a constitutional path, building bridges with other opposition parties, undermining the legitimacy of Nkrumah and the CPP, and circumventing the power structure in Accra. On May 1, a regional delegates conference of all opposition parties, including the NLM, was held in Kumase. Although there were no published reports of the outcome of the meeting, it was considered common knowledge that the "question of laying plans for a possible General Election before the close of this year was scrupulously examined."[52] According to the Executive's new strategy, there were only two ways to solve the crisis in Asante. There must be either a new election to establish a Constituent Assembly, or there must be an official committee of enquiry into the constitutional crisis. Both solutions necessitated the direct intervention of the British government and were predicated on undermining the power and legitimacy of the government in Accra.

From February to May, the NLM's newly aligned leadership had made much headway on its constitutional path. From the refusal to meet with Nkrumah to the conferences in Tamale and Kumase, it put many of Amponsah's "Proposals" into action. But to highlight only these developments is to ignore the equally important events occurring on the streets of Asante. Among the rank-and-file of the NLM, action, strategy, and propaganda seemed fired by a dynamic all their own. The leadership's constitutional path made great progress among the political opposition leaders in the Gold Coast. However, it did not serve to calm mass action on the streets of Asante. During the very months that the leadership of the NLM was offering a sober, diplomatic hand to fellow opposition groups in the name of constitutional change, Asante was rocked by some of the most devastating, widespread violence seen since the riots of 1948.

Asante Nationalist Propaganda and the "Reign of the Rabble"

While the dominant portion of the NLM leadership was busy selling the NLM as a national (Gold Coast) movement to other opposition groups in the country, on the streets of Asante, particularly in Kumase, the rank-and-file continued to act on and organize around an Asante nationalism no less meaningful than in the days surrounding Baffoe's murder. In the first months of 1955, mobilization, organization, and action continued to be fueled by appeals to the Golden Stool, to the glorious history of Asante and its right to self-determination. As John Tsiboe expressed it at an NLM rally in Nkawie: "The NLM was the Ashanti Nation and the Ashanti Nation the NLM. It was therefore the duty of every Ashanti to support it."[53]

Clearly, there was a fundamental contradiction between the propaganda and actions fueling the Movement in Asante and the desire of the newly aligned Executive to extend the NLM into the north and south of the Gold Coast as a national movement. Yet the leadership appeared adept at handling this contradiction during the first months of 1955. While propaganda within Asante continued to reinforce the Asante nationalism of the Movement, with appeals to the Golden Stool and Asante's glorious past, outside the region the "Asanteness" of the Movement was downplayed, and emphasis was placed on the NLM as a Gold Coast-wide movement aimed at saving the country from the "CPP's dictatorial tendencies."[54]

The Executive's handling of this contradiction in appeals was facilitated by "double entendre" propaganda. This was nowhere more evident than in the use of the name "National Liberation Movement." Within Asante, most people accepted John Tsiboe's above formulation that the "national" in "National Liberation Movement" meant "Asante." Outside the region, the leadership made every effort to convince potential supporters that "national" referred to the "Gold Coast" and that the National Liberation Movement was out to liberate the

Gold Coast from the "dictatorship" of the CPP. The use (and, indeed, usefulness) of the "double entendre" was evident in most all of the NLM leadership's leaflets and speeches. When Bafuor Akoto defined the NLM as "a crusade for the emancipation of this country from dictatorship and all those social evils . . . ,"[55] it was left up to the listener to determine which "country," which "nation," the NLM was out to liberate. But whether the appeals of the leadership were directed at Asantes, or the broader Gold Coast, or were a vague amalgam of both, the fact remained that the very "nationalism" the leadership had to reinforce in order to consolidate the NLM's position in Asante was the very "nationalism" capable of alienating the external, non-Asante support so essential to its constitutional strategy. And this nationalist sentiment could not be turned off and on—here today, gone tomorrow. "The ideology of nationalism," as Anthony Smith observes, "has a momentum of its own, once it has been generated . . . [and] finds 'bearer' groups within a society. Its particular force resides in its generalising and inclusive character."[56] Asante nationalism had fueled the political fires that swept through Asante in September and October, and there was little the newly aligned leadership could do during the first months of 1955 but watch the fire burn.

It is not an overstatement to say that terror, purposeful and political, reigned on the streets of Asante, particularly Kumase, from February through May. The Legislative Assembly devoted a good portion of its proceedings in late February to addressing the crisis by considering proposals to amend the Peace Preservation Ordinance to include the prohibition of carrying "bows and arrows" and "clubs and cudgels" during times when the Ordinance was applied. As Minister of the Interior A. Casely-Hayford argued, "Experience has shown that even when the weapons now listed in the definition are prohibited, there is a danger of disturbances taking place in which bows and arrows, or clubs and cudgels are used, effectively and dangerously, as offensive weapons."[57] The Assembly was greatly concerned by the number of assault cases in Asante since the founding of the NLM. From September through the end of December, 853 cases of assault were reported, 244 had been tried, and 32 awaited trial. During the month of January alone, a further 100 cases of assault were entered in the books.[58] In addition, the police in Asante reported 16 cases of arson since the inauguration of the Movement.[59]

The violence was sometimes a direct response to government

statements, which were perceived by the rank-and-file as direct assaults on the glorious heritage of the Golden Stool. Primary among these "assaults" was the CPP dominated Assembly's consideration, in February, of a petition brought forth by various Brong chiefs for government recognition of a separate Brong-Kyempim Council. Members of the council (known as the Brong-Kyempim Federation from 1951–54) had seceded from the Asanteman Council for reasons which included resentment against Kumasi clan chiefs' ownership of land originally belonging to some of the Brong states and a belief that the Asanteman Council was no longer a "voluntary" association of "free" states, but a vehicle for Asante domination of the Brong.[60] The Brong chiefs justified their rebellion against the Golden Stool on the grounds of "oppression, suppression, persecution, injustice and tribal segregation."[61] That full consideration of the Federation's demands was advocated by an Asante—the CPP's Krobo Edusei—only intensified the rage of people in Asante. In their eyes, the CPP was embarking on a plan to undermine the historic unity of the nation. Although it was not until 1959 that the Brong chiefs won their demands for a separate council and a separate regional administration, the government's consideration of the issue in 1955 was a clear indication to Asantes that the nation was about to be assaulted on all fronts.[62]

CPP members of the government were not the only ones in Accra to arouse the rage of the NLM's rank-and-file. Some British officials, most notably Governor Arden-Clarke, added to that rage and became its victims. On February 21, during a visit to Kibi in Akyem Abuakwa, the governor had made public his opinion of the NLM and its demand for a Constituent Assembly:

> It seems to me inappropriate to talk of a 'Constituent Assembly' . . . before the Gold Coast has achieved its independence and before it is capable of altering or framing a political constitution without reference to any other authority or power. . . . This surely is not the time to throw the *whole* constitution into the melting pot. There is much talk, too, of 'federalism' or 'regionalism.' As a practical administrator, I am very suspicious of '-isms.' . . . Frankly, I do not know what 'federalism' or 'regionalism' means in terms of practical politics and I don't believe the ordinary voter or the man in the street does either.[63]

With these words, Arden-Clarke not only revealed his insensitivity to the gravity of the situation in Asante, but publicized his stern unwillingness to consider the demands of the NLM worthy of attention. Indeed, in one of his most paternalistic speeches, the governor managed to belittle the passions of Asante nationalists, to declare their demands vacuous, and finally to question their very ability, as mere "men in the street," to formulate a political or constitutional demand.

For his remarks, Arden-Clarke directly suffered the consequences. The MAP immediately issued a statement, forwarded to the secretary of state for the colonies, charging the governor with having "failed to hold the balance evenly between the people and the Government. . . . He has prejudged the controversy without himself taking opportunity to hear all sides." It was in the interest of the country, the statement continued, "for Sir Charles to withdraw from the Gold Coast scene [and] for an impartial representative of the Crown to take his place."[64] Meanwhile, a week after the Kibi statement, Joe Appiah declared at a Cape Coast rally that "the Governor of this country, by his political acts, has laid himself open to attack. If he chooses to make himself a propaganda secretary of the CPP, we of the NLM take his challenge; this is politics."[65] A stormy variety of "politics" awaited the governor when he arrived in Kumase on March 21.

"Unlike the former days," wrote a *Pioneer* reporter, "when on such an occasion a Governor rode in a stately form along the Ahenboboano Road, Sir Charles, escorted by a Police Station wagon, came by a zigzag route at top gear amidst a raucous din of hooting, booing and catcalls of more than 10,000 demonstrators."[66] *West Africa* reported that the governor had to "lie flat on the seat of his car to escape stones rained on him by fanatics of the NLM."[67] Many of the demonstrators that day were women dressed in mourning cloth to underscore the gravity of the situation. At the Asantehene's palace, the governor was greeted by another 10,000 holding placards which declared, "Governor Must Go!" and "Give Us Federation or Give Us Death!"[68] They demanded that the governor call for a commission to inquire into the CPC, that Nkrumah's government resign, and that plans begin for the setting up of a Constituent Assembly.[69]

The irreverence shown by the people in Kumase that day for the highest ranking British official in the Gold Coast was unlike any seen since 1948. It was topped off during the minutes Arden-Clarke spent greeting the Asantehene. During that time, "one of the NLM boys," recalled K. A. M. Gyimah, "went and sat in his [Arden-Clarke's] car. And he said that the car belonged to us!" Gyimah remembered that it took much persuasion to get the youngman to leave the car before he

FLASH!

All Ashanti Youth Organization

(MOTHER of N.L.M.)

Calling a Historic General Meeting

For Major Decisions

AT THE

KUMASI STATE COUNCIL HALL

On Wednesday April 27, 1955

AT 5 p.m.

This is a critical moment in our lives. The Great Ashanti Nation with the whole country is in flames. There is a Danger, There is woe, but the dragon must be crushed. The time for our country's destruction and doom is at hand.

We the Youth must not therefore rest on our oars. We must be resolute, we must be firm, we must do or die. All are invited to attend in thousands to let our voices be heard that nothing but

CONSTITUENT ASSEMBLY AND FEDERATION

ARE OUR ONLY DEMANDS

AWAY WITH KWAME NKRUMAH'S

SELECT COMMITTEE

ADDRESS by M. G. K. Addai and
Dr. F. A. Kufuor

CHAIRMAN: Opaning Yaw Tufuor

FLOREAT N.L.M.

God Save the Asantehene

LONG LIVE CHIEFTANCY

We shall never be Slaves

YATE YE HO

N.E.P. KSI

Ossei A. Mensah &
Frank Alex Tawia

An anti-Nkrumah leaflet

was arrested.[70] The meaning of his actions was clear: by siding with Nkrumah on the nature of the postindependence state, the governor had thrown in his lot with the CPP and would be treated as other CPP members in Asante had been treated. Thus, neither he nor his vehicle were sacrosanct. Indeed, the youngman's action stood in stark contrast to the position taken by the Asantehene at a meeting of the Asanteman Council several days before the visit. When the Edwesohene declared that no one should have anything to do with the governor on his upcoming visit, the Asantehene asserted that "His Excellency was the Queen's representative and [any] invitations should be accepted."[71] But the youngman's occupation of the governor's car stood as a popular declaration of Asantes' right to confiscate the very symbol of colonial officialdom—the governor's limousine. "The denseness of the fog [surrounding] . . . the national consciousness of common men and women," aptly described by Hobsbawm, was briefly penetrated that day.[72]

The remainder of Arden-Clarke's visit to Asante was no less eventful. When he arrived in Bekwae, the Bekwaehene refused to greet him.[73] "The irresponsible elements of the NLM," reported the district commissioner, "comprising the majority of the inhabitants of Bekwae, demonstrated their feelings immediately after the governor's departure from the Ahenfie. I am informed that they proceeded to perform 'war dances' in the street and to proclaim loudly that 'they had driven the Governor from Bekwae.' "[74] On March 24, as the governor made his way back to Accra through Kumase, he again had to pass through hundreds of demonstrators, mostly women, dressed in mourning cloth. The NLM rank-and-file in Asante had issued its own response to the governor's remarks at Kibi. Representative of the Crown or not, the governor was no longer welcome in Asante.

The responses by the rank-and-file, from mourning cloth, to "war dances," to shouts of defiance, were evidence of the development and flourishing of a popular culture of resistance in Asante. While much of this resistance garnered strength from Asante tradition, it was not simply a resurgence of old values or a veneration of the past exploits of the nation. The popular culture of resistance which took shape in the first months of 1955 was a dynamic response to the new political and social climate of the decade. It was a strange tapestry of old and new, unmistakably Asante, undeniably contemporary. It combined the palanquin and the propaganda van, the gong-gong and the megaphone, the "war dance" and the rally.

The women of Asante stood in the forefront of this popular resistance. They donned traditional funeral cloth to symbolize a nation in mourning. They designed, and most wore, a special blue and white cloth for the NLM using the traditional colors of victory and rejoicing.

Later, that cloth would bear the faces of Busia and Danquah.[75] The women attended NLM rallies in forceful numbers, lending them a cultural vibrancy often lacking in straight political banter. As Maame Yaa Baa recalled, "We did everything. We would often go with *kete* drums to rallies and play and dance at the rallies. I could throw soda bottles, too!" Moreover, the women played a central role in bridging relations between the NLM and the other major opposition group in the region, the MAP, helping to forge a broad front of resistance. Asante women often attended the MAP rallies. "We were together," Maame Yaa Baa remembered, " 'Islam!, Islam!' all of them—the Suame women, the Asante Nkramo [Asante Muslims]—all of them. . . . We used to have a drumming and dance group called 'Papa Bi' and we would go there and play for their rallies."[76] There would have been no culture of resistance in Asante were it not for the women who gave the Movement its color, its depth, its energy, and its vibrancy.

The NLM Action Groupers, though not assuming a role as central as that of the women in the development of a culture of resistance, did stand as strange and often eccentric symbols of that resistance. A reporter from the U.S. journal *New Republic* was both amused and confused by the Movement's Groupers at an NLM rally he attended: "They dressed in the movie version of American cowboy costumes, black satin with white fringe, and they wore high-heeled black, Texas boots brilliantly studded with the letters NLM and the words 'King Force.' They were called to the platform . . . and sang a song. I was told that their throwing arms were not impeded by their tight clothing, and that most of the bomb damage in Kumase, rightly or wrongly, was attributed to them."[77] One can only hypothesize on the symbolism of the Groupers' attire. To a Western journalist it may have appeared incongruous, gaudy, perhaps even ridiculous. But the brilliant outfits of the Action Groupers were part and parcel of the new popular resistance in Asante, a marriage of old and new. The attire befitted the modern-day Asante warrior.

The chiefs of Asante did not exclude themselves from the resistance culture flourishing on the streets. On May 9, the Kumase State Council, with all the appropriate pomp and circumstance, held a mock public trial of Kwame Nkrumah. The complainants were Bafuor Akoto and Kofi Buor, and the charges were fraud and "stealing the farmers' money." The Asantehene presided over the trial as the chiefs of the Council acted as jury. Needless to say, Nkrumah was not present; nor was he represented by counsel. The verdict, after a lengthy presentation of the charges and a swift decision by the Council, came as no surprise: Nkrumah was found guilty on both charges.[78]

Manifestations of this popular culture of resistance were not limited to dancing and song, to NLM cloth and Grouper cowboy suits, or to mock trials and momentary confiscations of government vehicles. As the February debates in the Legislative Assembly revealed, the culture of resistance found expression in (and was emboldened by) direct actions—assaults, bombings and assassinations—which placed Asante off-bounds to any official or supporter of the CPP. May, 1955, was probably the most violent, tumultuous month Asante had witnessed since Yaa Asantewa, Queen Mother of Edweso, led the rebellion against the imposition of British colonial rule in 1901.[79] It was perhaps appropriate that the catalyst for May's wave of violence was centered in Edweso, in the *ahemfie* of the Edwesohene—grandson of Yaa Asantewa.[80]

On May 14, the CPP attempted to hold a rally in Edweso, an NLM stronghold and home of one of the most vehement supporters of the Movement, Edwesohene Nana Kwasie Affranie. Before the rally even began, a clash occurred between supporters of the CPP and supporters of the NLM. The clash escalated into a riot which left twenty-three wounded (twelve CPP men, eleven NLM men) and one CPP member, Kofi Banda, dead.[81] The shots which struck Banda came from the second floor of the Edwesohene's palace. A prime suspect, Nana Kwasie Affranie was arrested and charged with murder on the 19th of May. Yet, as the Asante chief regional officer stated in his weekly report to Accra, "no one seems to doubt he will be found innocent."[82] In fact, some three months later, partially due to insufficient evidence, the Edwesohene was acquitted, and no other suspects were charged.[83]

Though the Edwesohene's trial led to no conviction, the incident in Edweso set off an unprecedented chain of violence in Asante, violence directed primarily at supporters and symbols of the CPP. A dusk-to-dawn curfew imposed on May 15 did little to curtail the action in the streets. On the very day the curfew went into effect, some four hundred people "many of them armed with sticks, stones and bottles collected round the mortuary awaiting the arrival of the body of [the] CPP member killed at Ejisu." On that day, seventy-two people were arrested in Kumase on charges ranging from rioting, to throwing stones, to violations of the curfew.[84] A colonial official's minute of May

17 observed that "the town of Kumasi in particular resembles an occupied city, with police manning check points . . . and with a considerable force of police deployed in pairs every night throughout the urban area." The official's greatest concern was the use of firearms: "I have been apprehensive for some time of the possibility that there might be organised in Ashanti a strong-arm group using firearms who would be prepared, if the need arose, to take to the forest. The country is such that it would not be difficult for 200/300 youngmen suitably armed to stage a Mau Mau of their own."[85]

On May 18, fearful of "another Mau Mau," the government sent police reinforcements and a company of soldiers from the First Battalion of the Gold Coast Regiment stationed at Tamale to Kumase to help "curb down the present political crisis in the Ashanti capital."[86] A ban was issued on public meetings from May 20 to 26.[87] The tension only mounted. Fifty-six were arrested in Bekyem during a riot between NLM and CPP forces.[88] Finally, on May 24, the government enacted an ordinance—Proclamation Eight—prohibiting the possession of arms and munitions, all of which had to be surrendered to the police at Prempeh Hall in Kumase.[89]

But by May 24, the wave of violence was no longer limited to Kumase and the surrounding villages. On the very day Proclamation Eight went into effect, the leader of the Akyem Abuakwa Action Groupers died of stab wounds inflicted by a member of the CPP. Not only was the victim, Kwasi Ampofo, a staunch supporter of the NLM, he was an *oheneba* (prince) of the Akyem Abuakwa stool. His murder was viewed by NLM supporters as a direct attack both on the Movement and on the Omanhene of Akyem Abuakwa, Nana Ofori Atta II, who, with his Council, had enthusiastically endorsed the NLM in November, 1954. Though the murder of Ampofo occurred outside the borders of Asante, it was perceived as another vicious assault on the NLM and, thereby, on the Asante nation. Again, action on the streets of Kumase only intensified.

During the first months of 1955, many within the NLM prepared for battle, gathering up munitions, stockpiling arms, and lending credence to colonial government fears of "another Mau Mau." When it came to struggling against the CPP, as Alex Osei matter-of-factly recalled, "When one finds people so bad and so worse criminals . . . , [despite the NLM's] strong advisors, . . . one couldn't resist. . . . Well, you just used dynamite."[90] By "strong advisors," Alex Osei was undoubtedly referring to those in the Executive who preferred taking the constitutional path. But there were many, either outside the Executive or on its fringes, prepared to escalate the campaign for Asante self-determination into an armed struggle by taking "to the forest."

In late February, long before the incident at Edweso, the chief regional officer reported to Accra that a thief had been discovered at the mines in Obuasi with "53 sticks of dynamite, together with fuses and detonators." The thief reported that he was "taking it to Seidu Hausa—linguist to the Serikin Zongo (Obuasi) who has ties with Amadu Baba in Kumasi."[91] Amadu Baba, the Serikin Zongo in Kumase, was a long-time opponent of the CPP and leader of the MAP. He had worked closely with the NLM since its inauguration. In late March, two NLM Action Groupers, Abu Bukari and Kwasi Ntua, were arrested near Asante New Town for transporting four hundred rounds of army ammunition in their car.[92] After the assassination in Edweso and the ban on arms under Proclamation Eight, the chief regional officer reported to Accra that "gelignite and fuses (possibly several hundred sticks) were stolen from two underground magazines at the Ashanti Goldfields Corporation at Obuasi."[93] Alex Osei later recalled that most of the dynamite used by the NLM was obtained through this connection.[94]

During these early months of 1955, colonial officials in Asante became increasingly alarmed by the possibility of armed insurrection in Asante. "Security Schemes" were developed, an Asante Zone Intelligence Committee was established, and plans were made for the British evacuation of the region should the crisis escalate into a civil war. According to the only extant "Security Scheme," "the basic risk to internal security in Ashanti arises from Ashanti nationalism . . . [which] has as its object a Federal System of Government or, if this is not conceded, the overthrow of the Government." The Asante "Security Schemes," authored by the chief regional officer, revealed local officials' fears that the NLM had the support and the munitions necessary to escalate the struggle. At the same time, they point to local officials' frustrations with Accra and with the government's inability to appreciate the broader ramifications of Asante nationalism's resurgence.[95]

From March through June, fears of an escalating crisis echoed in colonial offices from Accra to London as no one seemed sure how to avoid what appeared to be the inevitable: the outbreak of civil war. After returning from a tour of the region, R. J. Vile, a representative of the Colonial Office, offered his appraisal of the situation. "There appears to be," he reported,

> a core of very determined people in the NLM whose main object will remain the destruction of the CPP Government. So little is known about the internal politics of the NLM that it is very difficult to know the importance of this core of determined people, or the kind of control exercised by the Asantehene over them. It is, however, clear that they have a fair amount of dynamite at their disposal and presumably can easily obtain fresh supplies by theft from the mines. . . . Reports were current in Kumasi a fortnight ago that the NLM had been smuggling in rifles and machine guns, and there were other reports that small bands of people were being trained with the object of sending them to Accra to attack, and possibly murder Gold Coast Ministers. Another report was to the effect that at the beginning of the next cocoa season Ashanti farmers would load lorries with cocoa and send those lorries in convoy to the French Territories. . . . It has so far proved impossible to get any Special Branch Officer near the inner circles of the NLM and no informers have been found willing to sell information for money.

In Vile's opinion, the governor was correct in assuming that "there is a good chance of achieving independence for the Gold Coast, . . . [but] the picture at the moment looks blacker than it ever looked before."[96] Even Arden-Clarke was forced to admit in his semiannual report to London that the NLM had "extended its influence to a point where the Government can no longer regard it as a negligible force."[97] Indeed, the Colonial Office considered the situation serious enough to warrant discussions with the War Office about the reinforcement of the West African Command. As a result, one brigade was "placed in a state of 'planning readiness,' " although "no other preparations of any kind" were contemplated at that point.[98]

For the first time, colonial officials began to appreciate the concrete ramifications of *Asante Kotoko*'s resurgence. It was no longer a situation of isolated, random or spontaneous confrontations between individual members of the CPP and the NLM. As bad as the violence had been at the close of 1954, by May, 1955, the crisis had escalated further into a state of terror. The Asante rank-and-file supporters of the NLM completely denied the legitimacy of government authority, a denial captured in the epithet so popular at the time: "*Yate yen ho!*" Literally, it meant, "we have separated ourselves"; in reality, it signified the NLM's refusal to recognize the government in Accra. Those very "men in the street" considered by Arden-Clarke incapable of comprehending the "-isms" of regionalism or federalism showed the governor just what "ism" they did understand—Asante nationalism. They made Asante, for all practical purposes, ungovernable.

And even when the violence ebbed, the threat of terror remained. The CPP's *Sentinel* frequently characterized life in Asante as an existence behind "Manhyia Curtain" before it was itself forced to cease publication in June, 1955.[99] In Kumase, the street which bounds Asante New Town and Manhyia was popularly referred to as "No Nonsense Street." It was the site of near daily clashes between NLM members and what was left of CPP support in Kumase.[100] Indeed, by May, 1955, a wall of terror surrounded Kumase. Travelers journeying from the North to the Colony would go miles out of their way to avoid having to pass through Kumase.[101] Not until after independence in 1957 would (or, better, could) leaders of the CPP, including Nkrumah, enter Kumase.

The response of the Executive of the NLM to the terror reigning in Asante by May, 1955 was not unlike its response to the violence surrounding the murder of Baffoe. It did little to quell the storm, but rather used the chaos to buttress its own position vis-à-vis colonial authorities in Great Britain. The ungovernable situation in Asante could only serve to underscore the gravity of the crisis, thereby providing justification for the Executive's constitutional demands and opening up the way for Britain to intervene. In late May, the Executive wired the secretary of state demanding that a Royal Commission be sent to examine the crisis in Asante.[102] Authorities in Accra were duly bypassed. The crisis provided the Executive with the ammunition it needed to take its demands directly to London.

The CPP's *Sentinel* argued that the NLM was "deliberately . . . committing crimes with a view to justifying" its demands.[103] While the crisis in Asante was certainly used by the leadership to justify the demand for a Royal Commission, the *Sentinel* probably gave the Executive more credit than it deserved. Those who held the balance of power within the leadership, though they would be the first to admit that their position vis-à-vis Britain was strengthened by Asante's ungovernability, were not the instigators. In fact, when the chiefs of the Kumase State Council considered encouraging a "general refusal to comply with Proclamation Eight," the Asantehene, as the dominant member of the newly aligned leadership, "persuaded them that compliance was the better course."[104]

For the time being, those wielding power within the NLM's Executive were intent on making the most of a chaotic situation over which they had little control. Through May, they maintained steady progress on their constitutional path by rallying country-wide support for a boycott of Nkrumah's Select Committee and laying plans for a possible general election. And the reign of terror in Asante only reinforced their strategy by providing concrete justification for circumventing the government in Accra and appealing directly to Great Britain: the government was no longer capable of governing Asante.

But as May drew to a close, it was unclear how long the Executive could proceed on this precarious road, exercising little control over the "reign of the rabble" but using that "reign" to justify constitutional appeals to Great Britain. Could the fury on the streets of Asante become a liability? Could the rank-and-file opt for a different path entirely, rejecting the legitimacy not only of the government in Accra but the colonial authorities in Great Britain? Indeed, might they challenge their own leadership and the viability of its constitutional path? Probably no one was more unsure of the answers to these questions than the Movement's ex-CPP leaders as they surveyed the ashes of May, 1955.

The Atwima-Nwabiagya Question: "Movement" or "Party"?

At the end of May, 1955, a circumstance of fate presented the leadership of the NLM with new possibilities for gaining a firmer footing on its constitutional path. On May 30, John Baidoo, the CPP member of the Legislative Assembly for Atwima-Nwabiagya constituency, was killed in a car accident.[105] A by-election was necessary to fill his seat in the Assembly. The NLM's Executive was thus faced with a complex question. Heretofore, they visualized their constitutional path as bypassing the Legislative Assembly and circumventing the powers-that-be in Accra in its direct course to the seat of colonial power in London. But the by-election at least presented the possibility of a new dimension in their struggle: the option of challenging the CPP at the polls and taking the battle into Parliament.

Yet the question was not as simple as whether or not to compete in the election. Despite successful overtures to other opposition parties in the Gold Coast, and despite the fact that it issued membership cards and bore the other requisite symbols of a political party, the NLM still maintained that it was not a political party but a "movement." Indeed, the outspoken support of the chiefs was justified on the basis of this differentiation between "movement" and "party." This conflict of semantics obviously posed a problem for the Executive, but not an insurmountable one. In the same ambiguous way that it was able to present itself as both an Asante nationalist movement and a Gold Coast-wide Movement, the NLM was able in June, 1955, to participate in an election and remain an apolitical "movement." The Executive decided to put forward a candidate to compete in the by-election, but the candidate would stand as an NLM-supported candidate, not as an NLM candidate. He would run as an independent.

But this subtle differentiating between an NLM candidate and an NLM-supported candidate was quickly lost in June through early July. The NLM presented B. F. Kusi as its "supported" candidate. Kusi was an excellent choice for the NLM's first venture into parliamentary politics. He had gained the Atwima-Nwabiagya seat in 1951 as a CPP member, but crossed the carpet later that year in what Austin calls a "protest against the [CPP's] rate of advance towards self-government."[106] In the 1954 election, he lost the seat to John Baidoo, but was now prepared, with NLM backing, to regain it. Nuances in terminology aside, Kusi recalls that he stood as the NLM candidate in 1955: "What we decided was that the candidate should be *sponsored* by the NLM instead of saying he *is* an NLM candidate. The government wouldn't like to accept that, so we put up a candidate, sponsored the candidate, organized for the election for and on behalf of the candidate and, in fact, he was regarded throughout the country as the candidate for the Movement . . . I was the candidate."[107] Indeed, all considered the election to be NLM versus CPP. It was a contest of political strength in Asante, the first constitutionally sanctioned confrontation between the CPP and the NLM since the Movement's inception ten months earlier.

Many colonial officials feared that electioneering would only serve to escalate the violence that had rocked Asante for so many months. In late June, all of the police who had been on temporary transfer to Kumase were asked to stay on for "protection in case of disturbances." A new police measure made it an offense to shout any provocative political slogans like "Freedom" or "Federation."[108] Yet in retrospect, many of these precautions were unnecessary. The campaigning, rather than leading to further acts of violence, calmed the political climate, at least temporarily. Everyone focused on the election. A few days before it took place, a giant political rally was held in Nkawie. Appiah, Amponsah, and Owusu, as well as Bafuor Akoto, were there to galvanize support for B. F. Kusi. Moreover, longtime political opposition leaders like Dombo, Danquah, and Busia stood on the NLM platform to endorse the NLM-supported candidate.[109] Their presence underscored the fact that anti-CPP forces were still gravitating toward the NLM as the group presenting the best possibility for a successful challenge to Nkrumah's government within the existing constitutional framework.

This possibility appeared all the more promising on July 15 when Kusi won a resounding victory over the CPP's B. K. Kufuor, polling 3,998 votes to Kufuor's 1,758.[110] To the dominant power bloc within the NLM, the election victory confirmed beliefs that the Movement was now capable of challenging Nkrumah on two fronts: indirectly, through appeals for Britain's intervention and directly, through a face-to-face confrontation at the polls. In a public message to Nkrumah, Bafuor Akoto summarized the Executive's new-found faith in its electoral abilities: "My supporters and I have won our first victory, the forerunners of many more and crushing victories. We have defeated you and your supporters and will continue to defeat you whenever . . . we meet you at the polls."[111] The NLM and the CPP met head-on, and the NLM emerged the winner. On the wings of victory, gone were the protestations that the Movement was above party politics; gone was the charade that Kusi, though enjoying NLM support, was not an NLM candidate. Indeed, many believed that gone were the days when the NLM's battles were fought on the streets of Asante. The NLM's electoral victory was heralded as the turning point in the constitutional crisis. *West Africa* declared that the victory "should convince those in the NLM who despaired of defeating the CPP through the ballot box that the place to fight the Government is in the Assembly."[112] The chief regional officer reported to Accra that "the NLM considers that it has established a supremacy . . . so that it has no need for violent measures, secondly it has deliberately eschewed violence as likely to do harm to its cause, but thirdly, and most importantly, it believes that politics played in a big way is now more likely to yield results."[113] The governor, in turn, informed the Colonial Office that "The Movement is now disposed to adopt constitutional methods as being more effective than violence as a means of bringing its dissatisfaction with Government to public notice, and there is a fair prospect that the leaders of the Movement will publish in concrete terms what they mean by a federal form of government."[114] And the Asantehene, still clinging to the notion that the NLM was not a political party, announced to the Asanteman Council:

> In normal circumstances, it should be of no particular concern to us whoever wins an election or by-election since we, as chiefs, are above party politics; but the victory of B. F. Kusi, an independent candidate, has been received by us with gratification and unbounded jubilation as his candidature was supported by the National Liberation Movement with which we are associated. . . . As far as a by-election can reflect the climate of public opinion, this victory justifies the condemnation of the manner in which the affairs of this country are being handled by the present Government and strengthens the demand for a federal constitution.[115]

From London to Accra, from Manhyia to the Executive office of the NLM, one could almost detect a huge, simultaneous sigh of relief. The NLM saw the challenge of the ballot box and seized it. The terror of the preceding months seemed a distant memory.

But was it? Those whose voices have been preserved for posterity in newspapers, minutes, and security briefs all heralded the NLM victory as the turning point, the juncture at which the NLM began to envision itself as a political party, not as an extraparliamentary organization, and promised a viable Gold Coast-wide opposition within the bounds of the constitution. Yet as future events would demonstrate, and as the recorded protests of nameless "men on the street" would show, not everyone was prepared to substitute the ballot for the cudgel. As an anonymous writer to the *Pioneer* asserted, "It is the height of folly to say that the NLM stands for mere opposition to the CPP. . . . [T]hose fervent declarations of allegiance to the stools were no idle babbling. They came straight from the heart. They clearly indicate that that sort of British parliamentary practice . . . is absolutely foreign to our soil."[116] But for the moment, anyway, the Executive's dominant power bloc controlled the day. Emboldened by the by-election victory, they pressed on with their constitutionalist strategy so confidently articulated by Amponsah only five months earlier. Indeed, before the votes were even cast, the Executive used the election as a pretext for taking its campaign directly to London. Busia and Amponsah were sent to plead the Movement's constitutional case at the seat of the empire.[117] Busia returned to London the week before the election as the NLM's official spokesman, meeting with the Secretary of State for the Colonies Lennox-Boyd, and requesting that a "constitutional expert come to examine the claims of the various regions."[118]

After the election, the Executive's pace on the constitutional path only quickened. Calls were made for a general election,[119] and a conference held in Kumase two days after Kusi's victory began to outline the opposition's alternative constitution.[120] Attended by representatives of the NLM, GCP, TC, MAP, ARPS, GNP, NPP, and GAP, the conference unanimously adopted what became known as the *Proposals for a Federal Constitution for an Independent Gold Coast and Togoland.* The authors of the *Proposals* were listed as "Movements and Parties other than the Convention Peoples' Party," a designation underscoring, at once, Gold Coast-wide support for federation and the isolated opposition of the CPP to that demand. Individual signatories of the document included Akoto, Dombo, Antor, Sekyi, and Danquah.[121]

The *Proposals'* publication in August, 1955 coincided with the release of Nkrumah's Select Committee *Report*. To no one's surprise, the committee concluded that federalism was impractical for the Gold Coast. It argued that because the Gold Coast was too small, federation too costly and economic inequities between the regions too great, a system of regional councils would better address the problems raised by the opposition.[122] The opposition's *Proposals* counterargued that nothing short of federation could address the problems of diversity—economic, ethnic, social, or historic—plaguing the Gold Coast:

> [T]he territories and peoples now comprised in the Gold Coast and Togoland were brought together without any regard for ethnic, social, historical or other affinities by the forces and events generally referred to as the scramble for Africa. . . .
>
> The peoples of these territories, belonging as they do to different tribes, have different structures of society, and are at different stages of adaptation and adoption of western culture.
>
> The . . . Proposals . . . allow for the making of domestic laws by the peoples of the four territories best suited to their environment and stage of development and thus for the necessary diversity in unity.[123]

The *Proposals* thus called for a federation of the Colony, Asante, the Northern Territories, and Togoland in a parliament consisting of a lower house (elected on the basis of population) and an upper house (made up of chiefs). Each region would have a bicameral parliament. The powers of the federal government would be limited to defense, foreign affairs, commerce, higher education, and communications.[124]

If Asante nationalism was the cement which bound together the popular front in the first days of NLM mobilization, the *Proposals* of August, 1955, were the adhesive binding the NLM to the Gold Coast-wide opposition to the CPP. They were a concrete realization of the goals Amponsah outlined in his attempt to reorganize and redirect the Movement. On August 8, when Nkrumah moved in the Assembly for the adoption of the Select Committee's *Report* and for steps to be taken toward the setting up of regional councils, the parliamentary opposition walked out.[125] Two days later, they returned to the Assembly carrying an NLM banner.[126] Albeit by a circuitous route, the NLM had made it into the Legislative Assembly.

"A Halo of National Repute"?

On the heels of the July election victory, the process of transforming the NLM from an Asante-based movement into a Gold Coast-wide party was well underway. An NLM rally in Cape Coast at the end of August saw 20,000 spectators cheer enthusiastically as Akoto declared, "You need our cocoa; we need your fish."[127] A few days later, the GCP, the GAP, the GNP, and the AYO boldly announced they had "merged identities with the NLM" and would constitute the Colony branch of the Movement.[128] In their words, they opted to disband and become part of the Movement because they were "conscious of the urgent need to effect a total unity of our forces and to liberate the country from the threat of dictatorship, the excessive taxation on cocoa, the extravagant expenditure and un-essential and unproductive services, the mal-administration of public funds [and] the premium placed on ignorance, divisionism, nepotism and corruption."[129] Two weeks later, the chiefs of the Colony's Joint Provincial Council voted to support the NLM. Putting aside any historic hostility which existed between the chiefs of the Colony and Asante, the Council announced that it now realized the Movement was "after a national readjustment in the good interest of the whole of the people of the Gold Coast."[130]

An NLM editorial in early September proclaimed that the merger of opposition groups with the NLM removed "the insidious and unjustified stigma that the NLM is tribalistic, and clothe[d] the movement in a halo of national repute. . . . "[131] Although the writer probably overstated the case, it was true that, as September drew to a close, Nkrumah and the government in Accra were no longer facing the same opponent they encountered nine months earlier. The entire opposition in the Gold Coast was emboldened and consolidated by the NLM and posed a more serious challenge both to the CPP government and to the Colonial Office in London.

Since the inauguration of the NLM, the Colonial Office had chosen not to intervene in the crisis. As R. J. Vile remarked, the governor "is naturally very anxious indeed that Dr. Nkrumah's success should continue and he has hitherto relied on the fact that the Secretary of State saw no reason to intervene. It is therefore likely that he may tend to resist quite strongly any suggestion of outside intervention."[132] Such sentiments notwithstanding, in July the secretary began to reconsider his position. At a July 22 Colonial Office meeting, he "explained the doubts and hesitations he now felt about the present Gold Coast situation" and noted what he termed the "complete failure" of Gold Coast ministers to "understand the importance of the Ashanti situation when it first developed, and their continued failure to bring about any relaxation of tension."[133] A few days later, in a dispatch to the governor, the secretary proposed that a mediator be sent to resolve the crisis and warned Arden-Clarke to advise Nkrumah, "to consider very carefully what the repercussions are likely to be if he should choose not to make the proposal for a mediator."[134] Two days later, Arden-Clarke informed the secretary that Nkrumah was willing to invite the assistance of the UK government with regard to a constitutional mediator.[135] Given the secretary's veiled threat of "repercussions," Nkrumah had little choice but to acquiesce. On September 19, Nkrumah announced to the Legislative Assembly that a constitutional advisor had been invited to come to the Gold Coast to "help formulate an acceptable constitution for the country and also to advise on the devolution of powers and functions to the Regions."[136] The constitutional advisor was Frederick Bourne, a long-time veteran of the civil service in India.[137] The Colonial Office was wasting no time. Bourne would arrive the following week.

The NLM leadership was uncertain how to handle the announcement of Bourne's arrival. On the one hand, Busia had been sent to London in July to ask the secretary of state for a constitutional expert to be sent to the Gold Coast. Now, an expert was coming. On the other hand, because it was Nkrumah who made the announcement, the Executive suspected Bourne was being sent to rubber-stamp the Select Committee's findings. Again, circumventing Accra entirely, the NLM cabled the secretary of state and announced its refusal to meet with Bourne because of its opposition to the Select Committee's idea of regional councils. The secretary of state replied immediately, assuring the NLM that Bourne was a constitutional advisor sent to resolve the differences between the CPP and the opposition, not to implement regional councils.[138] Shortly after his arrival, Bourne tried to reassure the NLM directly by announcing that he considered his position to be that of a "free agent."[139] The NLM then recabled the secretary and announced that it would meet with Bourne, but on the condition that his "precise terms of reference and his exact status should be published in the *Gold Coast Gazette* before he begins his work."[140] Two weeks later, those "terms of reference" appeared in the *Gazette*.

Thus, as the NLM prepared to celebrate its first anniversary, a peaceful resolution to the constitutional crisis appeared imminent. Those controlling the Executive—the ex-CPP stalwarts, the Asantehene, and several of his palace officials—had placed the Movement squarely on a constitutional path of struggle, and much of the Movement's early ambiguity had disappeared. "Clothed in a halo of national repute," the NLM took on more of the trappings of a political party and, as a result, the Colonial Office was more optimistic about resolving the crisis posed by the Movement. It was certainly much easier to deal with the known than the unknown, to contend with a political party having a recognized Executive, a set of "proposals," and a constitutional strategy than with a broad-based popular front representing the diverse interests of many, bearing no platform and fueled by a nationalist sentiment anathema to the British empire's nation-building strategy. Moreover, the Colonial Office now knew those with whom it was dealing. They were the very men who helped bring the CPP to power in 1951. As the dominant force within the NLM, they directed the Movement through a process of reorganization, molding it into a close replica of the very party they had deserted. Indeed, their constitutional strategy, which aimed at challenging the mandate of the CPP government, bore a striking resemblance, as Andoh argues, to the CPP's arguments for self-government in 1949.[141] In short, the new intelligentsia now stood at the helm of both the governing party and its most forceful opposition.

While the Movement's transformation was by no means complete by September, 1955, the scaffolding was in place. The NLM had a reorganized Executive representing the constituencies. It had local branches, some of which, for example in Cape Coast, were simply old GCP branches converted to the Movement's cause. It had its constitutional proposals in print and in the hands of the governor and the secretary of state for the colonies. It had its first representative in the Legislative Assembly. In March, it matched the CPP's Women's Section with a Women's Section all its own,[142] and by August, it had organized its own youth wing, the NLM Crusading Youth.[143] In September, it began publishing *The Liberator* to rival the CPP's *Sentinel* and *Evening News*.

The speed and intensity of changes occurring within the Movement were rivaled only by those occurring among the opposition groups at large. The new Movement leadership reached out to opposition political parties, from Tamale to Cape Coast, in an effort to consolidate the opposition country-wide, while that same opposition gravitated toward the NLM as the major force of opposition in the country. Indeed, some went so far as to merge their identities completely with the Movement. Those who did not realized nonetheless that their fate was inextricably tied to the NLM's, that no one could oppose the CPP and yet distance themselves from the challenge posed by the NLM. The Movement had become, for all intents and purposes, the vanguard of political opposition in the Gold Coast.

Writing a month later, the *London Times* might very well have reported that the opposition groups had been "properly guided" and were on the verge of coalescing into "Her Majesty's Loyal Opposition." The dominant power bloc within the NLM had demonstrated its willingness to confront the CPP through existing constitutional channels and through the ballot box and had revealed its unwillingness to challenge the authority of the British colonial government. Indeed, its very strategy for confronting the CPP rested on acceptance of the rules of the game as set out by the colonial government and on a belief that the only way to undermine Nkrumah was to win the support of the Colonial Office in London.

But what of the nameless Asantes who had "reigned" on the streets of Asante for the last year—the men and women who made Asante ungovernable? As Smith has written of the broad ranks of nationalist movements, we must recognize "they play a part in their own right, perhaps the central role of historical inauguration, even if their influence is sometimes invisible."[144] Certainly the youngman who "confiscated" the governor's car, the men who smuggled dynamite, the women who danced and demonstrated by the thousands in the streets of Kumase, and the man who scoffed at that "sort of British parliamentary practice" posed no idle threat to the CPP, the British government or, for that matter, to the NLM's Executive. They were evidence of those very "regional and class fissions" the *Times* reporter feared might "degenerate into a revolutionary movement." Their grievances were many and their actions often contradictory, but from them had sprung a popular culture of resistance fueled by Asante nationalism. Were they now, as the Movement prepared to celebrate its first anniversary, willing to entrust their futures to the ex-CPP stalwarts and the Asantehene—the dominant forces within the Executive? The Colonial Office predicated its strategy on the assumption that they were and developed a plan for resolving the constitutional conflict that hinged on a successful meeting between Bourne and the Movement's newly aligned Executive. But little did the secretary realize that the leaders of the CPP had their own agenda—one that would disrupt the very delicate machinery of negotiation and bring the colony that much closer to the brink of civil war.

5

Off the Streets and into Parliament

The Ascendancy of the Politicians and the Defeat of the Popular Front

On August 12, 1955, the Gold Coast Legislative Assembly, supporting Krobo Edusei's motion in a 58 to 13 vote, resolved to "request Government to introduce a Bill to amend . . . the State Councils (Ashanti) Ordinance, 1952, . . . to allow a Chief below the status of Paramount Chief, to appeal in a constitutional matter, from the decision of a State Council to the Governor." In support of his motion, Edusei argued that the Asanteman Council was "constituted as a Constitutional Body to advise the Government on both political and constitutional matters; but the Asanteman Council whose head is the occupant of the Golden Stool, has come out openly to state that it supports a political party, the National Liberation Movement, which is demanding [a] federal form of government. Thus, those Chiefs who are opposed to the Asanteman Council in their demand for a federal form of government are suffering under the [existing] provisions. . . ."[1] The passage of such an amendment would mean that the state could intervene in any stool dispute. The government, not the Asanteman Council, would be the ultimate arbiter, and one of the last vestiges of chiefly autonomy would be undermined.

In all probability, the very men the Colonial Office hoped to draw into negotiations would perceive the legislation as a calculated assault, and one can only speculate why the CPP chose to introduce it at this crucial juncture. Drah maintains that it was the direct result of "political blackmail" which centered on stool affairs in Bekyem. The

Bekyemhene was declared destooled by the Kumase State Council in 1954 and subsequently joined forces with the Brong-Kyempim Council. His supporters argued that the destoolment was a "reprisal for refusal to join the NLM." In an October, 1955, petition to the government, the elders and youth of Bekyem threatened to withdraw support from the CPP if the government did not "take prompt action on the twin issues of . . . recognition of the BKC and the secession of Bechem from the Kumasi division." The government's response, according to Drah, was passage of the State Councils (Ashanti) (Amendment) Ordinance in November.[2] While Drah is right to highlight Bekyem affairs in explaining the *content* of the Amendment, the *timing* of the Amendment—it was introduced two months before the Bekyem petition—is not so easily explicated. Not inconceivably, party leaders were less confident than the Colonial Office that Bourne would succeed in his mission and that those supporting negotiation in Asante would maintain the upper hand. Perhaps they believed the legislation would force a rift between chiefs and commoners in the Movement, thereby undermining opposition unity on the eve of discussions with Bourne. Or perhaps they were simply angered by Colonial Office intervention in Gold Coast internal affairs and were intent on demonstrating their determination to address the resurgence of Asante nationalism in their own way. Whatever the CPP's motivations, the negotiating mechanisms carefully built by the Colonial Office in the preceding months would be disabled with the government's decision in August to challenge *Asante Kotoko* by supporting the particular interests of chiefs in rebellion against the Golden Stool.

Despite the obvious implications of Edusei's motion, the bill's initial introduction met with minimal resistance and, in fact, received little attention in Asante. There was a brief report on the Assembly's proceedings in the August 15 *Pioneer*, but there were none of the inflamed editorials which usually accompanied coverage of legislative events in Accra, particularly when they directly affected the economy or politics of Asante. A strange sort of calm hovered over the region. The Executive of the NLM seemed preoccupied with consolidating a country-wide political opposition to the CPP, distributing its *Proposals*, and preparing for the promise of a general election. With Nkrumah's public announcement in mid-September that he had invited Sir Frederick Bourne to come to the Gold Coast as a constitutional advisor, the leadership became immersed in internal deliberations over whether or not to meet with Bourne and how to win assurances that Bourne would act as an independent advisor in the constitutional crisis. Through the remainder of August and most of September, it seemed as though Edusei's motion had passed unnoticed. The priorities of the NLM leadership now lay in consolidating the transformation of the Movement into an opposition political party, not in protesting CPP legislation. Plans had to be made for the future, for a general election, and for the assumption of political power.

But while most in the Executive busied themselves with politicking, murmurs and grumblings began to shake the illusory calm of August. If the leadership's intelligentsia had priorities more pressing than legislative events in Accra, many of Asante's chiefs did not. At first the murmurs of discontent were barely audible. A state council here, a state council there sent resolutions to the governor protesting the Legislative Assembly's resolution. The Kumase State Council, in mid-August, was the first to submit a letter of protest, declaring that the "Bill wished to introduce 'Government created' chiefs into the Gold Coast and [that] this constitutes a fundamental change in and an attack on our cherished traditions and culture."[3] Other state councils soon followed suit. From Edweso came the resolution that "since the Asanteman Council is the recognized authority in our Native Customary Laws and Culture we find it difficult to understand why the Governor who is strange to our customs should be made the highest arbiter in cases pertaining to our native customs. . . ."[4] Soon the trickle of protest resolutions became a flood.[5]

With the Movement's intelligentsia preoccupied with strategic planning and unmoved by events in Accra, the time was ripe for the youngmen of the NLM to seize the initiative, to grasp the political moment. Exactly one year before, the youngmen transformed the discontent of farmers over the fixing of the cocoa price into an Asante-wide national struggle whose professed aim was the preservation of Asante autonomy. The NLM was born. Now, in 1955, the youngmen, as they listened to the grumblings coming from the *ahemfie*, prepared to seize upon the discontent generated by Edusei's motion. They knew they had lost the upper hand the day the Asantehene declared that Amponsah would be the NLM's general secretary. The youngmen's political zeal and tireless efforts at organization and mobilization had proven no match for the political savvy of the ex-CPP stalwarts and the omnipotence of the Asantehene. But Edusei's motion reopened the door, and the youngmen, with their fingers on the pulse of the *Asanteman*, prepared to reassert their authority in the Executive.

The groundwork was first laid by the youth associations throughout Asante who, in September and October, joined their respective state councils in condemning the Assembly's August resolution. The Edweso Youth Association wrote to the governor proclaiming that "the palpable intention of Mr. Krobo Edusei is iniquitous and solely to cripple the Asanteman Council." They warned that any such attempt to destroy "the Great Ashanti Nation . . . would be viewed seriously by us, the Youth of Ashanti and the sole inheritors of this dear Nation."[6] Other associations, including the AYA, registered strong protest statements, as well. But despite this groundswell of opposition, the Executive of the NLM, by late October, still had not issued a statement of protest against Edusei's motion.

It was N. B. Abubekr, writing from Obuasi, who took the Executive to task for failing to address the issues raised by Edusei's motion and, in the process, formally initiated the youngmen's bid to recapture the Movement. Abubekr and many of the other youngmen believed that the proposed amendment and the chiefs' responses to it had to be politicized. The NLM had to respond, and it had to respond with fury. On October 22, the *Gold Coast Gazette* published for the first time the government's proposed amendments to the State Councils (Ashanti) Ordinance. Three days later, in a letter sent to General Secretary Amponsah, with copies to Bafuor Akoto and the Asanteman Council, Abubekr chided the Executive: "The agitation against the introduction of this bill has not been strong enough." He continued, "It is my candid opinion that we have an opportunity to stop this vicious bill becoming law. The objects and reasons of the bill give the opportunity because it is clear the cause of introducing it is political." Abubekr further argued that the question of whether or not to meet with Bourne had to be addressed within the context of this latest attack on Asante: "Sir Frederick Bourne is anxious to meet us. I think we must make it clear to the Government that in view of this bill we shall not be prepared to discuss anything with him. How can we meet Nkrumah round the table in the face of such glaring and wanton attack on the person of our Great Asantehene?" Moreover, Abubekr maintained that the bill and the necessity of "launching a mass protest against it" required that the Executive of the NLM be completely reconstituted. Implicit in his argument was the contention that the current Executive had lost touch with the chiefs and people of Asante and had become too preoccupied with constitutional negotiations and plans for a future election. It was no longer a leadership of the people and for the people of Asante. Summing up the aspirations of many of the youngmen, Abubekr therefore called for the "election of a new and more representative Executive Committee." He concluded with this exhortation: "This is the time to prove to the world and Nkrumah that we have an organization which can suppress evil. We must prove that we are true and loyal 'soldiers of the Golden Stool.' "[7] For Abubekr and many of the other youngmen, it was time to challenge the hegemony of the dominant power bloc and its constitutionalist strategy by driving a wedge between the new intelligentsia and the chiefs.

At a meeting of the Asanteman Council held on October 27 it was evident that Abubekr's seeds of discontent were sown in fertile ground. Despite the presence of the chief regional officer and Frederick Bourne as observers during the meeting's first hour, the chiefs did not hesitate to denounce the proposed bill as a direct political attack on the chiefs and people of Asante.[8] The Essumegyahene declared that the ordinance "attacked not only chiefs. It attacked the people also. It was an invasion by the Government of the sovereign right of the people to choose their own chief, of their right to destool a bad chief." He also argued that the government deliberately introduced the bill to "stultify" Bourne's work. In lengthy speeches, many others echoed the Essumegyahene's sentiments.[9]

After the CRO and Bourne departed, many of the chiefs pointed to the obvious political implications of the bill, arguing that the ordinance was a "challenge to both Ashanti and the National Liberation Movement"—a challenge that had to be met with force, if necessary. The Wenkyihene pulled no punches when he declared that "it was unnecessary for members to talk hot air, to vent their feelings and do nothing. Members should not just swear that they would not allow the Bill to operate. There were many ways of killing a cat, and no one was going to suggest what members should do if the Government did not heed the Council's remonstrations." He concluded by announcing that "if it was necessary for Ashanti to go to War to preserve its National identity, the Wenchi State was ready and prepared."[10] After several other chiefs had spoken, Bafuor Akoto, attending the meeting in his capacity as the national chairman of the NLM, reassured the chiefs that the Movement was opposed to the ordinance and had cabled a strong protest to the secretary of state for the colonies. He declared that the aim of the government was, "by one blind stroke, to cripple both chiefs and the NLM."[11]

But Akoto, a leading figure in the Movement's dominant power bloc, did not abandon the constitutional path entirely at this critical juncture. Indeed, his closing statement revealed the fundamental contradiction between the Movement's national (Gold Coast) rhetoric and its nationalist (Asante) foundations. "The NLM . . . was, so far as Ashanti was concerned, a National Organization . . . ," Akoto somewhat ambiguously declared. "It was determined to preserve the Ashanti Nation." And that preservation, he continued, was inextricably linked to the NLM's fight for a "federal system of Government," for a "Constitution for a Self-Governing Gold Coast . . . drawn up by a Constituent Assembly."[12]

If Akoto was hesitant to abandon constitutionalism and encourage the militant stance taken by many of the chiefs, the Asantehene was completely forthright in his declaration that he was against any form of extralegal resistance. He told the chiefs of the Council that although "he was very pleased to discover that the spirit of [the] Ashanti Nation was still abroad, . . . he disagreed with those who felt the Council should decide immediately to resist, with force if necessary, the operation of the Bill." Having confronted the militancy of the chiefs, the Asantehene then turned to denouncing those who had initiated the "reign of the rabble," broken the law and challenged the authority of the colonial government. "He added that he felt sorry," the *Minutes* recorded, "for the few Ashantis who would not understand the issues at stake. He regretted that for these people, the ideas of good and right had no meaning. He had decided that no ex-convict should have the privilege of shaking hands with him. This was, he hoped, to inspire into the youth, a sense of discipline; to make them do what was good and right through fear of going to prison."[13]

Though none were in attendance at the meeting, the Asantehene's message was aimed directly at the youngmen and was calculated to combat the arguments put forth in Abubekr's letter. The Asantehene, the dominant member of the NLM's power bloc, was responding in no uncertain terms. "The sense of discipline" he so wished to inspire in the youngmen was clearly an unquestioning acceptance of the hegemony of the NLM's leadership. He would not recognize anyone who had broken the law, anyone who dared to question the legitimacy of the constitutional path or the limits it imposed on popular resistance. With few words, the Asantehene denigrated the actions taking place on the streets of Asante, denied their importance to the NLM's growth and threatened those who dared escalate the struggle.

For the moment, anyway, the Asantehene had the last word. The Asanteman Council passed a very sober, moderate resolution of protest against the proposed ordinance on October 27 in which it regretted "the introduction of this novel procedure which constitutes quite a departure from the experience of the past when the Council's views were sought and respected by previous Governments on ordinance[s] touching on Local Constitutional matters and Customary Laws." It concluded with a warning that the Council would "protest vehemently" against the Ordinance and would request the Governor to "disallow the Amendment Ordinance if passed." It did not indicate by what means the chiefs would "protest vehemently," but it did report that the ordinance had "strengthened the Council's resolve to demand a Federal Constitution for the Gold Coast."[14]

If for the most part the Council's resolution was temperate in tone, it did acknowledge the possibility of violence—violence for which the chiefs could not bear responsibility if the Amendment passed. "In the interest of peace and order," they wrote, "this Government should be warned not to tamper with the cherished institution, culture and traditions of Ashanti."[15] And herein lay the irony of the resolution. Unwilling to challenge the authority of the colonial government, the Asantehene had assumed a characteristically moderate and compromising stance. Yet the only weight in his Council's temperate appeals came from the threat of violence posed by the youngmen, the "ex-convicts" who seemed prepared to challenge the dominant power bloc within the NLM. In short, the Council's resolution highlighted the Asantehene's untenable position vis-à-vis the youngmen: he could live neither with nor without them. But the question remaining was whether or not the youngmen dared challenge the Asantehene's authority and legitimizing role within the NLM in their bid to recapture the Movement.

Outside the NLM, few were aware of the crisis confronting the Movement's leadership in the wake of the ordinance's publication; few were aware of the opportunity it had created for the youngmen to initiate a realignment of forces within the popular front. However, none outside the Movement, but familiar with Asante, doubted there would be ramifications. Chief Regional Officer Russell, in his "Security Appreciation" to Accra, maintained that the ramifications would be far-reaching. It "provided just the provocation the Ashanti needed to occasion general disturbances," he wrote, "and the probability is that there would have been trouble . . . but for the presence of the Constitutional Advisor, Sir Frederick Bourne, and the moderating influence of the Asantehene." Despite this "influence," he concluded, "the publication of the bill has greatly helped to unite the Ashanti nation and it is doubtful whether since 1896 such a united and determined front has been shown to the Government of the day."[16] Throughout November, Russell waged a personal campaign against the ordinance and, as Arden-Clarke's biographer writes, "made desperate attempts to have the Ordinance repealed."[17]

Russell was not alone in believing the ordinance only fanned the flames of Asante nationalism. When it was being debated during the first days of November, Adam Amandi of the NPP warned, "If this Bill is passed into law, it will not kill the spirit of the people of Ashanti but rather strengthen it." He continued, "In 1939, when the British people felt that Hitler was threatening to destroy the British Empire, they fought and laid down their lives for the liberty of Britain; so also will the people of Ashanti fight to maintain the Golden Stool."[18] As Amandi's final question revealed with such clarity, those whose sympathies lay with the NLM were not the only ones fearing the ramifications of the amendment's passage: "If this Bill is acceptable to the country, why was it necessary to post more policemen than usual around the Assembly before the Bill could be introduced . . . why was it necessary to search individuals including even the Members of the Assembly when they were entering the Hall?"[19] The question was rhetorical, the answer obvious. On November 10, a week before the amendment was voted into law, an explosion occurred in Nkrumah's house in Accra. It was immediately assumed that the blast was related to the Asante ordinance. "The mystery regarding the Golden Stool, its symbol of feudal power," Nkrumah recalled, "has made the acceptance and practice of democracy in that part of the country more difficult than elsewhere."[20] Precautions had to be taken.

But those outside Asante most dreading the bill's ramifications were the colonial officials in London and Accra. The very fate of that delicate machinery of negotiation, so carefully constructed over preceding months, was now in question. In early September, the governor warned the Colonial Office that the ruling party felt "an increasing uneasiness at the evident growth of the Opposition and apparently intends to suppress this development, first by striking at the Asanteman Council." Arden-Clarke suggested that Nkrumah be invited to London in October to discuss the crisis with the secretary of state for the colonies.[21] The Colonial Office agreed with the governor, noting that the fact that the request came "just after the Constitutional Advisor was likely to arrive . . . impressed on us that you must feel the situation to be really one of difficulty and urgency."[22] An invitation was immediately issued to the prime minister, but Nkrumah's response put an abrupt end to the Colonial Office's plans for defusing the crisis. "I cannot visit you without attracting world-wide attention and speculation," Nkrumah wrote. It was essential that he and the secretary sort out ahead of time the precise goals of the meeting in order to make sure that they were "in line with the Party's stated goals" and that those goals included an announcement of the date for independence.[23] This was a condition the Colonial Office would not accept, and plans for the meeting were dropped.

At this juncture, the secretary of state began to reveal his frustration with the constitutional crisis in the Gold Coast, his increased intolerance of what he perceived as provocative attacks by the CPP on the opposition, and his growing resolve to take matters into his own hands. In a lengthy despatch to Nkrumah, the secretary of state warned that "if by any mischance it should be impossible for Sir Frederick to recommend proposals which are generally acceptable, then, as you yourself I know recognize, there would seem to be no choice but to seek the views of the people on this question by means of a General Election."[24]

In a private dispatch to the governor, he criticized the timing of the State Councils Amendment, claiming he found it "hard to understand why [the Gold Coast ministers] regard the merits of the Bill as outweighing the efforts of the Constitutional Advisor to bring about reconciliation."[25] Finally, in a much more harshly worded minute to his office, he both condemned the passage of the bill and questioned the very motives of the governor: "I have long been *sure* that we are in for real trouble here and I must frankly confess to a growing doubt whether the Governor is (as a neighbor said) 'whistling to keep his spirits up' or so influenced by the personal trust the CPP places in him as not to realise the extent of the forces on the other side. . . . It is surely criminally inept to introduce a Bill like this at such time. . . . I will *NOT* sanction this Bill."[26]

Evidence suggests that Arden-Clarke was aware of the secretary's wavering confidence in his abilities. He tried to assure the Colonial Office in his semiannual dispatch of December not only that he had tried to prevent the introduction of the bill, but that Nkrumah himself had no choice but to support its introduction: "I had flattered myself at one stage that I had persuaded the Government not to publish these Bills. But I was subsequently told that an incipient revolt by CPP back-benchers had only been averted by a hurried capitulation; in the Prime Minister's own words, he had to "publish or be damned.' Not for the first time, the tail had wagged the dog."[27] Even Arden-Clarke could not ignore the situation's inflammability. In his somewhat grim dispatch he admitted the ruling party had done little to resolve the constitutional crisis. "Over the past months," he wrote with some metaphoric flair,

> the ball has remained at the feet of the National Liberation Movement. In spite, however, of some spectacular individual play, warmly applauded by its supporters, there has been no score. This is due to the Movement's uncertainty regarding the goal to aim at, and on occasion to a coy reluctance to have a goal at all, rather than to any soundness in the Government defense. The Government team has preferred to make a series of inflammatory gestures, to quarrel with the linesmen, and to execute maneuvers which could only result in leaving the initiative more firmly than ever with the NLM. It only remains for both sides to turn and attack the referee for the analogy to be complete.[28]

Indeed, from Christiansborg Castle to the Colonial Office, from Kumase to Bawku, all now agreed that the passage of the State Councils (Ashanti) Amendment Ordinances, in contrast to its initial introduction, would have far-reaching ramifications. All waited and speculated, but probably none with more impatience than the governor, for Asante to react.

The Youngmen's Challenge: "We Are True and Loyal Soldiers of the Golden Stool"

With the introduction and passage of the State Councils Amendment Ordinance, the NLM leadership may have been confronting its greatest crisis in unity and hegemony, but to outsiders the Movement appeared as consolidated and determined to defend the sanctity of the Golden Stool as it had in the last months of 1954. Reporting to Accra, the chief regional officer expressed grave concern over the increasingly inflammatory speeches made by NLM members. "The question of prosecutions for sedition has to be considered," he wrote.[29] As November drew to a close, he offered a brief overview of the crisis for the benefit of officials in Accra: "Generally, the situation is more serious than it has been since the emergence of the NLM exactly a year ago."[30]

Indeed, word of the passage of the Amendment barely had time to reach Kumase before the city erupted. On November 17 a dynamite explosion rocked Central Market, and another blast devastated portions of Odumase Street. The *Pioneer* reported "rumours that there would be big trouble."[31] Two days later, Krobo Edusei's sister was killed when her home was dynamited. By the end of the month, few vestiges remained of a CPP presence in Asante. The party's Regional Office was shut at the end of the month,[32] and the managing editor of the CPP's *Sentinel* was forced to close up shop two weeks earlier "due to threats against workers."[33] And political violence was not limited to Kumase alone. From Sunyani came the district commissioner's report that "the amendment to the State Councils Ordinance was attended by the outbreaks of violence anticipated . . . the Magistrate has been faced with an ever-increasing number of political cases, and at the close of this quarter there were 29 outstanding criminal cases before the Magistrate and 83 under Police investigation."[34]

While newspaper accounts suggest that most of the violence during the last weeks of 1955 and the first of 1956 was perpetrated by NLM supporters against the CPP and its symbols of power, the battle was not entirely one-sided. During December two attempts were made to burn down the offices of the *Liberator,* and there were several explosions directed at NLM targets.[35] In late January, the Akyempemhene's house at Adum was dynamited.[36] However, these attacks appear to have been carried out by a small group and in no way signaled a resurrection of the CPP in Asante. In fact, the passage of the State Councils Amendment was the last straw for many Asante CPP members who only questioned some of their party's policies previously.

The *Pioneer* filled its November pages with one account after another of CPP defections: A. A. Owusu, chairman of the Kumase Municipal Council (KMC); W. K. Donkor, oldest member of the KMC;

Kofi Karikari, brother-in-law of Krobo Edusei; Kofi Senchere, regional propaganda secretary of the CPP; J. H. Asafu-Adjaye, regional chairman of the CPP . . . Overall, the paper reported, more than one thousand had quit the CPP and joined forces with the NLM by the close of November.[37] Like the murder of Baffoe, the Amendment only served to undermine support for the CPP and increase the NLM's membership and resolve. Thus, CPP attacks against the NLM in Asante must be seen as the last defensive acts of a few determined men rather than the offensive onslaught of a revitalized CPP.[38]

In early December, the party issued instructions to all its Asante members of the Assembly not to visit Asante without permission. Their safety could no longer be guaranteed. As the *Daily Graphic* reported, "any MLA who infringes the order by going to Ashanti without permission does so at his own risk."[39] As a rather sensationalized account in a British newspaper reported,

> Kwame Nkrumah, political wonder boy of the Gold Coast finds himself today face to face with that old bugbear of the British—an Ashanti rising. . . . The Ashanti are once more up in arms. Kumasi, their capital, might just as well be in a foreign country. It is only four hour's drive from Accra. Yet no Convention People's Party leader, let alone Nkrumah himself, dare nose up here. . . . An unseen stealthy backstreet war is being waged on Chicago lines, with gunmen in fast cars, rifles, shotguns, home-made bombs, broken bottles and knives.[40]

With the *Sentinel* offices shut down, the regional branch office abandoned, and CPP MLAs unable to travel to their respective constituencies, the Accra branch of the party called on the government to declare martial law in Asante.[41]

Yet this all-but-final routing of the CPP from Asante was not under the direct control of the NLM leadership, and the methods employed were clearly in defiance of the warnings made by the Asantehene in late October. Indeed, the evidence suggests that the Movement's leadership was in a deep quandary over how to contain the violence once again terrorizing the region. If in previous months, the leadership was able to utilize, though not control, the direct actions of its rank-and-file in legitimizing constitutional demands, by December, 1955 many in the Executive were overwhelmed by events on the streets and doubtful whether the latest nationalist upsurge—the most militant to date—would further their constitutional aims. Having repeatedly set back the date since mid-September, the leadership announced in late November that it had postponed the first anniversary celebration of the Movement indefinitely, due to "the uncertain state of affairs."[42] A few days later, fearing the militancy of its own membership and retaliatory actions by the CPP, the Executive canceled the planned inauguration of the NLM branch in Accra. Most of the Accra police had been sent to Kumase as reinforcements.[43] Even Bafuor Akoto felt compelled to write to the chief regional officer to complain about the level of violence. Though his letter obviously reflected the ulterior motive of assuring the colonial official that the NLM was not to blame for the wave of violence, it nonetheless revealed the leadership's genuine fear that things had gone too far: "Your honour, these atrocious acts are mounting higher and higher. . . . [I]f not checked [they] will eventually develop to civil war. . . . As peaceful and law-abiding citizens we have been complaining to the Police but I am sorry to remark that these acts of terrorism continue rather furiously without police intervention."[44]

If leading members of the Executive feared that the level of "terrorism" on the streets could jeopardize their constitutional path, they must also have wondered whether the youngmen's intensification of Asante nationalist propaganda might not undermine their attempts to forge a Gold Coast-wide opposition movement. As bombings and assaults continued unabated, the youngmen filled the *Pioneer* and the *Liberator* with statements and editorials that reaffirmed Asante nationalism's central role in the current struggle. Their appeals to all "true and loyal soldiers of the Golden Stool" and their unveiled threats of Asante secession stood in stark contrast to, if not in open defiance of, the Executive's earlier attempts to downplay the Movement's "Asanteness" by building opposition bridges to the north and the south.

The youngmen were certainly more sensitive to the pulse of Asante national sentiment than were the NLM's Executive and the Asantehene. Their words both reflected and helped to generate the direct action on the streets. In an early December issue of the *Liberator*, Joachim Osei wrote, "The so-called struggle of the CPP to obtain independence for the Gold Coast is not in anyway to make the Ashanti Nation free. Our future brothers will have to shed tears and probably their blood to rid themselves from the shackles of Nkrumah's black dictatorship."[45] In the same issue, E. T. Ohene-Duro published a lengthy poem which, as a vivid example of the youngmen's nationalist rhetoric during these weeks, deserves quotation in full:

The Ashantis shall rise.
Ashanti Kotoko shall rise,
To Retain the Golden Stool from Black Imperialists,
To Emancipate the Ashanti Nation from Political Slavery,
To Enjoy the fruits of their Labour,
To Organize as One Nation under the Golden Stool,
To Struggle and even shed blood for our Motherland
As Yaa Asantewa of Ejisu did in 1900.
Even a woman was she who ventured to be slain.
Such was first sampled by our Great Kings,
like Osei Tutu and Opoku Ware,
For the Emancipation of the Ashanti Nation.
Even unto death, they were despaired.
Awake, Awake from your long slumbering.
Ashanti's shall never sleep until the worse is seen.
Bafuo Akoto, invested with the Spirits of the Deads,
Shall lead the Ashanti Nation across Dictatorship.
Asika Dwa[46] is the Spiritual Guard of the Ashanti Nation.
Cocoa is the Beauty of the Ashanti Nation.
When the Golden Stool is robbed off,
The dignity of Ashanti Nation is trashed.
When Cocoa is ignored,
The Hope of the Golden Stool is frustrated.
In Rain, in Shine, Ashantis shall March on to War
Until the Best Federal Government is achieved.
Rise! Rise! All ye children of Ashanti,
A Nation once known not to know defeat.
Bafuo Akoto shall lead to victory.
Ashantis shall rise
Asante Kotoko shall rise.[47]

While Ohene-Duro's poem still pointed to federation as the ultimate goal of the nationalist rising in Asante, many of the youngmen during these weeks began to threaten secession, if not as the goal, then at least as the only viable option should the federalist demand be ignored. Shortly after the passage of the State Councils Amendment, Kwesi Agyarko, AYA stalwart and one of the founding members of the NLM, in a much-publicized telegram to Frederick Bourne, demanded, "Give us federation, that is unity in diversity, or do not be surprised to see another Pakistan in the Gold Coast."[48] A few weeks later, after Nkrumah publicly blamed the Asantehene for the violence in the region, the AYA sent a letter to Nkrumah, published in the *Pioneer,* which threatened, "Your repeated attack on Asantehene shall, if you don't put a stop to it, force us, the Asanteman . . . to reconsider the basis of Ashanti's association with the rest of the country."[49] In many ways, the AYA's letter highlights the conflicts inherent in the youngmen's stance during these crucial weeks. At once, the youngmen defied the Asantehene's demands for moderation, and posited themselves as his steadfast defenders. Their political struggle against the CPP was inextricably linked to the Asantehene as caretaker of the Golden Stool, but he, in turn, stood as the most formidable obstacle in their bid to recapture the NLM.

These ideological antinomies did not weaken the youngmen's resolve or immediately undercut their challenge. In mid-November, the chief regional officer sent letters to the Executive of the NLM and the Asanteman Council inviting them to meet with Sir Frederick Bourne to discuss "future constitutional developments in the Gold Coast."[50] Abubekr's sentiments, expressed a month earlier, were echoed in the replies of both the NLM and the Council to the invitation. Influenced by the youngmen's rhetoric and by the popular pressure mounting in the region, both announced that they would decline the invitation because of the Assembly's passage of the State Councils Amendment. The Council, in its letter to Bourne, maintained that passage of the bill "constitutes a major departure from the basis of Ashanti's Association with the rest of the Gold Coast. The probability of this departure being recognized by the Governor . . . must naturally be a matter of immediate and grave concern to the Chiefs and people of Ashanti. The prevention of this recognition as far as Ashanti is concerned must be ensured before it plays any part in finding a solution to the constitutional problems with which the Gold Coast is now faced."[51] The NLM replied that passage of the bill and the government's "disregard of protests" showed that it was "not prepared to respect the views of the territorial bodies and the public, especially in this matter which strikes at the very foundation of our culture and tradition."[52] Having successfully politicized the Amendment, the youngmen were again influencing, if not steering, the Movement's course, at least for the moment.

Frederick Bourne never met officially with the Movement, nor was he cognizant of the power struggles occurring within its Executive. However, he was convinced that his final report would have to go a long way toward satisfying the Asanteman Council or the Gold Coast's progress toward independence would be in serious jeopardy. In a letter to the governor before his departure, he wrote,

> so it was in England in the 17th century before the Great Rebellion. The 'small cloud' in the North which eventually enveloped the whole country was then situated over Scotland; here it is situated over Ashanti, and has already ceased to be small. If my proposals are to be of any service, they must be such as Ashanti can be reasonably expected to accept. Any endeavor to ride roughshod over the Asanteman Council would mean Civil War. The policy of subduing them by pin-pricks makes them progressively stronger.[53]

When his *Report* was issued a few weeks later, Bourne argued that the NLM's *Proposals* were basically a "revolt against excessive centralization" and that the sentiments embodied in the Movement's platform could best be addressed by a devolution of powers to the regions through the creation of regional assemblies within a wide range of delegated powers.[54]

With Bourne's *Report* in hand and faced with mounting violence in Asante, Nkrumah, in his New Year message, invited representatives of the NLM and the Asanteman Council, as well as other opposition groups, to a round-table conference at Achimota to discuss the issues raised by the constitutional advisor's recommendations.[55] The invitation came at a critical moment—a moment that would witness a true test of the youngmen's challenge. Would the leadership of the NLM accept the invitation or reject it? Would the NLM's commitment to a constitutionalist strategy be affirmed or undermined? And, most importantly, would the ensuing debate provide an opening for the youngmen to reassert their centrality to the Movement?

On January 8, the Executives of the NLM, NPP, and MAP met privately to discuss Nkrumah's invitation. They agreed to accept on certain conditions: (1) that the proposed conference "shall discuss all the constitutional issues over which the country is divided, and not merely the report of Sir Frederick Bourne";[56] (2) that the results of the Conference be considered by a new legislature; (3) that the results of discussion form the basis of a new constitution; and (4) that the State Councils Amendment be repealed.[57] Ten days later, the Asanteman Council released a similar reply, noting that the proposed conference was inadequate, "restricted as it is to discussing only the report."[58] Both the NLM and the Asanteman Council left open the door for further negotiation. At the end of the month, Nkrumah reissued his invitation with an additional notice that the "Government will have no objection to an enlargement of the terms of reference of the Conference."[59] However, he did not concede to the rest of the opposition's demands and announced that the conference would begin on February 16.

A little more than a week before the conference was to commence, the NLM and its allies issued a statement condemning the proposed constitutional discussions. The prime minister's invitation, they declared, "is ill-conceived, inadequate and superficial." They demanded the conference be called off and that a working committee be established to plan for a proper conference. "Never before," they added, "in the history of our country has so grave a situation been approached by Government in so reckless and so opportunist a manner."[60] Nkrumah responded that it was too late for such a committee to be established and the Achimota Conference began its proceedings as scheduled, but without the participation of the Asanteman Council, the NLM, or any of their allies from the North or the Colony. During a recess in the proceedings, a delegation from the Joint Provincial Council of Chiefs (JPC) traveled to Asante in an attempt to persuade the NLM and the Asanteman Council to reconsider their boycott of the proceedings. The NLM did not immediately dismiss the JPC's offer, but claimed it had to postpone making a decision until early March, after it had an opportunity to confer with its allies.[61] Back at Achimota, the delegates refused to delay proceedings, and the conference continued without NLM participation.[62]

Did the NLM's absence from the proceedings at Achimota herald the recapturing of the Movement by Asante's *nkwankwaa*? Did it symbolize the abandonment of Amponsah's constitutional path? In a word—no. The debate over whether or not to attend the Achimota Conference did fragment key blocs within the NLM's Executive—a situation seemingly ripe for the youngmen to initiate a realignment of forces. Years later, Cobbina Kessie, a prominent member of the old-guard intelligentsia and an ex-officio member of the Asanteman Council, recalled that he had urged the Movement to attend the conference and that many of the Asanteman Council's chiefs also wanted to attend but, "in this case, they were influenced by the National Liberation Movement."[63] But the youngmen were not able to take advantage of the conflicts raised by the invitation. They were not able to act as a united bloc and initiate a realignment of forces out of the discord, for they, like the old-guard intelligentsia and the chiefs of the Council, were themselves deeply divided over whether or not to attend. Some, like Osei Assibey-Mensah, came to embrace the position of the ex-CPP stalwarts and held, as Amponsah, Appiah, and others did, that Accra and Nkrumah should be by-passed in all constitutional discussions. "The NLM," Assibey-Mensah recalled, "relied solely on the Secretary of State. . . . We shouldn't be dealing with Nkrumah at all. He was from the South. We had conquered the South! We should be dealing directly with the government that conquered us in 1901!"[64] Other youngmen disagreed. As Kusi Ampofu later recollected, "In fact, we had *proposed* this meeting. The people agreed to meet us. So why stay away? We must all go. But it was Amponsah and Appiah who were insisting that we should not go, we should stay out. And it was there that we made a hell of a mistake! . . . That is why Nkrumah was given power. It was our own making. We ought to have attended that Achimota Conference."[65] Indeed, the only bloc within the leadership that stood united in the face of Nkrumah's invitation were the ex-CPP stalwarts, the new intelligentsia, who were in common opposition to attending.

But the roots of the youngmen's failure to recapture the Movement ran much deeper than disunity at this critical juncture. Never had Asante's *nkwankwaa* been able to maintain control over the very alliances they forged or the forces they unleashed. Since the late nineteenth century, they had served as catalysts of change, as rabble-rousers, but they never had the power, economically or politically, to go it alone. Never were they the decisive factor, and in the early months of 1956 it was once again clear that the youngmen were not to transcend their historical impotence as a class. Indeed, in their ideological formulations they "imagined" themselves to be elevated above class antagonism. They were the "people," the *Asanteman*. Like the petite bourgeoisie in Marx's "Eighteenth Brumaire," "With the rest of the nation, they form the people; what interests them is the people's interests. Accordingly, when a struggle is impending, they do not . . . examine the interests and positions of the different classes . . . [and] do not . . . weigh their own resources too critically."[66]

Because they envisioned themselves as the "people," Asante's *nkwankwaa* were able to articulate a nationalist ideology which embraced the varied and conflicting aspirations of Asantes on the eve of independence. But this ideological potency remained inextricably bound up with their impotence as a class. The youngmen's nationalist ideology denied the existence of their specific political and economic grievances within Asante society. Thus, when their central role within the Movement was usurped by the new intelligentsia, there was nothing the youngmen could do. The Asantehene had put his weight behind the once wayward sons. The only way the *nkwankwaa* could have challenged this alliance would have been to win the support of the dispossessed in a direct assault on the hegemony of the Asantehene. To do so would have meant rejecting the very basis of their own nationalist ideology. Herein lay the youngmen's historical predicament. Never an officer corps, they were destined to remain the loyal foot soldiers of the Golden Stool.

The Hegemony of the Asantehene and the Road to the Assembly

While the youngmen succeeded in politicizing the issue of the State Councils Amendment, they were unable to direct the course of the politicization and failed in their bid to recapture the Movement. The election of a more representative Executive—as demanded by Abubekr in the aftermath of the Amendment's publication—was never realized. Indeed, in the wake of Achimota, the dominant power bloc within the Executive only stood more firmly entrenched, and its constitutionalist strategy only proved more unassailable. The former CPP stalwarts had become the Movement's unquestionable strategists and policy formulators, backed at every turn by the Asantehene. Together, they would continue to steer the NLM along a constitutionalist path—one which would end, albeit via London, in the halls of the Gold Coast Legislative Assembly.

The decision to boycott Achimota, therefore, reflected growing confidence that success lay in appealing for British intervention. To negotiate with Nkrumah, no matter on what level, could only serve to legitimize the existing constitutional framework. The Executive believed, as it had since the June by-election, that if the colonial government were forced to call another general election, the NLM and its allies would capture control of the Assembly before independence was granted. During the very weeks Asante exploded after passage of the

State Councils Amendment, during the days the youngmen launched their bid to recapture the Movement and the constitutionalist strategy seemed abandoned, K. A. Busia was in London lobbying for another general election.[67] To all who would heed his warnings, he declared that the NLM would resist independence if it were granted before the holding of a general election.[68] As he spoke, the violence in Asante only justified his appeals in Great Britain.

Busia's warnings did not go unheeded. In early December, the secretary of state for the colonies, addressing the House of Commons, had uttered the very words the NLM's Executive had longed to hear, that "Her Majesty's Government, before granting Independence, must be satisfied that the constitution of the country is generally acceptable to all."[69] The secretary qualified his statement by admitting that he "did not look with favour on a constituent assembly in a country which already had a constitution, a Prime Minister and a Government."[70] However, as far as the NLM Executive was concerned, the secretary had placed his personal stamp of approval on their strategy. He had announced that the constitution must be "acceptable to all" and had implied that Nkrumah and the CPP would not have the last word. The NLM Executive heralded the secretary's announcement as a major victory.[71]

It was in this specific context that the Movement's intelligentsia convinced the Executive not to attend the Achimota Conference. The internal debate had little to do with agenda items or proposed participants, however much Movement replies to the invitations focused on those issues. The final decision was based on an assessment of how participation would hasten or impede progress toward a general election. In the end, arguments that a boycott of the proceedings would undermine the conference's legitimacy and speed the day of an election held sway. Significantly, the NLM arrived at this decision only after lengthy consultation with its allies.[72]

Fundamental to the dominant bloc's constitutionalist strategy was the building of a country-wide opposition capable of successfully challenging Nkrumah at the polls. If this strategy were to prevail, all of the Gold Coast's opposition groups had to respond to the Conference invitation in a united front, and that is precisely what they did. The solidarity of the opposition, first given expression in the *Proposals for a Federal Constitution,* was now fully activated. And those Asantes who had urged complete secession or had waged street battles against the

CPP were rapidly disarmed. The constitutionalist strategy was firmly entrenched, the national (Gold Coast-wide) dimension of the struggle now assumed preeminence, and the political kingdom loomed on the horizon.

In the opening months of 1956, it was a strange alliance, indeed, that was leading the NLM to the gates of the political kingdom. The Movement's dominant power bloc now brought together men who had been, at least on the political front, long-time enemies, but as Lonsdale has written, dominant classes often "get organized by the very institutions which their conflicts have created."[73] Men like K. A. Busia and I. B. Asafu-Adjaye thus linked arms with Joe Appiah, Victor Owusu, and R. R. Amponsah. On the one hand stood the old-guard intelligentsia of the UGCC; on the other stood the new intelligentsia who had broken with the conservative UGCC and succeeded, with Nkrumah, in building the Gold Coast's first mass nationalist party. Though they had been at political odds for years, in the context of the NLM their similarities came to outweigh their differences.

Unlike Asante's youngmen, they were both members of the Gold Coast's political intelligentsia whose aspirations were formed and legitimized by international experiences. While they were all sons of the Golden Stool, their shared political vision, the community they both "imagined," was never limited to Asante. They made their mark as the founders and articulators of a Gold Coast nationalism whose "territorial stretch" encompassed the "imperial administrative unit."[74] Unlike the youngman who "appropriated" the Governor's car, these men, former UGCC and CPP alike, accepted the rules of the game as set out by the colonial government. They clung faithfully to the notion of orderly progress toward Gold Coast self-government and to Britain's presumably pivotal role in effecting such progress. As Russell so pointedly asserted in early March, "the situation isn't worse because Ashantis believe in Britain."[75] Thus, based on their common political experiences, their shared faiths and fears, the stalwarts of the UGCC and the CPP joined hands in Asante to fight for a common goal: to capture political power from Nkrumah's party.

But simply to dissect this alliance does not provide an explanation for the intelligentsia's ultimate domination of the NLM. To understand that, it is necessary to comprehend the central, pivotal role of the Asantehene; for, in many ways, it was he who consecrated the marriage between the old and new intelligentsia and put the weight of the Golden Stool behind their every move. The Asantehene was key. As the caretaker of the Golden Stool, the ultimate symbol of the nation, and as the link personified between Asante's precolonial and colonial past, the Asantehene could legitimate and empower. Whoever received this recognition would become the Movement's indisputable leadership.

And at no time did the Asante's *nkwankwaa* stand a chance of gaining that recognition. The Asantehene knew that many of them did not possess unyielding faith, as he did, in the colonial power.[76] Indeed, he distrusted the youngmen and the "rabble" they could so easily rouse. Fearing the prospect that they might one day aim their grievances and frustrations directly at him, he saw the *nkwankwaa* as Emperor Francis II did his "faithful Tyroleans": " 'today they are patriots for me, tomorrow they may be patriots against me.' "[77] So, the Asantehene turned to the political intelligentsia, old and new, as those whose ideology and material interests closely reflected his own.

On the Asanteman Council of 1956 sat the Asantehene, Asante's paramount chiefs, and representatives of the old and new intelligentsia. The ties which bound them were, at once, political, familial, and economic. The intelligentsia members, though not chiefs, were all members of Asante's royal families. Victor Owusu was an Agona royal. I. B. Asafu-Adjaye was the grandson of Dwabenhene Nana Asafo Agyei. Joe Appiah's father served as secretary to the Asantehene and, later, as chief secretary of the Asanteman Council.[78] It is important, therefore, that we view the Asantehene and his paramount chiefs not as "distracted bearers of intercalary roles and values," as Lonsdale has written, but as "elements of a continually changing ruling class. . . . They may have propped up colonial rule," but their sons sought to inherit "its mantle of power."[79] Indeed, as it was constituted in 1956, the Asanteman Council symbolized, in no uncertain terms, the solidification of Asante's ruling class.[80]

Its members were bound together by a system of economic patronage probably as old as the Asante kingdom itself. An example which occurred in the context of raising funds for the NLM was recalled by one youngman:

> It was decided that Asantehene should give out certain plots in Kumase in the names of certain individuals in the Movement. . . . They were given for petrol stations. And the decision of the Executive Committee, which met in

the Asantehene's palace, presided over by the Asantehene, himself, was that . . . the money [received] from Shell or Mobil or any other petrol company should be paid into the funds of the Movement. And these plots were given over to certain individuals. I didn't get any.

The youngman claimed he was bitter not because he failed to receive a plot, but because Amponsah failed to "pay the money into the funds of the Movement." When the youngman challenged the Asantehene on this, the Asantehene "said [Amponsah] had some wards in Britain and he needed the funds to pay their fees."[81] For Asante's youngmen, it was a bitter lesson in ruling class solidarity.

And so it was, with common interests, and shared fears and faiths, that the dominant power bloc within the NLM—a power bloc centered in the halls of Manhyia rather than in the Movement's offices—developed its common strategy for challenging the CPP. It appealed to Great Britain, consistently circumventing the government offices in Accra, and patiently awaited the call for a new general election. It rallied together a Gold Coast-wide opposition that brought together leading anti-CPP politicians from throughout the country and reinforced the tendency, at least within the NLM, for important decisions to be taken by a narrow stratum of political intellectuals. Indeed, during the very days that the proceedings at Achimota were being concluded, General Secretary R. R. Amponsah was busy putting together his own version of a constitutional conference, inviting representatives from a host of organizations to come to Kumase to plan for an alternative conference.[82] As one colonial officer in Asante concluded, "It is the view in the circles of the leadership of the National Liberation Movement that a constitutional conference organized on the lines suggested by them and under the chairmanship of the Secretary of State would be able to solve the present political crisis in the country."[83]

By the opening of 1956, the NLM's dominant bloc had won the battle of ideas within the Movement. Only briefly, in early March, did anyone in Asante attempt to question the constitutionalist strategy and, as in the past, this challenge only served to strengthen the leadership's bargaining position vis-à-vis Great Britain. In late February, Nkrumah's minister of finance, K. A. Gbedemah, announced at a rally that the conditions for independence had been met at the Achimota Conference, and if Britain refused to grant independence, the CPP government "might be forced to declare themselves independent as the Sudanese did recently."[84] Gbedemah's remarks, though later recanted by Nkrumah,[85] resulted in numerous calls for Asante to secede from the Gold Coast should the ties with Britain be unilaterally severed.

The AYA, in a letter to the Asanteman Council, "strongly and seriously" suggested "that in view of the present Government's determined efforts to destroy Ashanti's national identity and in view of the Government's undenied intention to declare unilaterally, if necessary, an independent Gold Coast state, the Ashanti Nation should consider seriously the necessity for her seceding from the Gold Coast. . . ."[86] Similar sentiments were echoed in letters to the Movement's Executive from a variety of branch offices. The Kumase Asafo branch wrote to Akoto saying he should inform the world that "Ashanti will secede . . . at the very hour when the CPP declares unilateral independence," adding, on a practical note, that "access to the sea is no problem . . . [but] if worse came to worst Ashanti would rely on aeroplanes to transport goods to any part of the world at any time."[87] As one editorial in the *Pioneer* lamented, "From federation to separation, what a tale of woe! Yet the sombre indications are that the new Ashanti outlook is catching on fast. . . . The spirit of Ashanti secession is thus abroad. And definitely no joke."[88]

Talk of separation from the Gold Coast filled the *Pioneer* and the *Liberator* for weeks, and clearly those who called for secession did so earnestly. Even Bafuor Akoto added his voice to the secessionist choir when he declared that "without a general agreement on the constitution [before independence], Ashanti . . . would separate herself from the rest of the country."[89] But these calls for separation notwithstanding, the NLM Executive remained committed to its original strategy, confident that Great Britain would not pull out until a general agreement had been reached. Indeed, the secessionist demands would only serve to hasten the coming of a Gold Coast general election.

The steadfast confidence of the NLM's leadership was best exhibited in a May 7 meeting of the Asanteman Council called to discuss the publication of the government's White Paper on a new constitution and to consider recent calls for Asante secession. K. A. Busia, the former GCP stalwart who was beginning to play an increasingly important role in the Movement's leadership, was present to address the chiefs. In his opening remarks he sought to reassure the members of the Council that an election was imminent: "If the people of Ashanti were determined to get a good constitution, they would have it, not withstanding the CPP majority in the Assembly. It was certain that this country would go to the polls sooner than 1958, and he wished to impress on Nananom the necessity and importance of elections. All serious and important questions were being determined by elections, by the ballot box, and people should begin to appreciate the need for organization and education."[90] Few, if any, of the chiefs disagreed with Busia or challenged his confidence in the ballot box. Some were intrigued by the call for secession and argued, like the Akyempemhene, that "if the youth were thinking of secession and wishing to replace Federation with it, they should formulate the principles, delve into its implications and inform the Council."[91] Yet the majority reaffirmed their faith in the Movement's constitutionalist strategy and heralded the wisdom in Busia's remarks. They were in overwhelming agreement that the NLM should aim for the ballot box. The Essumegyahene summarized this consensus when he argued that

> he believed the country would go to the polls and wished to advise all Ashantis to be prepared and ready. . . . Secession involved several implications which had to be closely studied. . . . He felt the time was not yet when Ashantis should actively think of secession. If the Government proved adamant, of course, then secession could be resorted to as the last, even if unpleasant, measure. Meanwhile it was imperative that every Ashanti citizen should consider the question of organization for the polls very seriously. The strength of the Federal idea could be tested only at the polls.[92]

If Asante's ruling class was not prepared to take seriously the call for secession, the British colonial authorities were. In their view, the NLM was presenting the colonial government with two options: to call for a general election or to preside over the fragmentation of its model colony. The secessionist threats filling the newspapers in March, therefore, acted as the final straw. By April, newspapers in London were echoing opposition calls for another general election in the Gold Coast as the only way of avoiding Asante's secession from the colony.[93]

But by April, the die had already been cast. As early as October, 1955, the Colonial Office had begun to consider the possibility that another general election was the only viable means for resolving the constitutional crisis. The secretary of state for the colonies warned Nkrumah in late October that should Bourne's mission fail, there would be no option but to hold another election.[94] A month later, the governor informed the Colonial Office that he believed another election was necessary and that he was "gradually instilling this idea into the minds of Ministers."[95] Before the Achimota Conference took place, Nkrumah even informed the governor that he was prepared to hold another election if it were immediately followed by a mandate for independence.[96] However, after the NLM and the Asanteman Council refused to attend the conference, Nkrumah changed his position, arguing that "there is no guarantee that the National Liberation Movement and its supporters would change their present attitude even after a General Election." As far as Nkrumah was concerned, the NLM had shown itself unwilling to negotiate. "It is now clear to me," he continued, "that the National Liberation Movement will take advantage of a General Election campaign to cause riot and bloodshed and general confusion in the country, knowing full well that it has no chance of winning.[97]

But by mid-March, the secretary of state was convinced that a general election had to be held. Moreover, he was prepared to make the grant of independence contingent upon another election. "There will be no alternative to the holding of a General Election," he informed Nkrumah, "if HMG is to be in a position to proceed with the introduction into the UK of a bill providing for the transfer of power."[98] And while he waited for a reply from Nkrumah, the secretary, in a dispatch to Acting Governor Hadow, asked what the chances were that Nkrumah would refuse another election and declare unilateral independence, and the Colonial Office explored the legality of the governor dismissing CPP ministers and suspending the constitution should "Nkrumah do something drastic."[99] In short, the NLM's constitutionalist strategy, backed by the vague, but no less threatening, call for secession, was beginning to achieve concrete results.

Having sensed which way colonial winds were blowing, Nkrumah sent Kojo Botsio to London in late March to present the CPP's case against another general election.[100] Botsio carried a detailed brief from the prime minister which, in the end, accused the Colonial Office of emboldening the NLM: "Nothing has encouraged the NLM more than the statement of the Secretary of State that there must be a 'general agreement' before self-government is granted. The NLM are saying that unless they agree and unless the Asantehene endorses any constitution for the country, we cannot get our independence. If this interpretation by the NLM is correct, then we will have a distorted form of democracy whereby a minority opinion can be used to vet the expressed will of the overwhelming majority."[101] Despite Botsio's impassioned arguments, the secretary was not convinced. In a letter to Nkrumah in early April, he informed Nkrumah that, although he suspected the CPP would win another general election, it was the only way to avoid the government being "faced with a determined and obstinate opposition."[102] Botsio told Nkrumah that he was "impressed by the sincerity of Mr. Lennox-Boyd and . . . felt sure that he was genuinely out to help the Gold Coast gain its independence." "But," he added, "it looks as if a general election is the only answer."[103]

And then the negotiations began. Nkrumah had no choice but to agree to confront his opposition at the polls one last time before independence would be granted. As he explained to the secretary of state, his only options were to declare unilateral independence—"a revolutionary step"—delay independence until the next scheduled election in 1958 and face the wrath of his supporters, or hold an election in 1956. He agreed to call for another general election contingent upon the secretary's promise to accept a motion for independence passed by a reasonable majority in the new legislature.[104] At this point, according to the governor, Nkrumah "encountered powerful opposition" from his Cabinet and the only way to appease that opposition was for the secretary of state to make the announcement of another election, "thus enabling them [members of the Cabinet] to escape the odium of voluntary recourse to this expedient."[105] The secretary of state agreed. He would make the announcement of the election and present it as the final step toward full self-government.

On May 11, Lennox-Boyd made his address to the House of Commons—the address so anxiously awaited and so confidently foreseen by the NLM's Executive:

> I have been in close touch with the Prime Minister of the Gold Coast on these matters. It is the considered view of his Government that the time has now come for the Gold Coast to assume full responsibility within the Commonwealth for its own affairs. I have made my view clear to him that because of the failure to resolve the constitutional dispute we can only achieve our common aim of the early independence of that country within the Commonwealth in one way and one way alone; that is to demonstrate to the world that the peoples of the Gold Coast have had a full and free opportunity to consider their Constitution and to express their views on it in a general election.[106]

A week later, Arden-Clarke, speaking in the Legislative Assembly, recounted the secretary of state's speech to the House of Commons.[107] He informed the Colonial Office that his statement, "was received with general applause from members on the Government benches for whom the dissolution would have been the occasion for violent recrimination had it appeared to have arisen from the initiative of the Government."[108] On May 22, the Legislative Assembly envisioned by Arden-Clarke as leading the Gold Coast to independence was adjourned. Obviously frustrated by the havoc the NLM had brought to bear on his timetable for an orderly transition to self-government, yet ever faithful that transition would occur under his personal guidance, Arden-Clarke lamented in a letter to his wife: "I never realized what a prolonged battle I would have with the politicians and chiefs and people of this country in order to give them the independence for which they have been clamoring all these years. Now they are going to have it whether they like it or not."[109]

Arden-Clarke was not alone in his frustration or in his determination. Colonial officials both in Accra and London viewed the election as the final step before independence, the last gesture of accommodation to Nkrumah's opposition. They had assured Nkrumah that, if there were violence during the election, the British government "would not use this as an excuse to delay independence."[110] From Christiansborg Castle to the Colonial Office in London, all agreed that no matter what the outcome of the election, no matter what the circumstances surrounding the election, independence was forthcoming. The last obstacle standing between the Gold Coast and full self-government would finally be surmounted.

Meanwhile, the leadership of the NLM concentrated its sights solely on the election, slated for mid-July, not on what would come after. The NLM's eggs all lay in one basket—the election. Granted, most of the leaders were confident of victory at the polls and thus were not too concerned with the timetable for independence agreed upon by the CPP and the colonial government. Yet none of them considered the implications, none dared think the unthinkable—that the NLM might not emerge from the polls victorious. If the opposition in the Assembly remained a minority to the CPP's majority, then what would the Movement's long-term strategy be as the Gold Coast marched the last steps toward independence? As far as Arden-Clarke was concerned, the "politicians and chiefs and people" of the Gold Coast—

Asantes included—were going to have their independence "whether they liked it or not."

The Last General Election: A Victory for the NLM's Leadership and the Defeat of Asante's Popular Front

That the dominant power bloc within the NLM had won the battle of ideas within the Movement was decisively illustrated by the frenzy of political activity overtaking Asante in the days following Lennox-Boyd's announcement. There was no debate over whether or not to participate in the forthcoming election. There was no sober consideration of previous protests that the NLM was a "movement" and not a political party. There was no formal inauguration to herald the metamorphosis of the "movement" into a "party" or to mark the day the NLM decided to move off the streets and into parliament. That the NLM would compete in the election—the last election before the granting of full self-government—was a given. Smoothly and effortlessly, the Movement was transformed into a political party within hours of Lennox-Boyd's announcement. In fact, the process of transformation had begun over a year before, during the weeks in which the ex-CPP stalwarts outlined their long-term strategy for the Movement. The alliances, the structures and the propaganda necessary to transform the Movement were developed over the preceding months. When the election announcement was made, therefore, the Movement was prepared, and it burst on the scene as the unquestioned vanguard of political party opposition to Nkrumah's CPP. The long-awaited battle at the ballot box was about to begin.

The first indication of the Movement's election strategy came only two days after the Legislative Assembly formally adjourned, when a May 24 conference of the NLM and its allies elected K. A. Busia as parliamentary leader of the opposition forces,[111] a position he had held as a member of the GCP in the 1951–54 Legislative Assembly.[112] Since the closing months of 1955, he had come to play an increasingly central role in the NLM's leadership. Now Busia was the man chosen to present the platform of the 1956 Gold Coast opposition to Nkrumah. During the weeks preceding the election, he traveled throughout the country addressing rallies, and his pronouncements appeared daily in all the country's newspapers. Indeed, the continuity in Gold

Coast opposition politics, so disrupted with the emergence of the NLM, suddenly appeared restored. Party names were different, but the faces were the same. They were the faces of those who had dominated the political scene in the Gold Coast since the close of World War II.

It was Busia who presented the opposition's platform to the Gold Coast and to the world abroad. He provided the public with an innocuous definition of federation, declaring that "it meant cooperation, friendship and equality, but did not mean separation."[113] It was Busia who represented the opposition in a political debate with the CPP's Gbedemah—a debate which filled the pages of the *Daily Graphic*, the *Pioneer*, and the *Evening News* in the days preceding the election.[114] And it was Busia who announced to the governor on the eve of the election that, "in accordance with constitutional practice in the United Kingdom, the National Liberation Movement and its allies will expect Your Excellency to call upon Doctor K. A. Busia, their Parliamentary Leader, to form a Government should they (together with the independents supporting them) win more than 52 seats at the election."[115] With several of his old GCP cadre—John and Nancy Tsiboe, J. B. Dan-

A NLM election postcard. It included the caption: "The porcupine has driven away the fish, Osagyefuo [a praise name often associated with Nkrumah] a.k.a. CPP has been defeated."

quah, and M. K. Apaloo—it was Busia who set the dominant tone for the NLM's country-wide election campaign. These long-time political activists believed that the NLM had gained a firm footing in Asante and that efforts should be concentrated on the Colony, the CPP's stronghold.[116] But a concerted drive into the south required that the Movement downplay, if not deny, its origins. Thus, much of the Movement's countrywide campaign emphasized the corruption of the CPP and the necessity of having safeguards written into the constitution prior to independence in order to protect the Gold Coast from centralization and dictatorship. "The Ashanti appeal," as Austin writes, "was understandably kept at a minimum."[117] When the Movement inaugurated its Colony campaign in Accra on June 24, Bafuor Akoto assured his audience of over 20,000 that "The NLM [was] not for the Ashantis alone, but for all."[118]

But in Asante, this sort of tailoring of political appeals would not go far, so there the election campaign, like the original NLM mobilization in 1954, remained rooted in loyalty to the Golden Stool and in the right of Asantes to determine their own destiny, While campaign leaflets aimed at a Colony audience made the sober plea to

> VOTE FOR NLM AND ITS ALLIES
> For they are the Countries [*sic*] most
> trustworthy and patriotic servants who
> hold your mandate . . .
> VOTE FOR NLM
> For better Administration for our
> dear country[119]

those aimed at an Asante audience appealed to Asante national sentiment:

> VOTE FOR NLM
> . . . AKOTOISM . . .
> VOTE FOR NLM
> For the Nation wants you to do your duty,
> Death unto the red cockerel
> FEDERATION—YA TE YE HO[120]

According to Austin, "Almost every NLM meeting [in Asante] emphasized the need for loyalty to the Asantehene and the Golden Stool in order to protect Ashanti interests."[121] Just as in the early days of the

Movement, rallying cries centered on the economic importance of cocoa to Asante, the sanctity of chieftancy, the historic autonomy of the nation, and the invincibility of *Asante Kotoko*. It was every Asante's historic and national duty to vote for the NLM. And it was in the context of local election rallies that this duty was brought home. "The familiar setting of the NLM campaign," writes Austin,

> was an open clearing before the chief's palace or the nearby lorry park, where the start of a 'mass rally' was heralded by local propaganda vans playing the NLM highlife tune—*akoko suesue* [red cockerel—shoo!]. The chief and his elders would arrive and take their seats on the platform, to be followed by a succession of local speakers who proclaimed their readiness to die for the Golden Stool while demanding a higher cocoa price. . . . There would then follow supporting speeches from an MAP leader in his long white Islamic robe amidst cries of *Yate ye ho!* and *Islam!*, the pouring of libations, the swearing of oaths, affirmations of loyalty to the NLM.[122]

Within Asante, the CPP tried to counter NLM appeals with accusations that Asante nationalism was a manifestation of "tribal feudalism," an obstacle to independence. In its election manifesto, *Operation Independence,* the CPP argued that the voter had a simple choice to make: "Do I want Freedom and Independence NOW—this year . . . ? Do I want to revert to the days of imperialism, colonialism and tribalism?" The manifesto continued, "If you are faint-hearted enough and your spirit of nationalism is so pitiably deficient that you incline your mind towards the second question, then you are no concern of ours. . . . "[123] But the NLM was ready to respond to the CPP's charges that, by supporting the Movement, Asantes had chosen tribalism and colonialism over freedom and independence. In leaflets, editorials, and speeches, members of the NLM challenged the CPP's own brand of nationalism—accusing members of the CPP of having no sense of traditional heritage, of being mere European-surrogates who, having stripped themselves of their cultural baggage, were now intent on extinguishing the true national spirit of Asantes. "We do not want to change ourselves into a nameless race," began a poem published in the *Pioneer,*

> Or rudely spurn the royal embrace
> For a mob of prodigal slaves . . .
> But however much we toil
> We can never succeed

In turning a royal African
Into one without a class
Anymore than farmers can
Turn cocoa trees into grass.
Republic or a Monarchy?
'Socialist' or Native?
Is your vote indicative
Of what you want to be?
What our forebears say to you is
'Natives be Real'
And if you want to scrap the real,
It will scrap you.
Vote to save your ancient soil,
Vote for your dignity,
Vote to redeem what the stranger stole,
Vote for the cocoa tree.[124]

Thus, Janus-faced, the NLM organized support for its election campaign. Outside Asante, a sober veteran Gold Coast politician, like Busia, appealed to voters in the Colony, the North and Transvolta/Togoland in the name of "better administration for the country." Inside Asante, NLM leaders appealed to loyal soldiers, in the name of the Asantehene, to save the Asante nation. This two-pronged strategy was absolutely essential if the NLM were to have any chance of entering parliament as part of an anti-CPP majority. There were 104 seats in the Legislative Assembly: 44 for the Colony, 13 for Transvolta/Togoland, 26 for the North and 21 for Asante. The opposition needed at least 53 seats in order to form the next government and determine the constitution of an independent Gold Coast. The leaders of the NLM believed that their allies in the North and in Transvolta/Togoland could gain control of 25 seats. They were also confident of gaining at least 16 of the 21 Asante seats.[125] Thus, it was essential that the opposition gain at least 12 seats in the Colony, and this meant that the NLM had to ameliorate the long-standing tension between Asante and the Colony in the period of a few weeks.

As Austin argues, in one of the most thorough analyses of the 1956 campaign, it was not completely out of the question on the eve of the election that the NLM might gain a solid footing in the Colony. "There were the three Akim Abuakwa constituencies, where Nana Ofori Atta and the State Council were campaigning for the NLM," he writes, and there was "the hope that internal disputes within the local branch and constituency executives would damage the CPP, as happened in 1954 . . . [when] the CPP had lost six Colony seats to Independents."[126] Thus, the NLM put up 21 candidates for the seats in Asante and 18 for seats in the Colony and relied on its allies in the North and to the east to cover the election battle in those areas.[127] Filled with optimism, the NLM and its allies looked to a narrow but nevertheless secure victory which would see them winning at least 53 of the Assembly's 104 seats on July 17. The march into parliament would be a march to victory.

To almost everyone's surprise, considering the violence which had plagued Asante since the inauguration of the NLM, the day of the election was strangely calm. Though two had died in a July 1 rally when the CPP launched its election campaign in Kumase, on July 17 there was not a single incident requiring police action in any of the twenty-four wards of Kumase.[128] Two days after the polling, the *Pioneer* brought the official results to Asante. A magnifying glass was required to find the story. After weeks of bold-type headlines foretelling an NLM victory, the *Pioneer* published the election results in a narrow, right-hand column under the somewhat misleading headline, "Two Former CPP Ministers Defeated." The Ministers had been defeated, but the full picture was given in a first sentence which somberly began, "Mr. Kwame Nkrumah's Convention People's Party has won the General Election which was held last Tuesday with an absolute majority and will therefore form the next government."[129]

For the NLM and its allies, the picture was bleak. The CPP won 71 of the 104 seats in the Assembly. The opposition forces did not win a single seat in the Colony and gained only 5 in Transvolta/Togoland, 15 in the North, and 13 in Asante.[130] In the Asante constituencies, the CPP captured 8 of 21 seats and 43 percent of the total votes cast.[131] Although country-wide the popular vote was not as disheartening—the opposition carrying 43 percent of the total—the reality was that Busia would not form the next government, and the NLM would not determine the course of events in the Legislative Assembly leading the Gold Coast to independence. The battle of the ballot box was decisively lost.

When the Legislative Assembly reconvened, there were only thirteen NLM men seated (including one who had, in name, stood as an MAP candidate): Cobbina Kessie (MAP), E. K. Kurankyi-Taylor, R. R.

Amponsah, C. Ntoso, A. W. Osei, B. F. Kusi, J. A. Owusu-Ansah, Victor Owusu, Joe Appiah, I. B. Asafu-Adjaye, J. D. Wireku, R. B. Otchere and K. A. Busia. Ironically, with the exception of Kessie, none of these men were involved during the early days of NLM recruitment and mobilization in late 1954. None were from among that original group of Asante's youngmen who gathered at the source of the Subin River. Yet all three of the men who left the CPP in February, 1955, were now seated in the Assembly.

But why were the NLM seats so few? In no small part, the answer to this question lay in the liabilities inherent in the leadership's political strategy. In the final analysis, the Movement could not be, at one and the same time, the vanguard of the Asante nation and the country's UGCC reborn. Voters in the Colony, no matter what their grievances against the CPP, were not going to forget their long-standing suspicions of Asante in the course of a few frenzied political rallies. Though the Executive's watering-down of the "Asanteness" of the Movement paved the way for the forging of alliances with the leadership of other opposition groups in the country and served to justify the decision to contest elections in the Colony, it was not sufficient to allay wider Colony fears of an "Asante invasion." Even the common bond of cocoa was not enough upon which to build a bridge of reconciliation across the Pra River. As Austin writes, the Colony cocoa farmers, "as they listened to the propaganda coming out of the Ashanti capital and saw the preparations being made for the extension of the party into the Colony . . . saw the NLM not as the farmers' friend but as the spearhead of a new Ashanti invasion of the south."[132] And the CPP successfully capitalized on this fear in the weeks prior to the election. Looking back at the NLM's resounding defeat in the Colony, Bafuor Akoto recently recalled, "The CPP was *very* strong there. And the people in the South, they fear Asante. They think that if they join the NLM, then Asante will become once again a very powerful nation and will rule over them like we once did. They [the CPP] encouraged opposition to us on this basis. . . . Before the election, I went all over the country. In the South the CPP was saying to the people, 'They only want to rule you like their ancestors did.' "[133] From October, 1954, headlines which proclaimed that "the Asantehene may be made Monarch of the Gold Coast" to March, 1956, headlines announcing that the Asantehene, Akoto, and several others were conspiring to assassinate Nkrumah and Governor Arden-Clarke, voters in the Colony were constantly reminded of the ever-present "imperial" threat posed by Asante.[134]

Yet it is misleading to put the full blame for the NLM's overwhelming defeat in the Colony on historic suspicions and fears. Only a year earlier, there were indications of potentially fertile ground for mobilization among certain sectors of the Colony's working class. Since late 1955, several prominent political trade unionists, including Pobee Biney and Anthony Woode, had begun to question the fact that leadership positions within the Gold Coast Trades Union Congress (TUC) were dominated by non-trade-unionist CPP stalwarts. They challenged the party's insistence that "workers should wait til Independence Day before asking for their rights."[135] When Biney and others led the split in the CPP-dominated TUC in September and October of 1955, which led to the formation of the Congress of Free Trade Unions,[136] the NLM heralded the event as proof that the CPP was rapidly losing its footing among the working class, that "workers can't be fooled [by the CPP] all the time."[137] Yet despite these initial expressions of sympathy for the cause of rebel trade unionists, the NLM failed to capitalize on working-class disillusionment with the CPP.

Although the evidence is particularly muddy on this issue, it appears there was some attempt by the rebel trade unionists and certain members of the NLM to forge a working alliance in 1955. Early that year, colonial intelligence reported that Kurankyi-Taylor was in touch with Anthony Woode.[138] In September, Chief Regional Officer Loveridge reported that "Batsa, Anthony Woode and others have been around Kumasi visiting leaders, assessing the situation and apparently deciding to 'cash in' when the time was ripe."[139] A few weeks later, his successor, Russell, reported to the governor that the new Congress "had recently made approaches to the NLM." Although the "NLM and such trade unions can have little in common," he continued, "the outward appearance of friendship has no doubt lent encouragement to the NLM."[140] This was clearly a development the colonial officials found most disturbing, and Loveridge, before he left office, did everything he could to discourage such an unholy alliance:

> If really subversive elements choose to join the NLM (and the NLM accepts them) there is nothing much to be done except to reinforce the counter measures. The true Ashanti nationalistic feeling is, however, represented by

the Asanteman Council (and less and less by the NLM as the NLM spreads its roots), and it did seem to me that firstly it was dangerous for Ashanti nationalism to become the tool of really bad men and, secondly that there was a duty to stop such an association if possible. I consequently sounded the Asantehene on his appreciation of the dangers; I found that he had not appreciated them, but was very quick to do so. He used phrases implying that the Ashanti Nationalistic Movement must be kept pure.[141]

The events that followed suggest that the Asantehene took Loveridge's warnings to heart and that his suspicion of the rebel trade unionists came to dominate the NLM's mobilization strategy. There is little, if any, evidence of contact between the NLM and the CFTU after November, 1955. Moreover, it is probably safe to assume that the rebels had second thoughts about an alliance with the NLM after having thoroughly assessed the situation in Kumase. Perhaps initially intrigued by the actions and pronouncements of Asante's youngmen, the anti-CPP trade unionists eventually pulled back from a working relationship with the Movement because of the conservative nature of its leadership and the indomitable role of the Asantehene. No matter how disillusioned trade unionists had become with the CPP, they could not view the NLM as an alternative political outlet for organized labor in the Gold Coast.[142]

Only in the last days before the election did the NLM leadership hastily attempt to capitalize on worker disaffection with the CPP. Citing a host of strikes during the first months of 1956, a *Liberator* editorial proclaimed: "But the CPP Government who these workers voted to power disappointed them. Justice must have its course. . . . Workers, poor and suffering masses, the future is in your own hands. Get ready and go to the polls and demonstrate to the whole world that no political party can fool you forever."[143] For the most part, however, such political rhetoric fell on deaf ears. Even in Sekondi-Takoradi, where the CFTU was inaugurated and had its strongest base of support, the NLM was met with indifference at best, outright enmity at worst. The propaganda van which the NLM specifically purchased for campaigning in the area had to be kept in a garage for the duration of the campaign because of local hostilities.[144] "We know the CPP has squandered money," the railway and harbor workers told local opposition speakers, "[and] we will vote for them to squander even more. . . . It is the hungry man who eats. The present Assembly members are now satisfied. So we will vote them again."[145] Joe Appiah recalled similar sentiments being voiced by Takoradi workers. They told him the opposition " 'is full of lawyers, doctors, professors and too many wise men who may indulge in corruption too cleverly to defy detection. So in the end it might be better to vote in the not-too-clever Nkrumah and his CPP; at least we can always catch them out when they indulge in further corruption and bribery.' "[146] And vote for them they did. The results in Sekondi-Takoradi told the tale: the pro-NLM candidate received only 220 votes to the CPP's 8310.[147]

If the factors underlying the NLM's dismal showing in the Colony were fairly transparent, the reasons for the Movement's unimpressive results in Asante are not so straightforward. Granted, the NLM won the majority of Asante seats and polled a majority of the votes, but why, given its specific Asante nationalist appeal, did it lose eight of the Asante seats, and why were 43 percent of the votes cast for the CPP? Most political analysts, Austin included, point to the manipulation of local rivalries; that is, they argue that local rifts were translated into political party allegiances.[148] Such an approach certainly elucidates the losses in Wenkyi East, Sunyani West, Sunyani East, and Berekum. In these districts the Brong rebellion against the Golden Stool became an NLM/CPP rivalry. In its April, 1956, *White Paper on Constitutional Proposals,* the CPP government had announced its intention to create a separate Brong region and to recognize a separate House of Chiefs. In the July election, these four Brong constituencies voted solidly for the CPP.[149] Similarly, the CPP victory in Adansi Banka was due in no small part, as Austin asserts, to the "quarrel between the Adansi paramount chief (supported by the Asantehene) and the subordinate chiefdom of Akrokerri which solidly voted for the CPP." The victory in Sekyere East was rooted in the "rivalry between the Kumawuhene and the Asantehene."[150]

Indeed, the number of appeals filed by destooled Asante chiefs with the CPP's minister of local government under the newly amended State Councils Ordinance provides ample evidence of the CPP's success in undermining NLM support in certain key areas of Asante. In early March, 1956, the minister of local government forwarded to Asante's chief regional officer the first of the constitutional appeals under the new Amendment. Included among the ten cases were appeals from the Bekyemhene against the Asanteman Council's decision to destool him in 1955 and from the Akrokerrihene against the Asanteman Council's decision of 1954. In both Bekyem and Akrokerri, the CPP won decisive majorities on election day.[151] By making the government the final arbiter in local stool disputes, the CPP gained an important mechanism for penetrating into Asante. Local rivalries were transformed into political party contests. As Austin's 1967 discussion summarizes,

> Consider, for example, the so-called Ashanti-Southern conflict in the 1950s. At first sight, it might be thought to have been a tribal struggle: the Ashanti (represented by the NLM) versus the South (predominately CPP), and it did have something of that character. . . . On closer inspection the picture became more complicated, for it was also a Kumase-based NLM versus a western Brong-based CPP. . . . On a narrower view still it was *inter alia* a struggle among the Brong—between, for example, the Dormaa state and its allies on the one side (CPP) and a rival group based on the Wenchi chiefdom (NLM). And (to look yet more closely) the CPP-NLM conflict included a myriad of local disputes like that within the Dormaa state itself, between the paramount chief (CPP) and his local subordinate chief at Wamfie (NLM) and within the Wenchi state between the paramount chief (NLM) and candidates to the stool from the rival royal family.[152]

Yet this approach to the results of the 1956 election, emphasizing the paramountcy of local disputes in the outcome of parliamentary contests, tends to obscure other critical variables. It is important to look as well into the very dynamics of the NLM (and the changes undergone since the inauguration) and then to consider carefully what "mass politics" really encompassed in 1956. Although Austin emphasizes local rivalries, he also observes that on the eve of the election, "there was little to choose between the parties in respect of the candidates they put up—just as there was very little difference between the CPP and NLM constituency executives."[153] There were very obvious differences during the first months following the Movement's inception, but over the following year and a half, the popular front leadership of the NLM gave way, not without a struggle, to a leadership dominated by members of the intelligentsia, backed by the Asantehene—a leadership little different from that of the CPP.

And the similarities between the two parties—their candidates and their executives—clearly worked to the NLM's disadvantage in the context of the election. Faced with candidates who were more alike than different, many voters obviously decided not to vote at all. Only half of the country's registered voters cast their ballots on election day. Others, like the workers in Takoradi, must have taken into account that the CPP was the incumbent party, in control of the state apparatus, and able to allocate contracts and services. Though the Executive of the NLM tried to match the CPP in this regard—arranging loans for cocoa farmers through Cadbury and Fry to counter the influence of the CPP's Cocoa Purchasing Company and establishing open relationships with several expatriate firms—their efforts came to naught.[154] As one informant recently lamented, "In Africa, when you are the governing power, it is highly difficult to win an election from you. It is hard work."[155]

That the NLM's candidates were virtually indistinguishable from the CPP candidates, but lacked the clout of incumbency, was a major liability as the Movement entered the election. Compounding that liability was the fact that many supporters of the NLM began to question the very convictions of the Movement's candidates in the weeks before the election. Kusi Ampofu, the Movement's assistant general secretary, recently recalled that many doubted the sincerity of General Secretary Amponsah after he announced he would step down from his post in the Movement to run for office. According to Ampofu, many people questioned this decision: " 'You said you were coming to help build the organization. The organization is not built yet. Why should you leave at this stage to go and stand for election? Why?' So we found that he came out of personal ambition. Amponsah did. That was our impression and the impression of outside observers." But such criticisms were aimed not only at Amponsah. "Many politicians," Ampofu continued, "were attracted to this organization. They wanted to make it a political platform from which they could propagate their view, their ideas." "Personally," Ampofu concluded, "I think that our failure had to do with [the fact that] it was too much full of intellectuals—the leadership—who were not prepared to toe the line . . . everybody wanted to make himself show up so that he's the man automatically given all the coverage—the lead story. There were too many intellectual leaders."[156]

Such an analysis of the Movement's failings was not unique to Kusi Ampofu or the youngmen he represented. With a keen sensitivity to the limits of Asante nationalism and the liabilities and ambitions of its leadership, Abdul Alawa, a founding member of the Kumase MAP, highlights factors in the election often ignored by political analysts:

"The NLM members, you can't reckon that they're *all* strictly NLM members. . . . Some of them came to our side because they know that the Asantehene is the head of Asante and they know that the head of Asante likes the thing. So, though they are opposed to the Asantehene and they don't like the Party [the NLM], in reality . . . they seem as if they like the Party." Still others, according to Alawa, came to the Movement "for political office," and some came for money. "Those who came for money," he continued, "were really members of the CPP . . . but because of certain circumstances, they turned to the opposition. But these things are still in their veins. So when nobody is there, nobody will see them, they are still with Nkrumah. You put the ballot paper here and I am a member of the opposition and people know me, but I am still in the CPP. So, when nobody can see me, I put the ballot paper straight in the CPP box. Then, I come and tell you I have put it in the Opposition box. But, in fact, the ballot is in the CPP box."[157] One need not follow Alawa in imagining an NLM honeycombed with secret CPP supporters (or in charging conscious duplicity by Asantes who supported the NLM in highly charged rallies and opted for the CPP in the privacy of a voting booth) to appreciate the profound issues raised by the reminiscences of this veteran of mass mobilization who had witnessed the ascendancy of the ex-CPP stalwarts to the leadership of the NLM and the disheartening electoral results.

Indeed, the reminiscences of both Ampofu and Alawa provide insight into what was the larger and more crucial problem in 1956: the failure of *both* parties to mobilize mass participation in the final pre-independence election. Any unraveling of the polling results must take into account that only 50 percent of the Gold Coast's registered voters participated in the election (or 30 percent of the country's adult population). Thus the CPP's mandate was based on the electoral support of roughly 17 percent of the adult population (or 28.5 percent of registered voters). The NLM drew the votes of less than 13 percent of the adult population (or 21.5 percent of registered voters.) While these statistics alone paint a troubling picture of mass nationalist politics on the eve of independence, when compared to polling results in 1954, they are even more disconcerting. Despite two years of the most intense political battling the Gold Coast had witnessed, despite massive rallies, intense propagandizing, and the manipulation of local rivalries, a greater percentage of registered voters and a greater percentage of the adult population participated in the 1954 election! Unfortunately, none of these statistics can tell us why. They give no clue to the allegiances of the 70 percent majority of the adult population that did not vote, much less to the potentially decisive 50 percent who were registered in 1956 but did not cast ballots.[158]

It is impossible to determine whether the NLM was handicapped more by this low voter turnout than the CPP; it certainly proved no more effective in mobilizing for the ballot box. Alawa and Ampofu's recollections provide a partial explanation based on the indistinguishability of CPP and NLM candidates, doubts about the NLM leadership's sincerity, and questions about candidates' personal ambitions. But one cannot discount the fundamental difficulties inherent in attempts to transfer the energy and momentum of a political rally into the Westminster election process. In the context of large, energizing Movement rallies, replete with drumming and oaths of allegiance to the Golden Stool, Asantes either felt themselves to be a part of the collective strength of the Asante nation or feared the repercussions for not expressing such solidarity. These sentiments are not easily translated into electoral victories. In July, 1956, votes were not taken by open ballot at political rallies. Individuals, atomized and isolated from the collective strength of their "imagined community," made their choices. The vast majority cast no vote at all. If the Movement rallies of the previous years reinforced the collective, historical identity of Asantes (real and imagined) and underscored the vitality of Asante nationalist sentiment, the secret ballot reinforced both the rights and weaknesses of the individual outside the collective and revealed the very limits of Asante nationalism.

At the end of July, thirteen Movement men packed their bags and headed for the Legislative Assembly in Accra. They were individual victors in the battle of the ballot box, but they proclaimed to their party and to the Asante nation that their victories constituted a triumph for all. The results of the election, they protested, "When looked at regionally, as they must be, [showed] . . . that the case for the National Liberation Movement and its Allies has been established."[159] The opposition had won a majority of the seats in Asante, in the Northern Territories, and in the southern sections of Transvolta/Togoland. In the first days of August, as the Legislative Assembly opened, the opposition members continued to argue their case for federation on the basis of these regional statistics. Joe Appiah, in a lengthy and impassioned address, pleaded for members to consider the case of Great Britain: "Some Scotsmen [are] asking for home rule . . . Welshmen asking for some form of federation. . . . Would it be fair to the people, to the aspirations of the people of Scotland, and would it be fair to the aspirations of the people of Wales, if the question were put to the test on the basis of the overall majority of the votes collected at any general election to test that issue?"[160] Though Appiah and his comrades in the Assembly would not admit it, this was precisely the sort of test to which they had agreed when they decided the time was ripe to challenge the CPP at the polls. And it was on the basis of this very agreement that Nkrumah introduced a motion calling for independence on August 3. Busia, Appiah, Amponsah, and the rest of the opposition members of the Assembly walked out.[161] The motion passed 72 to 0. Yet the opposition exodus was only a weak gesture of defiance. With independence just around the corner, the NLM representatives had only one option: to walk back into the Assembly.

6

"And a Thousand More Will Come?"

The NLM's Demise and the Legacy of *Asante Kotoko*

When Nkrumah's motion for independence passed the Assembly on August 3, the immediate significance of the election results was brought home to all members of the Movement, from those conspicuously absent from their seats in the Legislative Assembly to those rank-and-file supporters who anxiously awaited word of events taking place in Accra. The agreement dictated that whoever won the battle of the ballot box would be empowered to form the next government and lead the Gold Coast to independence. Nkrumah and the CPP had won the voters' mandate (if not the broader mandate of the Gold Coast's adult population) and the British government, with an easy conscience, was now prepared to hand over power. The men who brought the NLM along the constitutional path and into the halls of the Assembly found themselves left with few options in the wake of the opposition's overall defeat.

Throughout most of August and a good part of September, the NLM and its allies in the Assembly refused to take part in the parliamentary proceedings—those very proceedings which, only a month earlier, they had heralded as the only means for safeguarding Asante's autonomy. For a brief moment, in early August, the politicians of the opposition appeared clueless on how to proceed, how to salvage their strategy. Meanwhile, the youngmen of the AYA, yet again, began to call for the total secession of Asante from the Gold Coast. Cabling the secretary of state on August 13, the AYA announced that "since CPP

Government have declared themselves unwilling to call for consultations before the Motion calling for Independence, [this] shall be considered by Ashanti as repealing the Order in Council of 1901 which annexed Ashanti to the British Crown. Ashanti shall then be a Sovereign and Independent State within the Commonwealth."[1]

The Asanteman Council, more drawn to such drastic appeals than in previous months, wired the secretary of state that it considered "the action of the Gold Coast Government in tabling a motion for Independence without an agreement on the future constitution of the country to be unrealistic, irresponsible and only likely to lead to undesirable consequences."[2] The Council gave no indication as to what those consequences might be, but on the following day it issued a bold reminder: "Ashanti has the right to state the terms on which she will associate with the other territories on the withdrawal of the British."[3] However, in contrast to the AYA, the Council was not yet prepared to assert that right.

As the youngmen talked of secession, the leadership of the Movement began to regroup. The members of the Assembly returned to Kumase to consult with the Asanteman Council and to consider what steps should be taken in the face of the CPP's majority in the Assembly. The decisions reached reflect little change in the leadership's strategy: it still held faith in the British government's ability to intervene. On August 12, Busia left for London to plead the NLM's case. Amponsah and J. A. Braimah (of the NPP) left to join him and the opposition's permanent representative in London, William Ofori-Atta, on August 23. Together, the four men would reenact the well-rehearsed scenario upon which the NLM leadership had relied time and again in the past: circumventing the government and the colonial officers in Accra and appealing directly to the Colonial Office in London.

With the delegation pursuing its task in London, the opposition members of the Assembly agreed to return to their seats in order to take part in the debate over the recently published results of the Commission of Enquiry into the Cocoa Purchasing Company. The Commission's *Report* concluded that the CPP did control the CPC, that loans were only given to pro-CPP farmers, that CPC vehicles had been used by the CPP in the Atwima-Nwabiagya by-election, and that bribery and corruption existed among CPC officials, including the company's managing director, A. Y. K. Djin.[4] If the delegation in London was not able to sway the secretary of state, so it was maintained, the results of the *Report* had just the ammunition the opposition seated in the Assembly needed to call for the resignation of the CPP government.

Thus, in the first two weeks of September, the leadership of the NLM and its allies launched a two-pronged attack against the CPP, challenging its integrity on the floor of the Assembly and appealing for British intervention in the London office of the secretary of state for the colonies. Yet the challenges were not being confidently launched, as had previous challenges, from an offensive position of strength. The opposition, as Austin writes, "was now on the defensive, and its leaders knew they had to secure the best terms they could" considering their minority position within the Assembly.[5]

On September 10, the opposition delegation met with the minister of state in London. Although the memorandum submitted prior to the meeting advocated "a federal union for the Gold Coast at independence" (based on the fact that " 'The Gold Coast' as a single state or colony has never existed and does not exist in law"[6]), during the course of the meeting the delegation argued for modified "constitutional safeguards," including Regional Assemblies, Second Chambers for chiefs, the "decentralisation of the police," and "security of tenure for the Judiciary." It also attempted to persuade the minister of state that the announcement of the date for independence should be postponed until a royal commission was appointed to work out an acceptable constitution for the country.[7] The following day, the delegates met with the secretary of state for the colonies. There they reiterated the need for "constitutional safeguards,"[8] and, realizing that their plea for a royal commission was getting nowhere, assured the secretary of state that if he "would consent to preside over a brief conference in the Gold Coast it might be possible to resolve the more important differences between Government and Opposition."[9] After meeting with the delegation at the House of Commons, a Fabian Colonial Bureau member remarked that the "delegation had come to London in a spirit of compromise and had to a large degree modified their earlier demands for federalisation."[10]

Although the Colonial Office, by its own admission, had "considerable sympathy with the views of the opposition,"[11] and was "impressed by their sincerity, the conviction with which their views are held and the moderation of their attitude,"[12] it stood firm in its position that the Gold Coast delegation had to work within the parameters of the Legislative Assembly. The opposition could not circumvent the government in Accra and expect to make headway in London. The Colonial Office could not delay announcing the date of independence without having such a delay attributed to the influence of the delegation, thus undermining the legitimacy of the Office in the eyes of Nkrumah's government.[13] While neither the secretary nor the minister of state dismissed out-of-hand the possibility of a visit to the Gold Coast, they agreed that such a visit would have to occur after the announcement of the date of independence.[14] Given the firm position of the Colonial Office, the opposition delegates announced they would be "reasonably satisfied if the provisions for Regional Assemblies and for Second Chambers . . . were written into the constitution."[15] On these grounds, the Colonial Office prepared to set the stage for the final resolution of the crisis.

Barely a week after meeting with the opposition delegation, the secretary of state announced on September 18 that he would introduce shortly an Independence Bill to the House of Commons, that the date for independence was set for March 6, 1957, and that the Gold Coast would thereafter be known as Ghana.[16] Despite the delegates' attempts to have the announcement postponed, the "spirit of compromise" they displayed in London affirmed the secretary's belief that the time was now right to proceed toward independence. In a letter to Nkrumah the day before he made his announcement, the secretary assured the prime minister that "the more responsible of the Opposition leaders have come at last to acquiesce in the impossibility of a federal constitution and now seek only to ensure that there are safeguards in the unitary constitution to meet regional susceptibilities. . . . I do honestly believe that in drawing up the constitutional documents it will be found that the difference between what they want and what you offered in your White Paper is really much narrower than either side at present realise or than I myself had believed possible."[17] On September 19, Nkrumah announced that the CPP government was prepared to discuss constitutional questions with the opposition before the official debate on the constitution began in the Assembly.[18] The "spirit of compromise" appeared infectious.

The date of independence announced, and the Colonial Office firm in its resolve not to intervene, the parliamentary opposition was now left to "secure the best terms they could."[19] In the Legislative Assembly, demands for Nkrumah's resignation in the wake of the *Report* on the CPC quickly subsided, and the Assembly members graciously accepted Nkrumah's offer to discuss the constitution in the prime minister's conference room. On October 16, talks began between eight members of the opposition and eight members of the CPP. However, after receiving complaints from the Asanteman Council that they, too, should be included in these preliminary constitutional discussions, Nkrumah, under some pressure from the Colonial Office, via the governor, extended an invitation to the Territorial Councils to send two representatives each to Accra for separate talks on October 30.[20] The Asanteman Council responded by demanding that the opposition representatives be allowed to attend the Territorial Council session. Nkrumah again agreed and the Asanteman Council's representatives, Victor Owusu and the Akyempemhene, Nana Boakye Dankwa, were dispatched to Accra.

Recently declassified minutes of the constitutional meetings in Accra provide ample evidence that the leadership of the NLM, aware of the opposition's minority position in the Assembly and cognizant of the compromising stance taken by the recent delegation to London, abandoned completely the concept of federation. Through most of October, as members of the AYA continued to call for total secession, leaders of the NLM, particularly members of the Assembly, talked of the need for "basic safeguards" in the constitution, focusing discussion on regional assemblies and regional control of local government and local constitutional issues. *Regional autonomy* was now the catchword; *federation* had been summarily dropped.[21] While the government and opposition failed to reach agreement on the need for an Upper House, provisions for amending the constitution, or the question of dividing Asante into two regions, on the central problem of decentralization there was a large degree of consensus. Indeed, in the counterproposals presented to the government in a meeting on October 19, the opposition delegation unequivocally announced, "We of the Opposition are prepared to modify our former position to allow the residuary powers to remain at the centre."[22]

Yet the "spirit of compromise" had not embraced everyone. Busia confided to the Colonial Office in early October that he feared "the extremists . . . may have gained ascendancy" in recent weeks.[23] Not everyone in the NLM had abandoned the concept of federation or believed the Movement now had to be satisfied with the best compromise it could achieve. Not everyone recognized the electoral agreement which now restricted the NLM's actions to parliamentary negotiations and compromises. Not everyone was resigned to defeat with honor. A denial of defeat, flowing just beneath the surface of calm, formed an undercurrent of resistance during the days of negotiation in Accra. Rumors circulated in mid-October that the CPP had no intention of incorporating the opposition's proposals into the constitution, that it had already sent its draft constitution to the secretary of state in London, and that the current negotiations were simply a means of quieting the opposition in the wake of the Assembly's passage of the motion for independence.[24] Despite the opposition delegation's contention that agreement had been reached on many important points, rumors began to spread that discussions had ended in a complete deadlock.[25]

On November 8, the government released its *Revised Constitutional Proposals for Gold Coast Independence*, and the results of the proceedings in Accra were revealed to all. The opposition's comments were limited to the appendix, thus lending substance to earlier rumors that the government's proposals were drafted and sent to London before negotiations in Accra began. The official parliamentary opposition immediately issued a statement asserting that there were "a few but very important discrepancies" in the government's White Paper.[26] However, unaware that the opposition delegation had gone into the proceedings conceding the retention of most powers to the central government (and unaware that the bulk of the White Paper had been drafted before those proceedings were undertaken), many must have considered "discrepancies" to be a major understatement. While the *Revised Proposals* guaranteed the position of the chief and allowed for a House of Chiefs for each region, the chiefs were limited to advising the central government only on matters pertaining to customary law and constitutional matters of a traditional nature.[27]

More importantly, while the government agreed that "there should be a measure of devolution of powers from the Central Government to the Regions" and advocated the establishment of Regional Assemblies, the powers of these Assemblies fell far short of even the most compromising formulations offered by the NLM leadership. The Assemblies' powers were to be "similar to those of the London County Council" and were vaguely limited to "all such matters as Parliament may from time to time determine."[28] Further, the government refused to state it had abandoned its notion of dividing Asante into two, arguing that "if it was possible to establish a second region in Ashanti to meet the Brong demands then consideration should be given to the setting up of the region."[29] In short, the government's *Proposals* made it absolutely clear that all power was to remain at the center, and that the sovereignty of parliament was to be supreme.[30]

While the parliamentary opposition decried the discrepancies between the government's *Proposals* and what they contended had been agreed to beforehand, in the *Liberator* the youngmen of Asante ran a daily half-page announcement from November 9 to the 15th declaring: "ASHANTI AND THE N.T.'S WILL SECEDE FROM GHANA." As these threats of secession filled the *Liberator,* the Legislative Assembly began to debate the government's *Proposals,* and after a marathon session on November 13 in which Nkrumah spoke for three and a half hours on the various aspects of the White Paper, the Assembly approved the draft constitution on the 14th by a vote of seventy to twenty-five[31] On November 16, the *Liberator* headline announced: "ALL ASHANTI YOUTH DECIDE ON DATELINE FOR SECESSION ASHANTI NATIONAL FLAG TO BE READY ON DECEMBER 26, 1956." The undercurrent of resistance during the negotiations in Accra now swelled to the surface and suddenly it appeared that the youngmen, once again, were not alone. After the passage of the government's *Revised Proposals,* the very members of the parliamentary opposition who earlier talked of discrepancies now began to echo the call for secession.

Secession: Threats, Plans, and Political Maneuvers in the Twilight of Colonial Rule

Never had secession been threatened with such outward determination. Since the early days of the movement, the NLM always maintained Asante's right to decide its relationship with the rest of the Gold Coast, but secession was never given full, serious consideration by most Asantes. In November, 1956, however, the threat of secession transcended the realm of political debate and rationalizations. For the first time, many made concrete plans to sever permanently Asante's relationship with the Gold Coast.

On November 18, the NLM and the NPP sent a joint resolution to the secretary of state announcing that "in view of the failure to reach agreement on the constitution, we now ask for separate independence for Ashanti and the Northern Territories and for a Partition Commission to divide the assets and liberties of the Gold Coast among its component territories."[32] The following day, the Asanteman Council endorsed this resolution by requesting that the United Kingdom take all steps necessary to grant a separate independence for Asante and the Northern Territories on March 6.[33] "The bonds to replace British control have not been fashioned," the Council argued, " . . . and the people of Ashanti therefore demand seperate [*sic*] independence for Ashanti."[34] Over the next two days, further endorsements followed from the AYA and the Asante Kotoko Society.[35] On November 26, the Executive of the NLM sent another cable to the secretary of state declaring that "Ashanti shall, on the basis of equality, seek union with the Northern Territories of the Gold Coast . . . pending the final withdrawal of British control, interim Governments shall be established before March 6, 1957 in Ashanti and the Northern Territories."[36] As Akoto informed a large rally in Kumase on November 25, "From today Ashanti and the North are one and have seceded from the Colony. Regard every N. T.'s man as your countryman."[37]

Never had the leadership of the NLM put such substance in their secessionist rhetoric. Not only was the secretary of state requested to initiate the necessary steps for a separate grant of independence for the Northern Territories and Asante, but preparations began for that separate grant. In mid-October, the Asanteman Council, the Nayiri (on behalf of the Northern Territories), and the Togoland Congress retained the services of the solicitors Coward, Chance, and Company in the event there was a failure to agree upon the constitution.[38] By the end of November, these solicitors submitted an eight-page brief to the Colonial Office, on behalf of the parties they represented, calling for the appointment of a Partition Commission.[39] Both Joe Appiah and R. R. Amponsah announced at several rallies that lawyers in London were engaged by the Movement to draw up the necessary legal documents for secession, and Appiah added on one occasion that these lawyers were also in the process of applying to the United Nations for membership on behalf of Asante and the Northern Territories.[40] By early December, plans were revealed for a £500,000 House of Parliament in Asante, and Amponsah announced that work on the constitution for an independent Asante and Northern Territories had begun.[41] Meanwhile, rumors widely circulated that Asante was in the process of purchasing arms.[42]

But did the call for secession, backed by elaborate plans though it was, represent a real break from the past strategy of the NLM leadership? Had the parliamentary forum finally been abandoned? Was total secession really considered a viable alternative by the leadership in the last weeks of 1956? Certainly, many Asantes believed then (and still believe to this day) that the leadership of the NLM was posing no idle threat in 1956 and that Asante was totally prepared to sever its links with the Colony. As Joe Appiah recalled, secession "wasn't an idle threat at all. Our people, the people were ready [and] . . . we knew how to move."[43]

And perhaps no one believed more in this preparedness than Asante's chief regional officer, A. C. Russell. Even before the NLM and NPP forwarded their secession resolution to the secretary of state, Russell wrote to Governor Arden-Clarke's secretary warning that a declaration of secession was imminent. He prefaced his remark by offering an overview of the deterioration of law and order in the region. He observed that thousands of Asante supporters of the CPP were now living in the Colony as exiles, that CPP municipal councillors had to have police guards to get them in and out of Kumase, and that Nkrumah had not been to Asante since August, 1954. Police reserves in Asante, usually numbering three platoons, had been increased to a permanent force of five and, on average, four additional platoons were stationed in the region. Thus, nearly 50 percent of the Gold Coast Police Reserve was stationed in or near Kumase. "Just as a nationalist and anti-imperialist wave has been sweeping the Gold Coast since 1948," he continued, "so has a nationalist and anti-Nkrumah wave been sweeping Asante." In concluding, he warned that "leading Ashantis are aware of the success of guerrilla tactics in Malaya, Kenya and Cyprus and of the fact that large numbers of disciplined troops are needed to deal with a much smaller number of rebels."[44]

For nearly a month, from mid-November to mid-December, Russell's fears that the NLM leadership had abandoned its constitutional path and that the nation was united in its support for secession appeared well-founded. Colonial officials in both Accra and London certainly operated under these assumptions. In a dispatch to Accra, the Colonial Office expressed grave concern: "Do you envisage it [the threat of secession] being backed by an appeal to force (or by civil disobedience which would challenge the Government to use force) either before or in the period immediately following the final transfer of power? If violence should occur on such an issue, could the present Government count fully on the police and local troops, bearing in mind their racial composition?"[45] The governor's office in Accra responded that "the intention to secede is seriously entertained by the Opposition leaders in Ashanti and by the Asanteman Council. . . . There is a distinct possibility that there will be sporadic outbreaks of violence in Ashanti leading up to non-co-operation with the Government at a point this side of Independence and to an unqualified declaration of intention to secede with effect from 6th March."[46] While a later dispatch sought to reassure the colonial authorities in London that there was little evidence that attempts would be "made to sabotage Government installations" and that there was "no firm evidence of preparations" for secession, it did warn that the "pattern of non-co-operation would depend very much on the Government's actions."[47]

After lengthy correspondence with colonial authorities in Accra, the secretary of state for the colonies responded to the demand for secession on December 10. In a measured, but firm statement, aimed at the more moderate leaders of the opposition, he wrote as follows:

> Her Majesty's Government do not consider that the partition of the Gold Coast is in the interests of the Gold Coast as a whole or of any of its component parts and cannot abandon their established policy which is directed toward the grant of Independence to the Gold Coast as a whole.
>
> Her Majesty's Government are now proceeding with the preparation of the necessary constitutional instruments having regard to all the circumstances of the Gold Coast and the efforts which were made to reach agreement locally. . . .
>
> The Grant of Independence to the Gold Coast is an act of good will which Her Majesty's Government trust will be received by the people of the Gold Coast in a spirit of responsibility which will command the respect of the world.[48]

Lennox-Boyd's words, reaffirming the position of the British government in no uncertain terms, pushed the NLM to the wall and shattered what was only a momentary illusion: the spectre of a united Asante nation prepared for total secession from the Gold Coast. As the secretary well knew, moderate forces within the Movement's leadership were not prepared to go that extra step, to take on the British government as well as Nkrumah's CPP. As soon as Lennox-Boyd let it be known that the British government would not tolerate any deviation from its blueprint for an independent Ghana, key NLM leaders quickly backed down.

The evidence suggests that the leaders of this retreat were K. A. Busia and the Asantehene and that the strategy for retreat involved reopening, by any means, negotiations on the constitution between Britain and the opposition which would allow the Movement's leadership to back down gracefully while retaining the support of the rank-and-file.[49] In their first reply to the secretary's announcement that there would be no partition of the Gold Coast, the NLM and its Allies responded that

> having regard to the fact that the Gold Coast is composite and to the incontrovertible evidence of incipient dictatorship, intolerance and corruption by the present Gold Coast Government, Ashanti will on no account accept the Gold Coast Government's Revised Constitutional Proposals. . . . Her Majesty's Government's policy to grant independence to the Gold Coast as a whole can therefore be achieved only if the Constitutional Instruments being prepared by Her Majesty's Government provide adequate safeguards and guarantee the legitimate interests and aspirations of the component territories of the Gold Coast.[50]

While this statement did not herald complete retreat, it did imply that other constitutional proposals would be welcomed and that the leadership was looking for a way out of the crisis.

A December 19 cable to the secretary of state from the Asanteman Council echoed similar sentiments:

> [T]he Council does not consider that autonomy to the component territories . . . conflicts with or frustrates established policy of Her Majesty's Government. . . . [T]he policy to grant independence to the Gold Coast as a whole shall . . . be achieved only if the Constitutional Instruments being prepared by Her Majesty's Government provide adequate safeguards and guarantee territorial autonomy. . . . As much as Ashanti would wish to be associated with other territories of this country . . . we wish to state that secession is an inherent right to which recourse may be had as a last resort by any nation whose liberties are at stake.[51]

Akoto, in his private cable, assured the secretary that independence for the Gold Coast as a whole could be achieved if the constitution embodied adequate safeguards.[52] Meanwhile, in a statement issued from London, Busia encouraged the leadership's retreat from secession and its search for a save-face settlement by assuring the Movement that the British government was able and ready to reconcile the differences between the CPP and the opposition.[53]

But as Busia and the Asantehene led the search for a peaceful solution and the retreat from secession in the last weeks of December, others prepared for civil war. Chief Regional Officer Russell reported in the first week of January that there was evidence of gun-running on a large scale into western Asante from the Ivory Coast.[54] Indeed, Russell was so concerned about the threat of civil war that he wrote to a fellow government agent in Cyprus for first-hand advice on countering guerrilla war tactics.[55] And while some in Asante began to arm themselves, colonial officials in Accra were compelled to discuss the precise tactics they would use in the event those guns were put to use. At a meeting in the governor's office on January 4, it was decided that the Special Branch needed to be trained in guerrilla warfare and that possible ways to undermine the forces in Asante might include the "systematic destruction of malcontents' farms," and the "denial of oil supplies [which] would automatically immobilize transport and stop the bringing of food into Kumase."[56] The governor argued that there were only two alternatives left open to the NLM: "sporadic violence, developing into wholesale attempts to annihilate political opposition or a full declaration of secession leading to open rebellion and civil war."[57]

Whether Arden-Clarke overestimated the lengths to which the NLM leadership was prepared to go or whether he underestimated its reluctance to challenge the secretary of state's declaration that there would be no partition, the governor certainly did not appreciate the final alternative open to the NLM leadership. Men like Busia and the Asantehene, whose dominance over the Movement was never successfully challenged from below, were more than prepared to lead a retreat from secession. All that was lacking were the circumstances which could veil such a retreat in a veneer of compromise.

Since mid-September, the Asantehene, Busia, Amponsah, and others pinned their hopes for a peaceful reconciliation between the NLM and the CPP on the expectation that the secretary of state would come to the Gold Coast and personally mediate the constitutional dispute. The secretary's personal intervention was essential for a retreat with honor. On December 19, the Asanteman Council wired Lennox-Boyd requesting that he either come to the Gold Coast or dispatch a parliamentary committee to help solve the constitutional deadlock.[58]

Shortly thereafter, Busia, as leader of the opposition, promised the fullest cooperation of the opposition if the secretary or some parliamentary group would come and mediate the constitutional dispute.[59] By early January, it was obvious the Movement's leadership and its constitutionalist strategy were still intact. Few were prepared to challenge the leadership's retreat from secession. A January 4 Asante Regional Delegates Conference of the NLM resolved that while it had "approved arrangements being made to establish a separate Independent government in [the] event of [a] failure to reach a constitutional agreement, . . . [it] endorsed efforts being made by the NLM here and abroad to make it possible to reach agreement on the Constitution before March 6, 1957."[60]

By mid-January, the secretary of state for the colonies was prepared to take the initiative, but not because of the series of requests issued by the opposition. In early December, the secretary had separated the Ghana Independence Bill from the Order in Council which would determine the essentials of the constitution. The House of Commons passed the Independence Bill with ease on December 8, but there was ongoing debate over the Order in Council as many members of Parliament argued that the future welfare of an independent Ghana rested on agreement over the constitution—agreement that had to be reflected in the Order.[61] The secretary realized that the Order in Council was the key to reconciliation between the CPP and the opposition. Thus, pressured by the misgivings voiced in the House of Commons, the secretary had already decided by mid-December that he had to personally intervene in the crisis. In a hastily written note to his office, he wrote: "Don't please think of 1,000,000 reasons why not. The Governor will do that for us. I feel very strongly about this and am about decided to go."[62] The following week, the governor was informed of the secretary's intentions and reassured that the "strong desire" he had to visit the Gold Coast was "formed quite independently of Busia's suggestion."[63]

Nkrumah was not easily convinced of the necessity of a visit by the secretary of state. His first reaction was to adamantly oppose the idea. He believed the visit would be "regarded as a triumph for the Opposition" and that the "whole Constitution would be thrown into the melting pot." He would be forced to make concessions "which would render [the] constitution unpalatable to his party and unworkable in practice."[64] After lengthy discussion, the governor was able to reassure Nkrumah on many points. He suggested that Nkrumah publicly issue an invitation to the secretary in order to avoid having the visit appear as a victory for the opposition. After much negotiation to make sure the visit was not "misunderstood or misinterpreted,"[65] Nkrumah issued his well-publicized invitation. "We are anxious," he wrote, "that the new constitution should be brought into being in an atmosphere of the greatest goodwill and if you consider that it would help you to finalise your White Paper if you paid a visit to the Gold Coast to have a personal exchange of views with me and my colleagues and with others, we shall be very pleased to see you."[66] Lennox-Boyd quickly accepted the carefully-worded invitation and prepared to set off on his mission. "If they [the Opposition] can be persuaded," Lennox-Boyd announced in early January, "that the Order in Council will contain the most important of the safeguards they have been asking for, they may be willing to withdraw from their present extreme position."[67]

Thus, on January 24, the secretary of state for the colonies arrived in the Gold Coast with one paramount goal: to convince the opposition that their interests would be safeguarded in the House of Commons Order in Council. It was not a formidable task. The secretary of state, by the very act of coming to the Gold Coast, succeeded in affirming and fortifying the NLM leadership's faith in its strategy and in the good intentions of the colonial government. Moreover, he created the very circumstances for which the leadership had searched, circumstances which would facilitate a retreat with honor from the secessionist demand. Even before he set foot in Asante, members of the Executive heralded the secretary's visit as a victory. Amponsah announced nearly two weeks before the visit that it might now be possible for the four regions to "enter Independence in peace, with unity, enthusiasm and hope." The secretary would now have "the opportunity," Amponsah continued, "of knowing the truth and of feeling justified in his decision to prepare a White Paper on the constitution not based on the Government's proposals."[68]

An Engineered Compromise, An Honorable Retreat, and a Loyal Opposition on the Eve of Independence

Lennox-Boyd arrived in Kumase on January 26. Over 5,000 were at the airport to greet him, and estimates suggest that over 70,000 lined the streets along the route to Manhyia Palace. Many had taken up their positions by 3:00 that morning. Though most in the crowd were dressed in mourning cloth, the jubilant atmosphere and the reception accorded the secretary were nothing like those Governor Arden-Clarke encountered on his visit to Kumase nearly two years before. Asante welcomed the secretary with open arms.[69] There was no hostility, there was no rock-throwing. This was the man to whom the NLM leadership had addressed its appeals for over two years as it bypassed the authorities in Accra. This was the man, they were convinced, who had the power to assure that Asante's interests were safeguarded in the constitution of an independent Ghana.

The Asanteman Council and the NLM leadership had one day to put forward their case to Lennox-Boyd and to justify their grievances and concerns with the government's constitutional proposals. They began their presentation to the secretary by assuring him that the chiefs and people of Asante were not motivated by hostility toward parliamentary institutions. "The position taken by the Asanteman Council," their prepared statement began,

> has been misinterpreted and therefore sadly misunderstood. The dispute itself cannot be presented as a struggle between traditionalism and modern democracy, especially as the Chiefs of Ashanti have accepted the introduction of British political institutions of Parliamentary and Local Government. . . . The dispute can best be presented as a struggle to protect chiefs against the concentration of power at the centre, a concentration which the experience of the past six years has proved to be highly dangerous and inimical to the liberties of individuals and minorities.[70]

Moreover, the Asanteman Council assured the secretary, the call for secession was made reluctantly. Asantes, given a degree of regional autonomy, looked forward to being part of an independent Gold Coast: "The aims of the Asanteman Council, therefore, have been a) the attainment of a degree of regional autonomy consonant with, on the one hand, the historical and cultural differences between the four territories and, on the other, our desire that the Gold Coast remain a single state; b) the introduction of a constitution which will tend to promote democracy and hinder the acquisition of absolute power by any single group or component territory." The resolution to secede, the statement continued, "and our request for a partition commission were the consequences of the Gold Coast Government's determination to frustrate the two aims stated above."[71]

The safeguards which the Movement leadership wanted to see included in the British government's Order in Council were then presented. The Order should, they argued, recognize the Asantehene as the natural head of Asante. It should provide that a Regional House of Chiefs alone be responsible for local constitutional and traditional matters. It should provide for one Regional Assembly and one Regional House of Chiefs for Asante, and it should guarantee that the Gold Coast's Regional Assemblies be established before independence. In response to the government's ambition to carve a Brong Region out of Asante, the leadership also urged that the Order "guarantee that the boundaries of Ashanti . . . remain inviolate" and that it dictate that constitutional amendment require more than a two-thirds majority.[72] With few exceptions—the primary one being the establishment of a separate Brong Region—the safeguards demanded by the Movement differed little from those suggested by Frederick Bourne in his *Report* of 1955, or by the Achimota Conference in its *Report* of 1956, or by the government, for that matter, in its *Revised Constitutional Proposals*.[73] The Movement was now advocating the very concept, regional autonomy, and those very structures, Regional Assemblies, which Bourne and the government had repeatedly offered for well over a year and which the opposition had repeatedly dismissed outright.

As he prepared to leave the Gold Coast four days later, Lennox-Boyd was filled with confidence that his mission was a success. There appeared to be little standing in the way of an agreement between the CPP and the opposition. Both groups supported the idea of Regional Assemblies as the means of addressing the problem of diversity in the country. Indeed, at a press conference at Christianborg Castle on January 30, the secretary remarked that he had been "more surprised by the underlying unity and the wide measure of agreement" than by the differences among the Gold Coast people on the constitutional issues.[74] He also reassured the NLM and its allies, the *Pioneer* reported, that "he himself . . . was a strong believer in tradition and felt that the Chiefs would still have a very important part to play in the affairs of this country for many years to come. . . . He said he would see to it that the institution of chieftancy was well-protected in the Order of Council."[75] Such reassuring statements encouraged many Asante to look toward independence with optimism, confident that the constitutional crisis was about to be settled. The *Ashanti Times* reported that a Gallup-style poll of political opinion taken in Kumase following the secretary's visit indicated "there are grounds for hoping that the constitutional issue will be settled amicably although there will be much 'palaver' on some very vital points."[76] Indeed, the governor later remarked that Lennox-Boyd had done the virtually impossible: "[y]our visit . . . allayed the worst misgivings of the Opposition parties regarding the shape of things to come, while . . . reassuring Ministers and the Government supporters of your own *bona fides* and that of HMG."[77]

As the *Ashanti Times* predicted, there was much "palaver" over the next few days, but it was centered in London, as the Colonial Office, aided by final discussions with CPP representatives Gbedemah and Botsio and opposition representative Ofori-Atta, prepared its White Paper on the Gold Coast's constitution. On February 8, the contents of the White Paper were published simultaneously in London and Accra and almost immediately both sides in the constitutional dispute heralded the paper as a great victory and agreed that an amicable settlement was about to be reached. In Asante, the *Liberator* headline for February 11 announced, "Kumasi Rejoices Over Contents Of White Paper."[78] The *Pioneer* reported that supporters of the NLM were jubilant over the White Paper, that there was much "merry-making" in Kumase, and that many people had smeared themselves with white clay—a symbol of victory and triumph. "General feeling," the report summarized, "is that the Opposition and Nkrumah will agree on it [the White Paper]."[79]

Considering the limited demands made by the opposition during the secretary's brief visit and the nature of the proposals put forward by the government over the past year (proposals which, in retrospect, met most of those demands), the Colonial Office's *Proposed Constitution of Ghana* contained few surprises. It included the division of the country into four regions, each of which would have a Regional Assembly and a House of Chiefs. It recognized a head for each region which, in the case of Asante, would be the Asantehene. The powers given to the Assemblies and to the Houses of Chiefs were essentially the same as those offered in the *Government's Revised Constitutional Proposals*.

The White Paper did, however, address several issues which had remained sources of contention between the leadership of the NLM and the CPP.[80] Paramount among these was the problem of amending the constitution. Throughout discussions, Nkrumah stood firm in his demand that the constitution be amended with a two-thirds majority. In the end, the Colonial Office acquiesced, but included specific safeguards to address the NLM's concern over Asante's boundaries and the threat of a Brong region being carved out of Asante. The White Paper stated that any alteration to the constitution which would increase the number of regions would require a referendum to be held in the region affected by the change. If passed, the proposal would then be put to the other regions, and if two-thirds passed it, it would then be sent to the National Assembly, where a simple majority would be required for the change to come into effect.[81] The White Paper further stated that any bill for the abolition or suspension of a Regional Assembly or for diminishing its powers would require the consent of the Assembly concerned.[82] Finally, the White Paper stated that in order for any basic clause of the constitution to be amended, the bill would first have to go to the House of Chiefs and then to the Regional Assemblies. Two-thirds of the Assemblies would have to approve such an amendment before it could have its third reading in the National Assembly.[83]

While safeguards such as these reflected the Colonial Office's willingness to address many NLM concerns and assured the participation of its leadership in the government of an independent Ghana, they far from symbolized an opposition victory in the constitutional dispute. The British government held firm to its blueprint for a unitary government for Ghana and a March 6 date for independence. The CPP similarly stood firm. The central government, the National Assembly, would retain most powers, a two-thirds majority would be required to amend the constitution, and the establishment of Regional Assemblies would be postponed until after independence. All significant shifts in position were made by the opposition. It was the leadership of that opposition which, in essence, took the 1956 proposals of Bourne and others and molded them into the opposition "demands" of 1957.

But the leadership of the opposition quickly heralded the White Paper as a major victory. On February 11, Busia announced, "We have made it difficult for anybody to be a dictator in the Gold Coast. . . . The NLM has achieved for all people in the country true Parliamentary democracy."[84] On the same day, at a meeting of the Asanteman Council, the Asantehene urged that all "Ashanti refugees domiciled in Accra and elsewhere . . . return home; they would be welcomed." He further announced that "Chiefs who as members of the Asanteman Council had refused to attend the Council's meetings and those of the unsuccessful Brong-Kyempim Council would also be received back into the fold."[85] There was victory in compromise; it was time to forgive and forget. Asante now prepared to march arm in arm with the rest of the Gold Coast to independence.

In the Legislative Assembly, the formal conclusion of the constitutional dispute was celebrated with full pomp and circumstance. Nkrumah, in his "Statement on the Ghana Constitution," proudly proclaimed: "The Leader of the Opposition and I are one in accepting the White Paper. . . . with mutual confidence and cooperation we are certain that the foundation of our Independence which is now being truly laid, will support firmly the superstructure of our political and economic life and lead to the greater happiness and progress of all sections of our nation." The leader of the opposition, K. A. Busia, was but slightly less enthusiastic about the contents of the White Paper. After he duly applauded the White Paper as a "workable compromise," Busia expressed concern that the divisions between the opposition and the CPP had run very deep over the past years and charged the Assembly with the responsibility of countering those divisions by providing a model of unity for the country on the eve of independence: "the Opposition have agreed to accept the United Kingdom's White Paper and the Order in Council to be based on it as a workable compromise. . . . I am painfully conscious of the deep divisions among the representative supporters of the Opposition and the Government which have resulted from our differences over the constitutional issue. I would appeal to all of both sides of this House to join together to work for the success and greatness of our nation."[86] Busia's concerns notwithstanding, from the perspective of the British colonial government, February 12 marked a crucial watershed in the political development of the Gold Coast. With independence less than a month away, the colonial power could now withdraw with an easy conscience and leave in its wake both a loyal majority and a loyal opposition.

Yet to gauge changes in political climate and to assess the efficacy of negotiations and compromises based on the pronouncements of parliamentarians can often result in a distorted political picture. Events in the Legislative Assembly certainly suggested that the constitutional crisis was over and that the demand for Asante self-determination had been adequately addressed once and for all. Indeed, even the Asanteman Council issued a resolution welcoming the statements made in the Assembly. "These proposals guarantee the territorial boundaries of

Ashanti and recognize the unity of the Asante nation," the Council proclaimed. "Now that there is agreement on both sides we hope that all in Ashanti will join in celebrating the achievement of Independence by the Gold Coast."[87] Yet events in Kumase reveal that some Asantes were not yet prepared to join in the festivities and were distrustful of the proclamations of victory and unity coming from Accra and from Manhyia. Indeed, some appeared unwilling to lay down their arms.

The first manifestations of this defiance came shortly after the February 12 session of the Legislative Assembly, when Nkrumah began to issue invitations for the independence celebrations in Accra. An equal number of invitations were sent to the Asanteman Council and the Brong-Kyempim Council—a clear signal that Nkrumah had not abandoned the Brong secessionists and was prepared, in due course, to make good his promise to establish a separate Brong region.[88] The following week, a new issue of the Gold Coast *Gazette* outlined proposed amendments to the constitution which would make it possible for the Brong chiefs of Dormaa and Tekyiman to appeal to the governor-general in constitutional disputes rather than to the Regional House of Chiefs, the Asanteman Council.[89] Shortly thereafter, rumors circulated in Asante that the CPP government intended to tear up the constitution as soon as the independence celebrations were over.[90]

Bafuor Akoto, aware of lingering resistance in Asante to the White Paper compromise, seized the opportunity presented by these events to resurrect the call for Asante self-determination. By his words and actions, Akoto brought about the first major split within the heretofore indivisible and indomitable power bloc whose constitutionalist strategy had guided the Movement for nearly two years. Less than two weeks before the scheduled date for independence, Akoto appeared before Chief Regional Officer Russell to announce that there would be no celebration of independence in Asante. All Ghana flags would be taken down and a partition commission should be summoned. In citing his reasons for renewing the secessionist call, Akoto pointed to the amendments appearing in the *Gazette*, the CPP's obvious intention to carve out a separate Brong region, and "several statements that had been made that the CPP would tear up the Constitution after Independence." Yet what was most telling about Akoto's visit was that he let it be known that the public call for Asante secession would not be made until after the British officially withdrew on March 6.[91] Implicit in this remark was an abandonment of faith in Great Britain and a conviction that the imperial power would no longer have a role in determining Asante's future. For Akoto, the time had come for *Asante Kotoko* to stand alone, rely on its own resources, and confront, on its own terms, Nkrumah's CPP.

Having long challenged the constitutional strategy of the Movement's leadership and the decision to wage Asante's battles within the halls of parliament, many youngmen echoed Akoto's sentiments. They questioned the leadership's acceptance of Regional Assemblies. As Ampofu recalled,

> I, myself, was pessimistic about the formation of regional assemblies. So, I told them that it wasn't actually autonomy that they had. The regional assemblies virtually had to work under the Minister in Accra. So, the Minister had the power to dissolve it or to do anything with it or to dictate to it. We had wanted autonomy, reasonable autonomy, a large measure of autonomy where we would be able to administer our own affairs, with the federal government centered in Accra, but not to be *under* a Minister who sits in Accra and dictates to us! So, we were very pessimistic about the whole affair.[92]

Outside Asante, some longtime NLM allies expressed similar pessimism, if not outright indignation, at the White Paper proposals and the concept of Regional Assemblies. S. G. Antor of the Togoland Congress denounced the White Paper on February 27 as a "Black Paper" which displayed total disregard for the wishes of the people of southern Togoland. A week later, on the day of independence, some members of the Togoland Congress took up arms in response to independence under the "Black Paper."[93] Such would not be the case in Asante.

Bafuor Akoto's threats to Russell, though echoing sentiments of disaffection similar to those expressed by leaders of the Togoland Congress, did not trumpet a new battle. For a brief moment, Akoto relinked arms with Asante's youngmen, but in 1957 not even Akoto was capable of moving the power bloc of chiefs and intellectuals who had dominated the NLM since the early months of 1955. Their only response to the provocative statements of the government in the days before independence was an expression of "concern" to the Colonial Office that the Order in Council be implemented in its entirety.[94] While Akoto's defection split the Movement's Executive into what Busia termed "the extremists and the ultra-moderates," it was a hairline fracture of little significance in both the long and short run. The balance of power still rested with the Asantehene and "the Asantehene," as Busia reassured Russell in late February, "is opposed to any immediate drastic action, wants to abide by the agreement to give the Constitution a fair trial and to pursue the Brong question constitutionally after Independence."[95]

As had been the case for nearly two years, the Asantehene and his allies within Asante's political intelligentsia—the "ultra-moderates," as Busia would have it—held sway. Those who refused to challenge British colonial authority and, one might argue, those whose power and position owed much to that authority, reigned supreme. Akoto's brief threat of secession was Asante's last flicker of extraparliamentary resistance to the British blueprint for an independent Ghana. On the eve of independence, less than two weeks after Akoto presented Russell with his demand for a partition commission, all was quiet in Asante. There was no evidence of the armed conflict, the nationalist resistance, which had rocked Asante for nearly two and a half years. Indeed, Russell was satisfied that "there was such a general desire for peaceful celebrations" that he removed most of the police reserves who had been stationed in Asante on an emergency basis for over two years.[96]

In his final dispatch to the Colonial Office, the governor wrote, "By and large, Ashanti . . . seems to have accepted its moral victory as adequate compensation for the abandonment of its claim for federal status. I have no doubt, however, that Ashanti will remain a thorn in the flesh of the Government for many years to come. There is good ground for hope that the responsibilities of nationhood will force the wilder politicians on both sides to a realisation that all parts of the country will have to swim together if they are not to sink separately."[97]

And on March 6 in Kumase, as throughout the rest of newly independent Ghana, the Union Jack came down and Ghana's Black Star was raised amidst cries of "Freedom!" The British were gone, but had much in Asante really changed? Asante's political intelligentsia—former-CPP and UGCC, alike—were in their rightful positions as members of the country's parliament and as representatives to the Asanteman Council. The Asantehene, the caretaker of the Golden Stool, stood firmly and indisputably in control of *Asante Kotoko,* living proof of Asante's historical tenacity. And the youngmen—those who had initiated the struggle for Asante self-determination—stood on the sidelines once again, amidst the "rabble" they so often roused.

Independence and Beyond: Asante Nationalism and the Fate of *Asante Kotoko*

Looking back over those critical months prior to Ghana's independence, Joe Appiah remarked in 1984, "Nkrumah, even in his grave, should thank [the Asantehene]. Now they are both on that side. Maybe they have discussed the matter over there. But he should be thankful to the gods-that-be. . . . If he had been one of the earlier fighting kings of Asante, I have no doubt at all what the outcome of it all would have been."[98] In many respects, Appiah was not overstating the case. Obviously, Nana Osei Agyeman Prempe II was not solely responsible for thwarting Asante's demand for self-determination and guaranteeing that Asante remained an integral part of an independent Ghana. Yet as the guardian of the Golden Stool, as the paramount symbol of Asante political authority and unity and as the focus of Asante national sentiment, the Asantehene cannot be cast as anything but the pivotal player in shaping the course of events between 1954 and 1957. It was the Asantehene who welded together the factions of Asante's political intelligentsia, endowing them with political legitimacy and empowering them to direct the course of the NLM. In an emergent Ghana, he consolidated Asante's ruling class—the "ultra-moderate" class of paramount chiefs, politicians, and large-scale cocoa farmers who were no more prepared to lead a mass-based challenge against Nkrumah's government after independence than they were prepared to challenge the British colonial government prior to independence.

While the British colonial government and the successive CPP government set limitations on the power of Asante's ruling class, neither managed to undermine its enduring hegemony within Asante. Such a challenge could only be launched from *within* Asante, from among those who could contest on Asante's national terrain the social and political hegemony of Asante's ruling class and its definition of national self-determination. While the political struggle of 1954–1957 was between the CPP and the NLM, it was, at the same time, a struggle, within Asante, within the NLM, over who would define the Asante nation.[99] The CPP was the victor in the first battle. The victors in the second battle were Asante's ruling class who, in the end, opted for the security of a sort of "indirect rule" under the CPP rather than face an open contest within Asante over the definition of Asante self-determination.

But in March, 1957, few were aware of the deep divisions which plagued Asante's nationalist struggle for self-determination; few understood the battles waged over control of that struggle or the long-term implications of that second victory. For most observers, March 6 was a day of triumph born of fruitful compromises beginning with Nkrumah's fateful decision in 1951 and ending with the opposition's acceptance of the British government's White Paper. Upon these compromises, many rejoiced, a foundation of stability had been built. The process of nation building and political integration had begun as the loyal opposition and the loyal majority, working within the bounds of a Westminster-style parliament, prepared to face the task of governing an independent Ghana.

Such was the momentary illusion. Such was the false sense of security engendered by unquestioning faith in the rules of the game. Granted, it was an illusion capable of easing the collective conscience of British colonialists, but it was not able to guarantee the security and stability of an independent Ghana. It only denied temporarily the dynamic, complex and oft-times explosive history of that society. It only veiled, for a brief historical moment, the deep class, ethnic, and national divisions that riddled Ghanaian society in 1957 and would continue to be sources of that country's instability in the years to come. It was only a matter of time before the celebrations and optimism of March 6 gave way to a haunting postcolonial reality.

In the Assembly, Asante representatives of the NLM attempted to safeguard their specific class interests while those upon whose shoulders they had victoriously ridden into the Assembly were left outside—the victims of depoliticization rather than the beneficiaries of a process of political empowerment or national integration. The mass popular front that was the NLM of late 1954 to 1955, a movement successful in mobilizing and politicizing so many in Asante, came to exist only in name after independence. Even the NLM's newspaper, *The Liberator,* ceased publication by 1958—only one manifestation of the complete disintegration of a movement whose strength had been in its broad, extraparliamentary appeal.

But it was not the case that Asante national aspirations had been sacrificed in the name of what some might deem a greater good—the creation of a strong, united, and loyal opposition to Nkrumah's CPP.

Far from constituting that "real Opposition" which so many had claimed would guarantee the stability of an independent Ghana,[100] the anti-CPP representatives in the National Assembly, of which the NLM was an integral component, were a weak, fragmented group which soon fell prey to internal strife and clashes of ego.[101] A shared dislike of the CPP did not a "real Opposition" make.

Yet in early November, 1957, three months after the CPP's annual conference adopted a resolution to ask the government to ban parties based on tribal or religious allegiances and a month before the CPP-dominated Assembly introduced such a bill,[102] the various components of the opposition came together in Accra, disbanded their respective parties, and inaugurated the United Party (UP), with K. A. Busia at the helm. The name belied the reality. As Nkrumah's CPP increasingly consolidated its position in the years ahead, the UP was incapable of meeting the challenge, falling victim to further internal fragmentation. As Austin summarizes, by 1960, "of the 32 opposition members at independence, 3 were being held in detention, 1 was in exile and 12 had crossed to the government side."[103]

But if the NLM representatives were doomed to being an impotent part of an even more impotent whole, their loss was not entirely Nkrumah's gain. Despite ineffectual representation in the Assembly and despite the continued unwillingness of the powers centered at Manhyia to challenge the CPP, Asante remained virtually as impenetrable to Nkrumah after independence as it had been since 1954–1955. Indeed, it was probably during that critical period that Nkrumah forever lost access to Asante's subaltern classes—the only ones who could have effectively mounted a challenge, from within, against the hegemony of Asante's ruling class. Thus, Nkrumah was left with only one option after independence: to try to reshape Asante from without, through consolidation of his own party's power, through infiltration of the traditional authority structures in Asante, and through outright repression. It was an option bound, in the long run, to fail.

The measures taken by the CPP to consolidate its power, particularly between 1957 and 1961, have been well documented,[104] yet some deserve recounting here as policies specifically designed to recast Asante's social, economic and political terrain from without. One of the initial actions taken by Nkrumah's independent government was the April, 1957 suspension of the Kumase Municipal Council and the assumption of its duties by a committee appointed by the minister of local government. Less than a week later, the Cocoa Purchasing Company, which had been the subject of so much controversy, was officially liquidated—something the NLM had been demanding since 1955. Yet the functions and duties of the company were taken over by the United Ghana Farmers Council, a body whose ties to the CPP were perhaps more explicit and direct than those of the CPC.[105] In essence, the CPP obtained full and direct control over the purchasing of cocoa, the foundation of Asante's economy.

But perhaps the CPP's most notable attempts to neutralize Asante were the attacks launched in 1958 on the Asanteman Council and on the Regional Assemblies, whose establishment was deferred until after independence. In February, 1958, the government appointed a special commission to examine the affairs of the Kumase State Council and the Asanteman Council, charging that over the past four years those customary authorities had abused their position, become involved in politics, and used money collected from rents on stool property for specifically political purposes.[106] The commission's final report found both Councils guilty as charged. In response, the government introduced the Ashanti Stool Lands Bill which made the governor-general the trustee of certain stool lands in the Kumase Division. Control of the rent or income deriving from those lands was transferred from the Asantehene's Lands Department to the government.[107]

Actions against the Regional Assemblies followed shortly. After appointing Regional Commissioners (all members of the CPP) to each of the regions, the CPP government passed legislation on the Regional Assemblies which, as Austin summarizes, "severely restricted the range of powers [suggested in the *Report* of the Regional Constitutional Commission] in effect reducing them to advisory bodies."[108] The opposition protested vehemently and boycotted the elections to the Assemblies, "thus opening the way," writes Austin, "for the revision of the 1957 constitution." In short order, the CPP-dominated Assemblies, including the one established in Asante, voted themselves out of existence, vesting all powers of constitutional change in the CPP-dominated National Assembly. In April, 1959, that Assembly easily passed legislation which divided Asante into two, creating a new Brong-Ahafo Region.[109]

The creation of Brong-Ahafo was but the most obvious manifestation of the CPP's attempts to undermine the structures of power in Asante. More subtly, and in continuation of its preindependence policy of manipulating local disputes, the CPP government supported destoolment proceedings brought against anti-CPP chiefs, upheld the position of pro-CPP chiefs and, early in 1958, proceeded to upgrade the status of chiefs who had been loyal to the party and to downgrade the status of those who had not. Thus, for example, the Duayaw Nkwantahene and the Offinsohene were downgraded from the status of paramount chiefs, while the Bekyemhene and the Akrokerrihene were upgraded to paramount status. Less than one year after independence, the government recognized the forced abdication or destoolment of several powerful pro-NLM chiefs, including the Edwesohene, the Kokofuhene, the Bekwaehene, the Berekumhene and the Bompatahene.[110]

While consolidation and infiltration were the primary means used by the CPP to recast Asante from without, of no less importance were the repressive actions taken against the leadership of the NLM/UP in the first four years after independence. Despite the obvious fragmentation of his opposition, despite the opposition's growing alienation from its diverse bases of support, and despite the obvious indications that the opposition, if left alone, would crumble of its own discord, Nkrumah launched a prolonged attack against the most prominent opposition leaders. First struck were those most vulnerable: two key leaders of the Muslim Association Party in Kumase, Alhaji Amadu Baba, Serikin Zongo, and Mallam Alhaji Alfa Lardan, head of the Zongo Volunteers. Both men were deported under the newly passed Deportation Act of August, 1957, on the spurious grounds that they were not Ghanaian citizens.[111]

By July, 1958, the government had the weapon it needed to censure and repress other leaders of the opposition: the Preventive Detention Act (PDA), which empowered the government, according to Boahen, "to arrest and detain for five years anybody suspected or found acting in a manner prejudicial to the defense of Ghana, to her relations with other states and to state security."[112] Under the notorious PDA, forty-one people were detained in November, 1958. A month later R. R. Amponsah was detained for allegedly plotting to overthrow the government,[113] and the following year he was joined by eight more prominent Asante members of the UP, including Bafuor Akoto.[114] Following the September, 1961, general strike by railway, dock, and transport workers—a strike supported by leaders of the opposition because it defied CPP-government demands for a return to work, and a strike bitterly crushed by the government—fifty leading members of the opposition were detained, including J. B. Danquah, Victor Owusu, Joe Appiah, Fred Sarpong, Kwame Boakye, and Osei Assibey-Mensah.[115] Busia obviously would have been on this list had he not gone into exile in June, 1959.

During these years, which witnessed the CPP's infiltration and undermining of customary authority structures, and its repression of the most prominent of Asante's political leaders, the Asantehene sat, for the most part, in silence. As early as February, 1958, the youngmen of Asante challenged the ambivalence of the Golden Stool's caretaker, deploring "the lukewarm attitude" of both the Kumase State Council and the Asanteman Council toward the CPP's policies and demanding to know "the action being taken . . . to check . . . [these] unconstitutional acts." The Asantehene and the Councils' response to the youngmen was issued in the form of a statement in March which unequivocally declared that the chiefs did not "support any political party in Ghana" and that they planned to "cooperate with the Government in power as they had cooperated with the former governments."[116] Perhaps what was most notable about this exchange was not the chiefs' declaration of noninterference, but the fact that the youngmen, in the face of everything, continued to look to the Asantehene for accountable leadership.

By 1961, the Asantehene was not only refusing to lead a challenge against the CPP, but was also denying that he had ever been a supporter of the NLM. In a January, 1961 broadcast on Radio Ghana, the Asantehene publicly abolished Akoto's family stool on the grounds that "he and his ancestors before him had always brought trouble upon the Ashanti nation." Akoto was then in detention. The Asantehene charged that Akoto had inaugurated the NLM without his knowledge or consent and that "this Movement had brought disaster upon the Ashanti Nation."[117] Obviously, the Asantehene's statement must be viewed in light of the pressure he must have been under to disassociate himself from those in detention. Yet one cannot help wondering what the Asantehene feared most: the power of Nkrumah's state or the loyal soldiers of the Golden Stool who, having brought such "disaster" upon their nation, now stood in foreboding silence.

In 1960 Nkrumah proclaimed, "The Convention People's Party is Ghana, and Ghana is the Convention People's Party."[118] There was little evidence in Asante to discredit Nkrumah's proclamation. The Regional Assemblies, which were the cornerstone of the NLM's compromise with the government in the months before independence, were gone. Asante had been divided into two separate regions. Much of its political intelligentsia had been silenced, and the Asantehene would soon deny that he had played any role in the struggle for Asante self-determination. By all appearances, Nkrumah's strategy of dismantling Asante from without was successful. By all appearances the CPP was, indeed, the victor in the struggle which had begun in 1954, or nearly so. In 1962, briefly and mysteriously, a clandestine group emerged in Asante calling itself the "Asante Unknown Warriors." The group wrote Nkrumah in July, 1962, warning him to "watch his step" when he visited Kumase.[119] Nothing came of this threat, and very little evidence exists of subsequent activities of the Warriors, who seem to have vanished as mysteriously as they appeared.[120] Although the Unknown Warriors did not shatter the illusion of Nkrumah's 1960 proclamation, they do stand as a telling omen that all was not as it appeared to be. On February 24, 1966, Nkrumah was toppled in a military coup, and *Asante Kotoko* seemed to emerge from hibernation to join in the jubilant reception of of the news.

But if *Asante Kotoko* lived on, sustained and protected by anonymous Warriors and loyal foot soldiers, those legions have not been the long-term victors in Asante's national struggle. Indeed, through thirty-five years of coups and countercoups, interspersed with periods of civilian rule, the real victor has been Asante's ruling class. And herein lay the legacy of the NLM. Asante's ruling class won the struggle within the NLM over the definition of Asante self-determination and thereby transformed a popular national struggle, an expression of the diverse aspirations of Asantes in an emerging Ghana, into a battle to retain, by constitutional means, its own hegemony. The security of Asante's ruling class, rooted in the precolonial past, was maintained through British colonial rule and has survived the policies of a succession of post colonial regimes since 1957. Indeed, if victory can be measured in continuity, in historical tenacity, and in enduring hegemony, the uncontested winner has been Asante's elite.

The noted American historian C. Vann Woodward once remarked that counterfactual history "liberates us from the tyranny of what actually did happen."[121] In concluding, it may be useful here to explore one critical counterfactual question. What if Nkrumah had agreed to the earliest demands of Asante's youngmen for virtual autonomy for

Asante? Clearly the terrain of struggle within Asante would have been much different. The fundamental social and economic contradictions among Asante's youngmen, the chiefs, and the old- and new-guard intelligentsia would have been brought into sharp relief as each group vied for control of an autonomous Asante. Indeed, by agreeing to the youngmen's demands, Nkrumah could have forced into the open the contest in Asante over definition and control of that nation—a contest heretofore distorted and overshadowed by the broader struggle against the CPP.[122] In such a contest, the victory of Asante's ruling class was not inevitable. The formal demand for self-determination having been addressed, it could no longer shape the terrain of political struggle within Asante. Nkrumah would have unleashed upon Asante's ruling class those very youngmen and that very "rabble" who had transformed the Gold Coast's political struggle in 1948. He might have forced the youngmen not only to rouse the rabble, but to help articulate and support their specific class demands. Indeed, if Nkrumah had conceived of national liberation in terms broad enough to accommodate the demands of the National Liberation Movement, perhaps the CPP would have found an "ideological insert" into Asante, as Roger Murray describes it, and could have linked itself "explicitly and concretely with poor farmers, the floating agricultural proletariat and Zongo dwellers *against* old and new privilege."[123] In such a scenario, perhaps Asante's *nkwankwaa* might finally have escaped their fate as loyal foot soldiers of the Golden Stool.

But Nkrumah's conception of national liberation, though broad enough to encompass the entire African continent, was not broad enough to encompass the demand, within his own country, for Asante autonomy. Thus, the social conflict within Asante has continued to take a back seat to Asante's broader struggles with the central government. The definition of Asante self-determination remains the definition offered by Asante's ruling class on the eve of independence, and Asante nationalism remains the province of a ruling class which has consistently used it to foster its own privilege. Asante's youngmen, the *nkwankwaa*—those who were the catalyst behind the 1954 resurrection of *Asante Kotoko*—remain locked in an historical limbo, prisoners of a nationalism so defined as to render them incapable of effectively challenging Asante's ruling class. Social and economic hegemony continues to be the preserve of those chiefs and political intellectuals who, since gaining control of the NLM, have held securely the reins of power in Asante. Those nameless, faceless men and women—the small-scale cocoa farmers, the *abusa* laborers, and the urban workers whose militancy and mass support made the NLM an imposing force—stand in foreboding stillness. They have not, as some predicted, been integrated into the modern civil state. They have been, quite simply, disarmed and silenced. And *Asante Kotoko,* unchallenged from within and unassailable from without, remains a force with which all Ghanaian governments must contend. In the words of Akoto, "even today, in the future, we can always secede if anyone troubles us."[124] All are reminded that "if you kill a thousand, a thousand more will come." But the question continues to be posed, as pressing now as in 1954: Who shall lead the thousands, and in what direction must they go?

Notes
Bibliography
Index

Notes

Preface

1. While it is impossible to offer a complete listing of works on precolonial Asante, a representative sample might include Kwame Arhin, "Rank and Class Among the Asante and Fante in the Nineteenth Century," *Africa* 53:1 (1983), 2–22; idem, "Peasants in Nineteenth Century Asante," *Current Anthropology* 24:4 (1983), 471–80; Thomas Lewin, *Asante Before the British: The Prempean Years, 1875–1900* (Lawrence, Kansas: Regents Press of Kansas, 1978); Thomas C. McCaskie, "Accumulation, Wealth and Belief in Asante History. I: To the Close of the Nineteenth Century," *Africa* 53:1 (1983), 23–43; idem, "Accumulation, Wealth and Belief in Asante History. II: The Twentieth Century," *Africa* 56:1 (1986), 3–22; idem, "*Ahyiamu*—'A Place of Meeting': An Essay on Process and Event in the History of the Asante State," *Journal of African History* 25:2 (1984), 169–88; and idem, "Komfo Anokye of Asante: Meaning, History and Philosophy in an African Society," *Journal of African History* 27:2/3 (1986), 315–39; Robert S. Rattray, *Ashanti Law and Constitution* (Oxford: Clarendon Press, 1929); Enid Schildkrout, ed., *The Golden Stool: Studies of the Asante Center and Periphery, Anthropological Papers of the American Museum of Natural History* 65:1 (New York, 1987); William Tordoff, *Ashanti Under the Prempehs, 1888–1935* (London: Oxford University Press, 1965); Ivor Wilks, *Asante in the Nineteenth Century: The Structure and Evolution of a Political Order* (Cambridge: Cambridge University Press, 1975); idem, "Dissidence in Asante Politics: Two Tracts from the Late Nineteenth Century," in Ibrahim Abu-Lughod, ed., *African Themes: Northwestern University Studies in Honor of Gwendolyn Carter* (Evanston: Northwestern University Press, 1975), 47–63, and idem, "The Golden Stool and the Elephant Tail: An Essay on Wealth in Asante," in George Dalton, ed., *Research in Economic Anthropology*, vol. 2 (Greenwich, Conn.: JAI Press, 1979), 1–36; Larry Yarak, *Asante and the Dutch, 1744–1873* (Oxford: Clarendon Press, 1990). See also Ivor Wilks and Thomas McCaskie, eds., *Asantesem: Bulletin of the Asante Collective Biography Project* 1–11 (1975–9).

2. For examples of scholarship focusing on British imperial policy and the transfer of power, see the following essays in Prosser Gifford and W. R. Louis,

eds., *The Transfer of Power* (New Haven: Yale University Press, 1982): Dennis Austin, "The British Point of No Return," 225–48; John D. Hargreaves, "Toward the Transfer of Power in British West Africa," 117–40; A. H. M. Kirk-Greene, "A Historiographical Perspective on the Transfer of Power in British Colonial Africa," 567–602. See also Richard Rathbone, "The Transfer of Power in Ghana, 1954–1957," (Ph.D. thesis, University of London, 1968). For a critique of the trend toward emphasizing the imperial variable in African history, see Richard Crook, "Decolonization, the Colonial State, and Chieftancy in the Gold Coast," *African Affairs* 85:338 (1986), 77–8 and passim.

Chapter 1. "Leaving the Dead Some Room to Dance"

1. See McCaskie, "Accumulation," II: 3 and 19. This article represents one of the first attempts to bring the weight of Asante's precolonial history to bear on the twentieth century.

2. See, for example, the works cited in note 1 of the preface. *Asanteman* is translated as the "Asante state."

3. In this bibliographical discussion, I limit my focus to those works which explicitly address the Asante National Liberation Movement. They are, of course, representative of broader currents in African studies, but the density of the literature precludes a full, comparative discussion here. For useful historiographical overviews of the extensive literature on nationalism, ethnicity and the state and the paradigms which have marked various trends over the years, see John Lonsdale, "States and Social Processes in Africa: A Historiographical Survey," *African Studies Review* 24:2/3 (1981), 139–225, and M. Crawford Young, "Nationalism, Ethnicity and Class in Africa: A Retrospective," *Cahiers D'Etudes Africaines* 103:26:3 (1986), 421–95.

4. Young, "Nationalism, Ethnicity and Class," 429. See also Anthony D. Smith, *State and Nation in the Third World: The Western State and African Nationalism* (New York: St. Martin's Press, 1983) for a general critique of modernization theory. Smith writes of modernization theorists that "their functional approach . . . to the role of ideology, with nationalism often being viewed as a form of 'political religion,' has tended to inhibit a more historical-causal analysis of the rise of nationalist movements and ideologies within the framework of colonial territories; with the result that current political and social structures assume the status of 'givens' of historically necessary outcomes—as they appeared to be in the West." (4–5)

5. Thomas Hodgkin, *Nationalism in Colonial Africa* (London: Muller, 1956), 23.

6. Dennis Austin, *Politics in Ghana, 1946–1960* (London: Oxford University Press, 1964), passim.

7. See Clifford Geertz, "The Integrative Revolution: Primordial Sentiments and Civil Politics in the New States," in Geertz, ed., *Old Societies and New States: The Quest for Modernity in Africa and Asia* (New York: Collier-Macmillan, 1963), 109–30 and passim. For Young's discussion of the impact of Geertz and primordialism on Africanist scholarship, see "Nationalism, Ethnicity and Class," 449–50.

8. See David Apter, *Ghana in Transition* (Princeton: Princeton University

Press, 1972); idem, "Ghana," in J. S. Coleman and C. G. Rosberg, eds., *Political Parties and National Integration* (Berkeley: University of California Press, 1966), 259–315; idem, "The Role of Traditionalism in the Political Modernization of Ghana and Uganda," *World Politics* 13 (1960), 45–68; and idem, "Some Reflections on the Role of a Political Opposition in New Nations," *Comparative Studies in Society and History* 4 (1962), 154–68. Austin offers a similar analysis in his "Opposition in Ghana: 1947–1967," *Government and Opposition* 2:4 (1967), 539–55.

9. Lonsdale, "States and Social Processes," 197.

10. Ibid., 150.

11. See Bob Fitch and M. Oppenheimer, *Ghana: End of an Illusion* (New York: Monthly Review Press, 1968), 53–80.

12. Ibid., 59–60. The term *Asante* is sometimes rendered as *Ashanti*. Arhin considers the latter to be the result of anglicization. See Arhin, "Peasants in Nineteenth Century Asante," 471 fn. Christaller suggested that the spelling resulted from the fact that "the interpreter of Mr. Bowdich (the author of a very important book on Asante) was an Accra man." See J. G. Christaller, *Dictionary of the Asante and Fante Languages*, 2d ed. (Basel: Basel Evangelical Missionary Society, 1933), 427.

13. LeRoy Vail, "Introduction," *The Creation of Tribalism in Southern Africa* (London: James Currey, 1989), 3.

14. David R. and A. C. Smock, *The Politics of Pluralism: A Comparative Study of Lebanon and Ghana* (New York: Elsevier, 1975), 1.

15. Ibid., 68, 204–5, and 154.

16. Peter Osei-Kwame, *A New Conceptual Model for the Study of Political Integration in Africa* (Washington, D.C.: University Press of America, 1980), passim.

17. Ibid., 195. K. C. Morrison offers a similar analysis in his "Ethnicity and Political Integration: Ashanti, Ghana" (Ph.D. thesis, University of Wisconsin–Madison, 1977).

18. Vail, "Introduction," 3.

19. Osei-Kwame, *A New Conceptual Model*, 98.

20. Richard Rathbone, "Businessmen in Politics: Party Struggle in Ghana, 1949–1957," *Journal of Development Studies* 9:3 (1973), 398–9. See also idem, "Opposition in Ghana: The National Liberation Movement," in *Political Opposition in the New African States* (University of London, Institute of Commonwealth Studies, Collected Seminar Papers Series, no. 4), 29–53; "Politics and Factionalism in Ghana," *Current History* 60:355 (1971), 164–7; "The Transfer of Power in Ghana." Cf. Crook, "Decolonization," 96–103.

21. Indeed, many of the nineteenth-century chroniclers, upon whose work historians base their reconstructions of Asante's past, frequently use the term *nation* in describing the nineteenth-century *Asanteman*. See, for example, the correspondence of T. B. Freeman, R. Brookings, and others associated with the Wesleyan Methodist Mission in the Gold Coast. Methodist Mission Society Archives [School of Oriental and African Studies], West Africa: Gold Coast, Correspondence, 1835–1896.

22. See, for example, Benedict Anderson, *Imagined Communities: Reflections on the Origin and Spread of Nationalism* (London: Verso, 1983); Ernest Gell-

ner, *Nations and Nationalism* (Oxford: Blackwell, 1983); and Eric Hobsbawm, *Nations and Nationalism Since 1780: Programme, Myth, Reality* (Cambridge: Cambridge University Press, 1990).

23. Political scientist Maxwell Owusu has recently argued that historically "the most influential nationalism of Ghana has been that of the Asante nation-state which became the prototype of later nationalisms of the region." See his "Kingship in Contemporary Asante Society," in Schildkrout, ed., *The Golden Stool*, 164.

24. Wilks, *Asante*, 668–74 and 720.

25. See, for example, Anderson's discussion of "official nationalism" in Anderson, *Imagined Communities*, 80–103; Hobsbawm's discussion of government or state-sponsored nationalism in *Nations and Nationalism*, 80–100; and Smith's discussion of bureaucratic or state-sponsored nationalism in *National Identity* (London: Penguin, 1991), 54–70.

26. Ivor Wilks, "What Manner of Persons Were These? Some Reflections on Asante Officialdom," in Schildkrout, ed., *The Golden Stool*, 129.

27. McCaskie, "Accumulation," I: 29–30. Most scholars of Asante history rely on notions of "Asanteness" or Asante "national sentiment" to explain Asante structural tenacity, but few have explored the content of that sentiment. For example, Tordoff writes, "Ties of sentiment to the Golden Stool . . . tended to attract rebellious member-states back into the Confederacy." See Tordoff, *Ashanti Under the Prempehs*, 14.

28. McCaskie, "Accumulation," II: 14–17.

29. Anthony D. Smith, *The Ethnic Origins of Nations* (Oxford: Blackwell, 1986), 137 and passim.

30. Smith, *State and Nation*, 68–9.

31. Gellner, *Nations and Nationalism*, 81–83; Hobsbawm, *Nations and Nationalism*, 71 and 137.

32. Anderson, *Imagined Communities*, 66.

33. Ibid., 40.

34. Ibid.

35. Young, "Nationalism, Ethnicity and Class," 453–4. Young argues that in contrast to the "debates raging over the nature of class," ethnicity enjoys a broad consensus which has been given "magistral summary" by Donald Howowitz in his *Ethnic Groups in Conflict* (Berkeley: University of California Press, 1985).

36. Barth, for example, views "boundary maintenance" as the key to ethnicity. See Fredrik Barth, ed., *Ethnic Groups and Boundaries: The Social Organization of Culture Difference* (Boston: Little, Brown, 1969), 15.

37. See, for example, Horowitz, *Ethnic Groups*, passim, and Vail, *The Creation of Tribalism*, passim. Lonsdale writes that "ethnicity is . . . seen as the bugbear of contemporary Africa." See his "African Pasts in Africa's Future," *Canadian Journal of African Studies* 23:1 (1989), 134.

38. Horowitz, *Ethnic Groups*, 55.

39. Smith, *Ethnic Origins of Nations*, 212, 18.

40. Lonsdale, "African Pasts," 134–5.

41. See esp. Lonsdale's "States and Social Processes," 201–5 and "African Pasts," 134–7.

42. Vail, *The Creation of Tribalism*, 6–7.

43. Gellner, *Nations and Nationalism*, 86–7.

44. Smith, *State and Nation*, 66–7.

45. See, for example, Rathbone's response to my recent article, "The Youngmen and the Porcupine: Class, Nationalism and Asante's Struggle for Self-Determination, 1954–57," *Journal of African History* 31:2 (1990), 263–79. The response and my reply appear in the *Journal of African History* 32:2 (1991), 331–8. "The argument is written," he argues, "from a discernibly 'Asante nationalist' position and a rather populist one at that" (333).

46. Gellner, *Nations and Nationalism*, 55. See also Hobsbawm, *Nations and Nationalism*, 9–10.

47. Gellner, Breuilly, and Hobsbawm emphasize politics in their definition, while Anderson and Smith devote more attention to the cultural content of the "imagined community" or the "ethnic core." See Gellner, *Nations and Nationalism*, 1–38; Hobsbawm, *Nations and Nationalism*, 9–14; John Breuilly, *Nationalism and the State* (Manchester: Manchester University Press, 1982), 1–5; Anderson, *Imagined Communities*, 11–40; and Smith, *Ethnic Origins of Nations*, passim; idem, *National Identity*, passim, esp. vii, 43, and 82.

48. See Lonsdale, "States and Social Processes," 201, and Allen Isaacman's discussion of ideology as contested terrain in his recent bibliographic overview, "Peasants and Rural Social Protest," *African Studies Review* 33:2 (1990), 49 and 55.

49. Lonsdale, "African Pasts," 141. The notion of "leaving the dead some room to dance" is drawn from Wole Soyinka's play, *A Dance of the Forests* in his *Five Plays* (London and Ibadan: Oxford University Press, 1964), 39.

Chapter 2. Cocoa and *Kotoko*

1. *Pioneer*, 18 September 1954.

2. For detailed descriptions of the inauguration festivities, see *Pioneer*, 20 September 1954, and *Daily Graphic*, 20 September 1954.

3. The "Aims and Objects of Liberation Movement" are published in full in the *Pioneer*, 20 September 1954.

4. *Pioneer*, 20 September 1954.

5. *Pioneer*, 4 September 1954.

6. For various descriptions and interpretations of the Positive Action campaign, the 1951 general election, and the CPP's assumption of power, see Austin, *Politics in Ghana*; Apter, *Ghana in Transition*; Florence M. Bourret, *Ghana: The Road to Independence 1919–1957* (London: Oxford University Press, 1960); Basil Davidson, *Black Star* (London: Allen Lane, 1973); Fitch and Oppenheimer, *Ghana: End of an Illusion*; C. L. R. James, *Nkrumah and the Ghana Revolution* (London: Allison and Busby, 1977); Manning Marable, *African and Caribbean Politics* (London: Verso, 1987); Kwame Nkrumah, *Ghana: The Autobiography of Kwame Nkrumah* (London: Nelson, 1957); George Padmore, *The Gold Coast Revolution* (London: Dennis Dobson, 1953); Rathbone, "Businessmen in Politics."

7. For an account of these alliances, see Austin, *Politics in Ghana*, 134–9.

8. For a brief description of several of these parties, see Austin, *Politics in Ghana*, 138–9. In addition, there are correspondence files relating to the People's

Democratic Party and the Gold Coast Labour Party at Manhyia Record Office (hereafter, MRO), Asanteman Council, Miscellaneous Files (hereafter, AC)/217/50 (People's Democratic Party) and 168/49 (Gold Coast Labour Party).

9. Austin, *Politics in Ghana*, 138. All of the small groups which proliferated prior to the 1951 general election supported the idea of self-government. They primarily differed with the CPP over when and how. For example, the National Labour Party, in alliance with the Gold Coast Labour Party in Kumase, declared its aim to be "Immediate National Independence," but argued that there had to be an "Organized Labour Structure in this Country to champion the cause of Labour." See Kwame Kesse-Adu, *National Labour Party* (Kumase, 1950, pamphlet). See, also, Austin, *Politics in Ghana*, 138–40.

10. See esp. Horowitz, *Ethnic Groups*, and Anderson, *Imagined Communities*.

11. Breuilly, *Nationalism and the State*, 168. For a useful retrospective overview of Africanist scholarship on "sectional" politics, see Young, "Nationalism, Ethnicity and Class," 442–50.

12. For detailed examinations of the MAP and politics in the *zongo* communities, see Jean Allman, " 'Hewers of Wood, Carriers of Water': Islam, Class and Politics on the Eve of Ghana's Independence," *African Studies Review* 34:2 (1991), 1–26; Enid Schildkrout, "Islam and Politics in Kumase," *Anthropological Papers of the American Museum of Natural History* 52:2 (1974), 113–37; idem, "Strangers and Local Government in Kumase," *Journal of Modern African Studies* 8:2 (1970), 251–69; idem, *People of the Zongo* (Cambridge: Cambridge University Press, 1978); J. H. Price, *The Gold Coast*, "Chapter 3," (unpublished manuscript, 1956).

13. *Pioneer*, 3 February 1954.

14. Austin provides a detailed account of the formation of the MAP, TC, and NPP and their struggles in the 1954 general election in *Politics in Ghana*, 184–94 and Chapter 5, passim.

15. For a tabulation of the results of the 1954 election, see Austin, *Politics in Ghana*, 243–4.

16. *Pioneer*, 1 December 1953. Indeed, Awooner-Renner was anything but a stereotypical "sectional" leader. Described by his biographer as an "unrepentant socialist" and denounced by George Padmore as a "prominent ideologist of Crypto-Communism," Awooner-Renner spent his early years as a writer for the NAACP's *Crisis* (edited by W. E. B. Du Bois). A staunch nationalist and internationalist, he spent the mid-twenties in the USSR and was the first President of the Pan-African Council of the West African Youth League. An early leader of the CPP, Awooner-Renner was imprisoned with Nkrumah during the Positive Action campaign of 1950. He broke with Nkrumah shortly after the 1951 CPP victory and entry into the Legislative Council. He became a founder of the Muslim Association Party and later converted to Islam, taking the name Mustapha. His biographer quotes him as remarking that he felt the need "to lead the down-trodden, unrepresented and unrepresentable." See S. K. B. Asante, "Bankole Awooner-Renner," in L. H. Ofosu-Appiah, ed., *Encyclopedia Africana Dictionary of African Biography*, vol. 1 (New York: Reference Publications, 1977), 208–9. Padmore's denunciation of Awooner-Renner is cited in Marable, *African and Caribbean Politics*, 115. See also Allman, " 'Hewers of Wood.' "

17. Vail, "Introduction," 17. Vail's approach contrasts markedly with that of

Ernest Gellner who, in his discussion of nationalism, argues that "the precise doctrines are hardly worth analysing" because the words of one ideologue can easily be substituted for those of another. "Nationalist ideology," he argues, "suffers from pervasive false consciousness." See Gellner, *Nations and Nationalism,* 123–5.

18. Gold Coast, *Report of the Commission of Enquiry into Representational and Electoral Reform* (Chairman: Van Lare) (Accra, 1953). Hereafter cited as Van Lare, *Report*.

19. For discussions of the Burns Constitution of 1946 which united the Colony and Asante under a common legislative body, see Apter, *Ghana in Transition,* 141–6 and Austin, *Politics in Ghana,* 3–11. For further background on Asante's decision to join the Legislative Council, see A. S. Y. Andoh, "The Asante National Liberation Movement of the 1950s in Retrospect," in Schildkrout, ed., *The Golden Stool*, 176–7.

20. Van Lare, *Report, 17*.

21. For a brief overview of the importance of the Golden Stool in Asante and Ghanaian politics, see Owusu, "Kingship in Contemporary Asante Society," 162–7. For an historical examination of the centrality of the Golden Stool to nineteenth- and twentieth-century Asante national discourse, see McCaskie, "Accumulation," I: 29–32, and II: 9–17.

22. Gold Coast, Legislative Assembly, *Debates,* 4–17 November 1953, passim. Also cited in Austin, *Politics in Ghana,* 178–9.

23. Austin, *Politics in Ghana,* 179. In the 1951 Assembly, there were eighteen "territorial seats," six of which were allotted to Asante. As Andoh summarizes, "the 1950 (Coussey) Constitution provided for the retention of the Asanteman Council and the Joint Provincial Council as electoral colleges" for these seats. A. S. Y. Andoh, "The Asante National Liberation Movement," 175. See Austin, *Politics in Ghana,* 103–48, for a full discussion of the mechanics of the 1951 election.

24. Austin, *Politics in Ghana,* 179.

25. Ibid., 201. See also *Pioneer,* 8 May 1954, for an account of local CPP officers' discontent over Nkrumah's appointing of candidates.

26. Nkrumah, *Autobiography,* 208.

27. *Evening News,* 2 May 1954. Excerpted in Austin, *Politics in Ghana,* 216.

28. Austin, *Politics in Ghana,* 210.

29. Ibid., 211.

30. See Young, "Nationalism, Ethnicity and Class," 431 and 447–50. Lonsdale, "States and Social Processes," 151–2.

31. Maxwell Owusu, *Uses and Abuses of Political Power: A Case Study of Continuity and Change in the Politics of Ghana* (Chicago: University of Chicago Press, 1970), 171. For D. R. and A. C. Smock's critique of Owusu's argument, see their *Politics of Pluralism,* 261.

32. Rathbone, "Businessmen in Politics," 392.

33. Ibid., 395.

34. Rathbone, "Politics and Factionalism in Ghana," 166.

35. Rathbone, "Businessmen in Politics," 397.

36. Lonsdale, "States and Social Processes," 151.

37. Young, "Nationalism, Ethnicity and Class," 450.

38. Gold Coast, Legislative Assembly, *Debates,* 12 August 1954, cols. 335–6.

39. Gold Coast, Legislative Assembly, *Debates,* 12 and 13 August 1954, pas-

sim. Although it would have been improper for him to declare so publicly, the colonial governor, Charles Arden-Clarke was a staunch supporter of the Cocoa (Amendment) Bill. In a memo to the Colonial Office, he characterized the freezing of the cocoa price as a "courageous act" on the part of the government. See Public Record Office, Colonial Office (hereafter PRO, CO.) 554/1162: Arden-Clarke to Colonial Office, "Gold Coast: Review of Events, July–December, 1954," dd. Accra, 22 December 1954.

Most of the Public Record Office materials upon which this study is based come from three collections: CO.96, *Original Correspondence, Gold Coast,* 1948–1951 (the collection ends in 1951); CO.554, *Original Correspondence, West Africa,* 1951–1957; and DO.35, *Original Correspondence, Dominions Office and Commonwealth Relations Office,* 1953–1958. Unfortunately, many of the later records in the CO.96 series and some of the earlier records pertaining to the Gold Coast in the CO.554 series (prior to 1954) were "destroyed by statute" and are no longer extant. Thus, much of the "behind-the-scenes" activity during this most crucial time in Ghanaian national history (1948–1951) will remain permanently hidden. In the CO.554 series for the period 1954–1957, approximately six files relevant to this study are currently being retained under section 3 (4) of the Public Records Act of 1958, "because the records contain highly sensitive information relating to national security or to the safety of individuals which cannot be released to the Public Record Office." Six files in the DO.35 series are being similarly retained. For a thorough investigation of the British government's policies with regard to the preservation and destruction of records and a brief, but provocative, discussion of the ramifications of these policies for the reconstruction of colonial and postcolonial African history, see B. Wasserstein, "Whose History Is It, Anyway?" *Times Literary Supplement,* 25 July 1986, 814.

40. For a thorough study of the United Ghana Farmers' Council, see Björn Beckman, *Organizing the Farmers* (Uppsala: Scandinavian Institute of African Studies, 1976).

41. *Pioneer,* 6 September 1954.

42. *Pioneer,* 4 September 1954.

43. For a description of this meeting, see *Ashanti Times,* 27 August 1954, and Austin, *Politics in Ghana,* 258–9.

44. Jean Allman, Field Notes: Interview with Osei Assibey-Mensah (FN/15/1), dd. Asante New Town, Kumase, 27 July 1984, 120.

45. E. Y. Baffoe was a former member of the CPP. He had participated in the Positive Action campaign and was jailed in 1951 for his role in the CPP's independence struggle. He later became the regional propaganda secretary for the CPP and was elected to the Cocoa Marketing Board. He also served as the director of the Cocoa Purchasing Company. In 1954, however, he stood as a rebel candidate in the general election and was, as a result, removed from his positions with the CMB and the CPC and expelled from the party. See *Pioneer,* 11 October 1954.

46. E. Y. Baffoe, "Cocoa Price Agitation" (leaflet; Kumase, 1954). Copies of all leaflets cited herein (unless otherwise noted) were given to the author by Osei Assibey-Mensah. Copies are on deposit in Northwestern University's Melville J. Herskovits Memorial Library.

47. The etymology of the term *nkwankwaa* is somewhat murky. Its root is undoubtedly *nkoa,* which can be translated as "subject" or "commoner." But as Busia

noted, *nkwankwaa* was often used synonymously with *mmerante* (literally, young men). Clearly, *nkwankwaa* has come to have a very specific meaning—much more limited than "commoner," and transcending, in many cases, the chronological or generational designation of *mmerante*. (During the 1950s, the youngmen active in the NLM ranged in age from twenty to fifty.) See Tordoff, *Ashanti,* 374fn., and Kofi A. Busia, *The Position of the Chief in the Modern Political System of Ashanti* (London: Oxford University Press, 1951), 10fn. In reference to the nineteenth century, Wilks defines *nkwankwaa* as "literally 'youngmen' and sometimes translated as 'commoner.' " Wilks, *Asante,* 728.

48. Wilks, *Asante,* 535. See, also, Austin, *Politics in Ghana,* xiii–xiv.

49. Wilks, *Asante,* 535–9 and 710–1.

50. Ibid., 535. Unfortunately, more precise data on the early *nkwankwaa* is not available. As Wilks points out, "The leaders . . . in the early 1880s, as is appropriate to a movement which although popular and mass-based had necessarily to be organized in secrecy, are not identified in contemporary reports" (p. 535). Thus it is difficult not only to pinpoint the *nkwankwaa*'s origins in time, but to examine their specific social and economic grievances.

51. Wilks, *Asante,* 530.

52. For a brief description of the Council or *kwasafohyiamu,* see Wilks, *Asante,* 540. For additional interpretations of the tumultuous events of 1880–1884, see Lewin, *Asante Before the British,* 69–76, 115–6, and passim, and McCaskie, "*Ahyiamu,*" 169–88.

53. Wilks, *Asante,* 710.

54. Great Britain, *Colonial Reports,* Ashanti, 1923–4, cited in Tordoff, *Ashanti,* 204.

55. Tordoff, *Ashanti,* 375–82.

56. After the British invaded Asante in 1896, they exiled the Asantehene, Nana Prempe I, to Sierra Leone and then to the Seychelles Islands, along with members of his family and several other chiefs. Prempe was repatriated as a private citizen in 1924 and then, in 1926, was recognized as the Kumasehene, paramount chief of the Kumase division. Prempe I died in 1931. With the British restoration of the Asante Confederacy Council in 1935, his successor, Nana Osei Agyeman Prempe II, would be recognized as Asantehene. For a discussion of Prempe I's exile, see A. A. Boahen, "A Nation in Exile: The Asante on the Seychelles Islands, 1900–24," in Schildkrout, ed., *The Golden Stool,* 146–60.

57. Tordoff, *Ashanti,* 268.

58. Ibid., 365–9.

59. MRO, Asante Confederacy Council, *Minutes of the Second Session,* 23 January 1936. See also Tordoff, *Ashanti,* 375–86 for a detailed discussion of the role of the *nkwankwaa* in local disputes and their opposition to taxation and communal labour.

60. For discussions of the role of the *Nkwankwaahene,* see Busia, *Position of the Chief,* 10, and Tordoff, *Ashanti,* 373–4 and 383.

61. Fortes was in Asante completing his "Ashanti Social Survey." Meyer Fortes, "The Ashanti Social Survey: A Preliminary Report," *The Rhodes-Livingston Journal* 6 (1948), 27.

62. Two years before the AYA was founded, Fortes observed that, despite the formal prohibition of the *nkwankwaa* ten years earlier, youngmen's associations

and self-help groups (modeled on the *nkwankwaa* organizations) continued to give expression to the "opinions of commoners." Fortes, "Ashanti Social Survey," 26–8 and esp. 26fn.

63. It is interesting to note that the four AYA members who played the most pivotal roles in the founding of the NLM—Kusi Ampofu, Sam Boateng, K. A. M. Gyimah and Osei Assibey-Mensah—were all journalists by trade.

64. This is not to suggest that in the Asante of the 1950s there were four neatly packaged social classes or groups—the chiefs, the *asikafo*, the *nkwankwaa*, and the *ahiafo*. The categories were not mutually exclusive, particularly with reference to the chiefs and the "big men," or *asikafo*. Many chiefs, particularly the Kumase Divisional chiefs (*nsafohene*), were wealthy landowners with an economic base in cocoa, transport, and trading. At the same time, many of the *asikafo* aspired to chiefly office, and much of their wealth and power depended on maintaining a close relationship with and courting the favors of the ruling powers. In an article dealing with wealth and political power in the nineteenth century that applies also to the twentieth century, Wilks notes that "the analytically distinct categories of the office holders (*amansohwefo*) and wealthy (*asikafo*) are, in terms of actual membership, largely overlapping ones; that is, office holders became wealthy through the exercise of their office, and persons of wealth acquired office through the use of their money." Wilks, "The Golden Stool," 17 and passim. Cf. Arhin who maintains that "one can only accept Wilks' 'classes' as heuristic constructs," and argues, instead, for a system of ranked "status groups" in late nineteeth-century Asante. Arhin, "Rank and Class," 2–13.

65. Wilks, *Asante,* 710 and Arhin, "Rank and Class," 2. McCaskie raises concerns similar to Arhin's in his critique of the "rational" or "positivist" approach to Asante history. See esp. his "Komfo Anokye," 371fn.; "Accumulation," I: 24–5; and "Asantesem: Reflections on Discourse and Text in Africa," in K. Barber and P. F. De Moroes Farias, eds., *Discourse and its Disguises: The Interpretation of African Oral Texts* (Birmingham: Centre for West African Studies, 1989), 72.

66. As Young remarked, Cabral has gone "furthest in confronting" the historic role of the petite bourgeoisie. See Young, "Nationalism, Ethnicity and Class," 441.

67. See Amilcar Cabral, *Revolution in Guinea* (London: Stage 1, 1969), 69–72 and passim, and Basil Davidson, "On Revolutionary Nationalism: the Legacy of Cabral," *Race and Class* 27:3 (1986), 21–45.

68. Young, "Nationalism, Ethnicity and Class," 469.

69. Crook, "Decolonization," 98–9 and passim.

70. This is a paraphrasing of Nkrumah's famous statement, "Seek ye first the political kingdom, and all things will be added unto it." *Pioneer,* 5 March 1949. See also Fitch and Oppenheimer, *Ghana,* 25, and Austin, *Politics in Ghana,* 131.

71. Allman, Field Notes: Interview with Sam Boateng (FN/6/1), dd. Adum, Kumase, 3 July 1984, 41 and 99.

72. Allman, Field Notes: Interview with Kusi Ampofu (FN/24/1), dd. Asante New Town, Kumase, 15 October 1984, 194–5. The testimony of both Ampofu and Boateng provides further evidence in support of Crook's argument that after 1951 the CPP became "a party with distinctive, and narrower, interests" and was "clearly associated with a modernizing, statist and hence centralizing, ideology which brought it into conflict with chiefs, farmers and unions." Crook, "Decolonization," 99 and 99fn.

73. Osei Assibey-Mensah Private Papers, "National Charges Against Mr. Kwame Nkrumah: Preferred by Moses T. Agyeman-Anane," mimeo, (no date).

74. Joseph G. Amamoo, *The New Ghana* (London: Pan Books, 1958), 80; Tony Killick, "The Economics of Cocoa," in W. Birmingham, I. Neustadt, and E. N. Omaboe, eds., *A Study of Contemporary Ghana*, vol. 1 (London: Allen an Unwin, 1966), 372.

75. PRO, CO.98/98: "Gold Coast Colony Reports: Report on the Labour Department for the Year 1952–53 (Accra, 1954), 11. The "Cocoa Labour Survey" included cocoa farmers who employed labor, those who maintained farms on land belonging to relatives, and those who worked on their own farms but without employing labor. The total number of farms involved was 12,905, the average size being less than three acres. The *1948 Census*, considered by many to be highly unreliable, places the number of adults in Asante (age 16 and over) at 388, 447. See Gold Coast, *Census of the Population, 1948* (Accra, 1950), 44.

76. For a detailed study of cocoa farm labor in Ghana and the various ways it is organized, see Polly Hill, *Migrant Cocoa Farmers of Southern Ghana* (Cambridge: Cambridge University Press, 1963).

77. See Gareth Austin, "The Emergence of Capitalist Relations in South Asante Cocoa-Farming, c. 1916–33," *Journal of African History* 28:2 (1987), 259–79. For a thorough examination of the role of northern laborers in shaping the relations of production in the south, see N. Van Hear, "Northern Labour and the Development of Capitalist Agriculture in Ghana," (Ph.D. thesis, University of Birmingham, 1982).

78. For example, the annual contract laborer received anywhere from £7 to £24 per year. The survey does not indicate whether these variations were based primarily on local discrepancies in payment or on yearly fluctuations in the price of cocoa between 1951 and 1954. CO.98/98, No. 12: *Report on the Labour Department*, 12–13. However, the fact that the producer price per load of cocoa went from 45s. in 1950–51 (when the "Cocoa Survey" began) to 80s. in 1952–53 and then down to 70s. in 1953–54 may provide a partial explanation for the vast fluctuations in pay to cocoa laborers. For a list of producer prices for cocoa from 1947 to 1959 see Beckman, *Organizing the Farmers*, 282.

79. Allman, Field Notes: Interview with Osei Assibey-Mensah (FN/15/1), dd. Asante New Town, Kumase, 27 July 1984, 119.

80. Cited in Austin, *Politics in Ghana*, 275.

81. Killick, "Economics of Cocoa," 366.

82. This percentage was obtained from figures available in Killick's table, "Financial Record of Cocoa Marketing Board, 1947–48 to 1960–61." See Killick, "Economics of Cocoa," 367.

83. Björn Beckman, "Government Policy and the Distribution of Cocoa Income in Ghana, 1951–1960," *Proceedings of the Cocoa Economics Research Conference*, (Legon, 1973), 277.

84. Killick, "Economics of Cocoa," 366, quoting Gold Coast Ordinance No. 16 of 1947.

85. National Archives of Ghana, Kumase, Regional Office Files, Asante [hereafter, NAGK, ROA.]/2097: Head Farmer, Nana Osei Kwabena to the Chairman, CMB, dd. Kumase, 28 August 1952.

86. Austin, *Politics in Ghana*, 172–3.

87. For detailed allegations against the CPC, see Gold Coast, *Report of the Commission of Enquiry into the Affairs of the Cocoa Purchasing Company, Ltd.* (Chairman: O. Jibowu) (Accra, 1956), 25–26 and passim. Hereafter cited as Jibowu, *Report.*

88. Gold Coast, Legislative Assembly, *Debates,* 3 March 1954.

89. In 1953–54, the producer price per ton of cocoa stood at £134.4, while the average selling price on the world market was £358.7. See Beckman, "Government Policy and the Distribution of Cocoa Income," 285.

90. Allman, Field Notes: Interview with N. B. Abubekr (FN/16/1), dd. Akowuasaw, Kumase, 28 July 1984, 124.

91. Allman, Field Notes: Interview with Sam Boateng (FN/6/1), dd. Adum, Kumase, 3 July 1984, 39.

92. Austin, *Politics in Ghana,* 261.

93. Excerpted from Osei Assibey-Mensah, "Save Your Nation, Oman Asante Kotoko" (leaflet; Kumase, 1954).

94. Austin, *Politics in Ghana,* 259.

95. Ibid., 260, and Andoh, "The Asante National Liberation Movement," 174. For further discussion of the powers of the chiefs under colonial rule, see Crook, "Decolonization"; Tordoff, *Ashanti;* K. A. Busia, *The Position of the Chief;* and Lord W. Malcolm Hailey, *Native Administration in the British African Territories, Part III* (London: HMSO, 1951), 229–55. For an examination of the internal workings of the Asante Confederacy Council under indirect rule (renamed the Asanteman Council in 1950), see Alessandro Triulzi, "The Asantehene-in-Council: Ashanti Politics Under Colonial Rule, 1935–1950," *Africa* 42:2 (1972), 98–111.

96. For reports, letters, and clippings on the abolition of the Native Authority system in Ashanti, see PRO, CO.554/231: (Reform of Local Government in the Gold Coast), passim. For the recommendations upon which the 1952 State Councils Ordinance was based, see Gold Coast, *Report of the Select Committee of the Legislative Council Appointed to Make Recommendations Concerning Local Government in Ashanti* (Chairman: Beeton) (Accra, 1951). Finally, for a recent, compelling analysis of why the British colonial government abandoned the Native Authority system (an analysis rooted in a fascinating discussion of the "crisis in colonial state-society relations after World War II), see Crook, "Decolonization," 75–105.

97. Austin, *Politics in Ghana,* 260. See also Andoh, "The Asante National Liberation Movement," 175. In addition, the chiefs lost control of the Native Authority Police. Under the Local Government Ordinance of 1952 and the Local Authority Police Power Ordinance of 1953, the Native Authority Police were disbanded and placed under the control of local councils. See David Killingray, "The Maintenance of Law and Order in British Colonial Africa," *African Affairs* 85:340 (1986), 428.

98. *West Africa,* 30 October 1954, 1010.

99. *Pioneer,* 6 September 1954.

100. Allman, Field Notes: Interview with Sam Boateng (FN/6/1), dd. Adum, Kumase, 3 July 1984, 39.

101. Cf. David Rooney, who maintains that Akoto was responsible for bringing the youngmen into the NLM. Rooney, *Kwame Nkrumah: The Political Kingdom of the Third World* (London: Tauris, 1988), 92.

102. Allman, Field Notes: Interview with Kusi Ampofu (FN/24/1), dd. Asante New Town, Kumase, 15 October 1984, 196.

103. For a brief, but useful, biography of Bafuor Akoto, see *West Africa*, 11 December 1954, 1161.

104. Osei Assibey-Mensah, "Arise! Arise!! Arise!!!" (leaflet; Kumase, 1954).

105. *Pioneer*, 7 September 1954.

106. *Pioneer*, 7 September 1954.

107. Bafuor Akoto made the call for separation. The next speaker, K. A. M. Gyimah, "called the day Ashanti Independence Day in view of their determination to be separated from the rest of the country." *Pioneer*, 7 September 1954.

108. *Pioneer*, 7 September 1954.

109. Allman, Field Notes: Interview with N. B. Abubekr (FN/16/1), dd. Akowuasaw, Kumase, 28 July 1984, 125–26.

110. *Pioneer*, 27 November 1954 (letter to the editor).

111. Prior to the September 19 inauguration, there was much debate over what to call the new opposition. Among the names suggested were "Ashanti Action Group," "Farmers Party," and "Ashanti Labour Party." Many were in favor of "Action Group" because of the parallels with Awolowo's opposition in Nigeria. Kusi Ampofu, future general secretary of the NLM, takes credit for suggesting the name "National Liberation Movement." See *Daily Graphic*, 15 September 1954; Allman, Field Notes: Interview with Sam Boateng (FN/6/1), dd. Adum, Kumase, 3 July 1984, 39–40, and Interview with Kusi Ampofu (FN/24/1), dd. Asante New Town, Kumase, 15 October 1984, 195–6.

112. Hailey, *Native Administration*, 254.

113. See Gellner, *Nations and Nationalism*, 1, and Hobsbawm, *Nations and Nationalism*, 9–10. Breuilly's definition is similarly rooted in politics: "Nationalism is used to refer to political movements seeking or exercising state power and justifying such actions with nationalist arguments." See Breuilly, *Nationalism and the State*, 1–3.

114. Gellner maintains that nationalism "is indeed inscribed neither in the nature of things, nor in the hearts of men, or in the pre-conditions of social life in general, and the contention that it *is* so inscribed is a falsehood which nationalism has succeeded in presenting as self-evident" in *Nations and Nationalism*, 125. See also Smith, *Ethnic Origins of Nations*, 18.

115. Geertz, one of the first to provide a full, theoretical elaboration of these attachments, argued that the creation of the new states stimulates "an obsessive concern with the relation of one's tribe, region, sect or whatever to a center of power" which is perceived as a "frightening new force with which to contend." The only way to assuage this concern is to channel it "into properly political rather than para-political forms of expression"—to initiate an integrative revolution. See Geertz, "The Integrative Revolution," 109–30 and passim.

116. Hobsbawm, *Nations and Nationalism*, 75–6, and "Introduction," to Hobsbawm and Ranger (eds.), *The Invention of Tradition* (Cambridge: Cambridge University Press, 1983), 14. While I agree with Hobsbawm's sentiments here, in the case of Asante, the characterization of this "historicity" as "proto-national" raises numerous problems. For alternatives to Hobsbawm's terminology, see Smith's discussion of "ethnie" in *Ethnic Origins of Nations*, passim, and *National Identity*, 19–98 and passim, and Anderson's examination of *Imagined Communities*, 11–40.

117. Anderson defines the nation as an "imagined political community." See his *Imagined Communities*, 11–16.

118. Kwame Arhin, "Chieftaincy Under Kwame Nkrumah," Paper presented at the Symposium on the Life and Work of Kwame Nkrumah, Institute of African Studies, University of Ghana (Legon, 27 May–1 June, 1985), 5.

119. Richard Wright, *Black Power* (New York: Harper and Brothers, 1954), 221.

120. Hobsbawm, *Nations and Nationalism*, 122.

121. Smith, *Ethnic Origins of Nations*, 173.

122. Anderson distinguishes between the "emerging nationalist intelligentsias" of the former colonies and the "vernacularizing nationalist intelligentsias" of nineteenth-century Europe. However, the terms appear equally suited for differentiating between the Gold Coast nationalist intelligentsia and its Asante counterpart. Anderson, *Imagined Communities*, 108–9.

123. Davidson uses this terminology in describing the political formation of the petite bourgeoisie in Guinea-Bissau, but it is applicable to the youngmen of Asante. See Davidson, "On Revolutionary Nationalism," 26–27.

124. McCaskie, "Accumulation," II: 9 and 17.

Chapter 3. The Dump Ablaze

1. *Pioneer*, 20 September to 9 October 1954 (assorted issues).

2. *Pioneer*, 23 and 30 September, 4 October 1954.

3. General Secretary Ampofu reported to the *Pioneer* on October 4 that thirteen branches of the NLM had been officially inaugurated outside of Kumase. They included Mankranso, Ofoase (Twedie), Dormaa, Wenkyi, Fumesua, Jacobu, Ahafo, Sunyani, Berekum, Nkwanta, Atwina Area, and Asekyerewa. *Pioneer*, 5 October 1954.

4. *Pioneer*, 9 October 1954.

5. *Pioneer*, 21 September 1954.

6. Cited in the *Pioneer*, 20 September 1954.

7. *Pioneer*, 20 September 1954.

8. *Pioneer*, 22 September 1954.

9. For the colonial government's confidential profile of Professor Busia, see PRO, CO.554/1060: "Dr. Kofi Abrefa Busia," no date (circa 1954?).

10. Cited in the *Pioneer*, 27 September 1954.

11. *Asomfo* chiefs head the various administrative offices within the Asantehene's palace. Traditionally, they hold appointive rather than hereditary stools. Thus, the chief of the physicians (*nsumankwaa*) is the *nsumankwaahene*, and the chief of the linguists (*akyeame*) is the *akyeamehene*. For a detailed discussion of the origins and role of the *asomfo* (administrative officials) see Wilks, *Asante*, 445–76.

12. The Nkofehene, though traditionally a palace official (*asomfo*) appointed by the Asantehene, also holds the stool for Atrama in the Kwabre II Area. Buasiako gained the stool in 1941 at the age of nineteen. He held it until he was detained by Nkrumah after independence. Since 1977, he has been an *okyeame* to Asantehene

Nana Opoku Ware II. See Allman, Field Notes: Interview with Nana Antwi Buasiako (FN/8/1), dd. Tophigh, Kumase, 19 July 1984, 58–60.

13. Austin, *Politics in Ghana,* 267. See Allman, Field Notes: Interview with Nana Bafuor Osei Akoto and Nana Antwi Buasiako (FN/4/1), dd. Asokwa, Kumase, 27 June 1984, 19, and Interview with Nana Antwi Buasiako (FN/8/1), dd. Tophigh, Kumase, 19 July 1984, 58–60.

14. *Pioneer,* 20 September 1954. The Kronkohene, like the Nkofehene, holds a traditionally appointive rather than hereditary stool which comes under the Gyaase Division (palace personnel) in the Kumase State Council. See Wilks, *Asante,* 469–70 and 727, and MRO, Kumase State Council, *Minutes,* 10 September 1956.

15. *Pioneer,* 21 September 1954.

16. Technically, the chiefs were unable to give the Movement their official endorsement at this meeting because the Asantehene was not present.

17. *Pioneer,* 21 September 1954.

18. *Pioneer,* 30 September 1954.

19. See McCaskie, "*Ahyiamu,*" 186–7.

20. The NLM and CPP offices were located in the same building in Asante New Town. See Allman, Field Notes: Interview with B. K. Owusu (FN/12/1), dd. Asokwa, Kumase, 23 July 1984, 96.

21. Allman, Field Notes: Interview with Alex Osei (FN/3/1), dd. Asante New Town, Kumase, 26 June 1984, 12.

22. For various descriptions of the events of October 9, see Allman, Field Notes: Interview with Alex Osei (FN/3/1), dd. Asante New Town, Kumase, 26 June 1984, 11–3; Interview with B. K. Owusu (FN/12/1), dd. Asokwa, Kumase, 23 July 1984, 95–6; *Pioneer,* 11 October 1954; and *Ashanti Times,* 12 October 1954.

23. See *Ashanti Times,* 12 October 1954, and *Pioneer,* 11 October 1954.

24. *Pioneer,* 8 October 1954.

25. A. C. Russell Papers (Rhodes House), "Security Appreciations," dd. 11 October 1954. Unless otherwise noted, all "Security Appreciations" cited are from the Chief Regional Officer, Asante, to the Permanent Secretary, Ministry of the Interior.

26. A. C. Russell Papers, "Security Information on Twumasi Ankrah," (no date). See, also, PRO, Dominions Office and Commonwealth Relations Office (hereafter, DO.) 35/6178: Deputy Governor to Colonial Office, dd. Accra, 17 July 1956. Neither of these documents provides concrete evidence warranting an indictment of Nkrumah. They do, however, given the details enclosed, raise the question of why the governor did not initiate a thorough investigation.

27. *Pioneer,* 12 October 1954.

28. Osei Assibey-Mensah, "Awake!" (leaflet; Kumase, 1954).

29. *Pioneer,* 12 October 1954.

30. On the day following the ban, the Senior Superintendent of Police in Asante was reported to have said, "the situation had got much settled." See *Pioneer,* 13 October 1954.

31. A. C. Russell Papers, "Security Appreciations," dd. 11 October 1954.

32. MRO, Kumase State Council, *Minutes,* 11 October 1954.

33. *Pioneer,* 12 October 1954.

34. As Andoh points out, under the 1954 electoral regulations, paramount chiefs were not allowed to seek "election to either a local government council or the Legislative Assembly. . . . In the prophetic words of the Watson Commission [1948], the chief . . . must either remain on his stool and take no part in external politics or forgo the office." Andoh, "The Asante National Liberation Movement," 175.

35. Not until after independence was the position of the chief vis-à-vis political parties investigated and potential abuse of power given full legal consideration. See Ghana, *Report of a Commission Appointed to Enquire into the Affairs of the Kumasi State Council and the Asanteman Council* (Chairman: Justice Sarkodee-Addo) (Accra, 1958), 91–118 and passim. Hereafter cited as Sarkodee-Addo, *Report*. In 1954, the line separating issues of customary concern, on the one hand, and political issues, on the other, was hazy at best. By calling the NLM a "movement" and denying that it was, in fact, a party, Akoto and the youngmen had the best of both worlds, at least temporarily: the full support of "nonpolitical" chiefs in a very political struggle against Nkrumah and the CPP.

36. NAGK, ROA/2619: "Kumase District Quarterly Report to 31 December 1954."

37. Cited in *Pioneer*, 13 October 1954. Two days after the NLM issued their request for a Royal Commission, the Asante Regional Branch of the CPP sent a cable to the secretary of state declaring that no Royal Commission was necessary. See *Sentinel*, 15 October 1954.

38. In addition to the Bantamahene, Amakomhene Nana Mensah Yiadom and Akyempemhene Nana Boakye Dankwa were listed as signatories to the cable and Executive members of the Movement. See *Pioneer*, 13 October 1954.

39. *Pioneer*, 19 October 1954.

40. Bafuor Osei Akoto Papers, "Memorandum from NLM to the Asanteman Council," dd. Kumase, 19 October 1954. For a more readily available copy of the "Memorandum," see PRO, CO.554/804. There is some irony in the fact that the Movement's appeal attacked Nkrumah's "communistic practices" yet readily borrowed the left-wing *comrade*, in describing Baffoe. If anything, it betrays the CPP roots of many NLM activists, particularly the members of the Asante Youth Association.

41. MRO, AC/006/54: General Secretary, NLM to Asanteman Council, dd. Kumase, 19 October 1954.

42. Agyeman Anane signed himself as the chairman of the "Ashanti Action Group," Sam Boateng as the secretary of the "Ashanti Ex-Servicemen," and Osei Assibey-Mensah as the secretary of the "Ashanti National Council"—a body which does not appear in any sources either before or any time after the October 19 Council meeting. See MRO, AC/006/54: passim.

43. *Pioneer*, 20 October 1954.

44. Three members of the Asanteman Council did not endorse the NLM—the Kumawuhene, the Asokorehene, and the Bekyemhene, who was later destooled. See *Daily Graphic*, 30 October and 6 November 1954; *Sentinel*, 1 November 1954. For further discussion of the Bekyemhene's destoolment, see Chapters 4 and 5.

45. PRO, CO.554/804: "A Resolution by the Asanteman Council Praying for a Federal Constitution for the Gold Coast," dd. Kumase, 21 October 1954.

46. Quoted in *Pioneer,* 22 October 1954.
47. *Pioneer,* 22 October 1954.
48. Osei Assibey-Mensah, "Royal Commission," (leaflet; Kumase, 1954).
49. *Pioneer,* 16 October 1954.
50. *Pioneer,* 16 October 1954.
51. *Pioneer,* 16 October 1954 (editorial).
52. See, Allman, Field Notes: Interview with Sam Boateng (FN/6/1), dd. Adum, Kumase, 3 July 1984, 39–40; Interview with Alex Osei (FN/3/1), dd. Asante New Town, Kumase, 26 June 1984, 41–44. The leaders of the Action Groupers included Sam Boateng, Kwaku Danso, and Fred Sarpong. A year later, when these men began to devote their time to the publication of the NLM's newspaper, *The Liberator,* the organization was taken over by Alex Osei.
53. Allman, Field Notes: Interview with Sam Boateng (FN/6/1), dd. Adum, Kumase, 3 July 1984, 40.
54. Allman, Field Notes: Interview with Boateng (FN/6/1), dd. Adum, Kumase, 3 July 1984, 40.
55. The Zongo Volunteers were founded in 1949 by several prominent Zongo residents, including Alfa Lardan (the group's president) and Alhaji Moru (the Volunteer's commander and chief). The original purpose of the Volunteers was to patrol the community and protect it from thieves. Since its inception, the Volunteers have sought to remain above party politics—recruiting members from both the CPP and its opposition. Nonetheless, many Volunteers did become Action Groupers. When asked if the Volunteers were the main component in the struggle against the CPP, Lardan responded, "No, but it is nearly true in this sense: the CPP tended to be the thieves and ruffians in the Zongo, so the Volunteers were fighting them . . . the Volunteers' main aim was to fight thieves, not the CPP. The Action Groupers' aim was to fight the CPP." For further discussion, see Allman, Field Notes: Interview with Alfa O. Lardan (FN/19/1), dd. Zongo, Kumase, 3 August 1984; Interview with Alfa O. Lardan (FN/19/2), dd. Zongo, Kumase, 25 September 1984; Interview with Alhaji Moru (FN/22/1), dd. Zongo, Kumase, 27 September 1984; and " 'Hewers of Wood,' " passim.
56. *Daily Graphic,* 25 October 1954 and *Pioneer,* 25 October 1954. The meeting occurred at the *Pioneer* office in Kumase. The NLM was represented by Akoto, Busia, Abubekr, and Ampofu; the MAP, by Awooner-Renner, Braimah, Tamakloe, and Lardan; the GCP, by Ollenu, Attoh, Nikoi, and Annan; the TC by Tamakloe, Djansi, and Nyagbodzo; the GNP, by Parker. The Douri-Na, representing the NPP, and Amadu Baba, the Serikin Zogo, sat in as official observers. See A. C. Russell Papers, "Security Appreciations," dd. 25 October 1954.
57. A. H. M. Kirk-Greene, "Interview with A. J. Loveridge and W. T. Beeton," transcript (Oxford, Rhodes House, 18 December 1968). Cited with the permission of A. H. M. Kirk-Greene and Rhodes House Library, Oxford.
58. PRO, CO.554/804: Governor to Secretary of State for the Colonies, dd. Accra, 22 November 1954.
59. *Pioneer,* 19 October 1954. The invitation is cited in full in the *Pioneer,* 21 October 1954.
60. Cited in *Pioneer,* 21 October 1954.
61. The letter is not extant, but its contents can be gleaned from Prempe's response. See fn. 62 below.

62. Bafuor Osei Akoto Papers, Asantehene to Prime Minister, dd. Kumase, 23 October 1954.

63. *Pioneer,* 12 October 1954.

64. *Daily Graphic,* 25 October 1954.

65. *Daily Graphic,* 25 October 1954; *Pioneer,* 26 October 1954; *Sentinel,* 27 October 1954.

66. *Pioneer,* 1 November 1954.

67. *Pioneer,* 3 November 1954; *Pioneer,* 15 November 1954.

68. *Pioneer,* 27 October 1954. See, also, PRO, CO.554/804: Governor to Secretary of State for the Colonies, dd. Accra, 22 November 1954.

69. *Pioneer,* 30 October 1954.

70. *Pioneer,* 8 November 1954.

71. *Pioneer,* 5 November 1954.

72. *Pioneer,* 11 November 1954.

73. PRO, CO.554/804: Governor to the Secretary of State for the Colonies, dd. Accra, 18 November 1954.

74. PRO, CO.554/804: Governor to the Secretary of State for the Colonies, dd. Accra, 18 November 1954.

75. A. C. Russell Papers, "Note of an Informal Meeting held in Governor's Office," dd. 26 November 1954.

76. *Daily Graphic,* 4 December 1954.

77. Cited in PRO, CO.554/804: Governor to the Secretary of State for the Colonies, dd. Accra, 3 December 1954.

78. PRO, CO.554/804: Governor to the Secretary of State for the Colonies, dd. Accra, 3 December 1954.

79. Cited in David Rooney, *Sir Charles Arden-Clarke* (London: Collings, 1982), 159.

80. PRO, CO.96/819: Governor to the Secretary of State for the Colonies, dd. Accra, 16 April 1951.

81. PRO, CO.554/298: "Note of a Meeting Held by the Secretary of State to Discuss Changes in the Constitution and Public Service of the Gold Coast Proposed by the Governor," 10 January 1952.

82. Joseph Appiah, *Joe Appiah: The Autobiography of an African Patriot* (New York: Praeger, 1990), 247.

83. PRO, DO.35/6172: Commonwealth Relations Office Representative (F. E. Cumming-Bruce) to Commonwealth Relations Office, dd. Accra, 21 July 1956.

84. PRO, CO.554/298: "Changes in the Gold Coast Constitution: File Minutes, 1951–1953."

85. PRO, CO.554/804: Secretary of State for the Colonies to the Governor, dd. London, 1 December 1954; A. C. Russell Papers, Deputy Governor to the Governor, dd. Accra, 2 December 1954.

86. A. C. Russell Papers, Deputy Governor to Governor, dd. Accra, 9 December 1954.

87. PRO, CO.554/804: Governor to the Secretary of State for the Colonies, dd. Accra, 18 November 1954.

88. See Gold Coast, *Report of the Commission for Regional Administrations* (Chairman: S. Phillipson), (Accra, 1951).

89. See A. C. Russell Papers, "Brief," no date, no author. The "Brief" is

attached to the December 9 letter from Hadow to Arden-Clarke (see fn. 85 above), which suggests that it was written by Hadow in early December. See PRO, CO.554/804: Governor to Secretary of State for the Colonies, dd. Accra, 21 December 1954, for a lengthy quotation on Nkrumah's memorandum.

90. See Kirk-Greene, "Interview," 44.

91. A. C. Russell Papers, Chief Regional Officer, Asante to Deputy Governor, dd. Kumase, 8 December 1954.

92. Ibid.

93. Kirk-Greene, "Interview," 51.

94. *Pioneer,* 6 December 1954.

95. *Pioneer,* 7 December 1954.

96. *Pioneer,* 10 December 1954.

97. MRO, AC/006/54: "Asanteman Council and NLM Reply," dd. Kumase, 17 December 1954.

98. Why did Nkrumah choose to write to the Asantehene rather than the NLM leadership? His letter implies an awareness of the Asantehene's central role in the struggle and perhaps reflects an effort to undercut the Movement's legitimacy by appealing directly to Asante's leading statesman.

99. MRO, AC/006/54: Prime Minister to Asantehene, dd. Accra, 29 December 1954. See also, PRO, CO.554/804: Governor to the Secretary of State for the Colonies, dd. 30 December 1954, and *Pioneer,* 31 December 1954.

100. Fabian Colonial Bureau Papers (Rhodes House), "Joint Statement Issued by the Asanteman Council and the National Liberation Movement on the Prime Minister's Reply of the 29th December 1954," dd. Kumase, 3 February 1955. For another copy of the "Statement," see PRO, CO.554/1061.

101. PRO, CO.554/804: Governor to Asantehene, dd. 11 February 1955. Also cited in *Pioneer,* 14 February 1955.

102. Andoh makes an important point when he argues that "Akyem Abuakwa's support was not based on any acceptance of Asante's desire for autonomy but rather on Dr. J. B. Danquah's implacable opposition to Kwame Nkrumah and the CPP." Andoh, "The Asante National Liberation Movement," 178.

103. Bafuor Osei Akoto Papers, Akoto to Nana Ofori Atta II, dd. Kumase, 17 November 1954. See also *Pioneer,* 19 November 1954.

104. Bafuor Osei Akoto Papers, "Minutes of a Meeting Between the Working Committee of the NPP and a Delegation of the NLM Held at the Headquarters of the Northern People's Party," dd. Tamale, 21 January 1955. The NPP said that it would take an official stand on federation after it had consulted with the Northern Territories Council and District Councils.

105. Bafuor Akoto Private Papers, Kofi Amponsa Dadzie to Akoto, dd. Cape Coast, 24 January 1955.

106. Smith, *Ethnic Origins of Nations,* 213–4 and Hobsbawm, "Introduction," 14.

107. *Pioneer,* 10 January 1955.

108. *Sentinel,* 7 January 1955. By this time, most CPP higher-ups who lived in Kumase had fled to Accra on Nkrumah's recommendation.

109. *Ashanti Times,* 11 January 1955.

110. PRO, DO.35/6213: Governor to the Secretary of State for the Colonies, dd. Accra, 8 January 1955.

111. Towns under the Peace Preservation Ordinance included Agogo, Agona, Akrokerri, Asokore, Attebubu, Bekyem, Bekwae, Berekum, Dormaa-Ahenkro, Dwaben, Effiduasi, Edweso, Fomena, Goaso, Juaso, Jakyi, Jamasi, Kintampo, Konongo/Odumase, Kumase, Kumawu, Mampon, Mim, Nkawie, Nkoranza, Obuasi, Offinso, Sunyani, Tekyiman, Teppa, and Wenkyi.

112. A. C. Russell Papers, "Security Appreciation: District of Obuasi," dd. Obuasi, 7 February 1955.

113. A. C. Russell Papers, Assistant Commissioner of Police to the Permanent Secretary of the Ministry of the Interior, dd. Kumase, 10 January 1955.

114. Bafuor Osei Akoto Papers, "Minutes of NLM Meeting Held at the Kumase State Council Hall," 25 November 1954.

115. See, for example, NAGK, ROA/2619: "Kumasi District Quarterly Report to 31 December 1954." The district officer wrote, "Though some of the opposition to the payment of rates can be attributed to the unsettled political situation in Ashanti and resentment against the cocoa price, there is no evidence of any concerted attack on rate payment by the National Liberation Movement. Although there have been sporadic attempts to place obstacles in the way of the smooth collection of the rate, it has not been possible to gain evidence of any cases of actual incitement."

116. MRO, Kumase State Council, *Minutes*, 6 December 1954. This was the second vote taken by the Council in favor of funding the NLM. The first vote resulted in the NLM being granted £20,000. The commission which enquired into the affairs of the Kumase State and Asanteman Councils did not investigate the £5000 loan to the Movement. However, the government used the issue of the £20,000 grant as the basis for its case that the Asanteman and Kumase State Councils had abused their customary power by using public funds for political purposes. See Sarkodee-Addo, *Report*, 7–9 and passim.

117. Osei Assibey-Mensah Papers, "Report of the Finance Committee," (Chair: Nana Kwabene Amoo, Kronkohene), no date.

118. Allman, Field Notes: Interview with N. B. Abubekr (FN/16/2), dd. Akowuasaw, Kumase, 10 October 1984, 188–9.

119. See Bafuor Osei Akoto Papers, "Administrative Report Filed by Kusi Ampofu," no date; Osei Assibey-Mensah Papers, "The Two-Point Programme by Kusi Ampofu," no date.

120. See the discussion in Chapter 2 of the events of 1883.

Chapter 4. "Revolutionary Movement"

1. *Daily Graphic*, 15 August 1955, citing front page of the *London Times*, 12 August 1955.

2. See Nkrumah, *Autobiography*, 48–63, and Appiah, *Autobiography*, 163–71.

3. While these three were the best known and most influential to leave the CPP in early February (and the ones having the most profound impact on the leadership of the Movement), they were by no means alone. During the same week, Dr. E. K. Kurankyi-Taylor, J. D. DeGraft-Johnson, Enoch Edusei (a noted Ku-

mase merchant and member of the National Executive of the CPP), and A. R. Dennis (of the CPP's Cocoa Purchasing Company) also announced their resignations. See *Pioneer,* 8 and 9 February, 1955.

4. *West Africa,* 12 February 1955, 127.

5. *Pioneer,* 7 February 1955.

6. For a full and fascinating account of his life, see Appiah's *Autobiography,* passim. For a Colonial Office profile of Appiah, see, PRO, CO.554/1062: "Brief for the Secretary of State," no author, 1954.

7. Allman, Field Notes: Interview with Joe Appiah (FN/11/1), dd. Mbrom, Kumase, 23 July 1984, 86. See also Appiah, *Autobiography,* 160–71.

8. Appiah, *Autobiography,* 197–210.

9. See Nkrumah, *Autobiography,* 108 fn., and Allman, Field Notes: Interview with Joe Appiah (FN/11/1), dd. Mbrom, Kumase, 23 July 1984, 83–4. Plange was elected to the Legislative Council in June, 1950. He was one of the principal forces behind the establishment of the franchise for those youth between the ages of twenty-one and twenty-five. After battling a long, serious illness, he died in 1954 at the age of twenty-nine.

10. Allman, Field Notes: Interview with Joe Appiah (FN/11/1), dd. Mbrom, Kumase, 23 July 1984, 83. See also Appiah, *Autobiography,* 207 and 232.

11. PRO, CO.554/1062: Secretary of State for the Colonies to Governor (description of a meeting between the Secretary and Joe Appiah), dd. London, 23 November 1954. See also Appiah, *Autobiography,* 235.

12. Allman, Field Notes: Interview with Joe Appiah (FN/11/1), dd. Mbrom, Kumase, 23 July 1984, 83–5. See also Appiah, *Autobiography,* 235–7.

13. Appiah, *Autobiography,* 238.

14. PRO, CO.554/1062: Secretary of State for the Colonies to Governor, dd. London, 23 November 1954.

15. Allman, Field Notes: Interview with Joe Appiah (FN/11/1), dd. Mbrom, Kumase, 23 July 1984, 84.

16. PRO, CO.554/1062: "Press Statement by Joe Appiah," dd. Kumase, 3 February 1955. (Appiah's *Autobiography* misdates the press statement as 23 February 1955, but includes a full transcript of the official statement on pp. 240–42.)

17. See esp., Andoh, "The Asante National Liberation Movement," 179; Owusu, "Kingship in Contemporary Asante Society," 168–9, and S. K. B. Asante (cited in Owusu's article), "Law and Society in Ghana," in T. Hutchinson, et al., eds., *Africa and Law: Developing Legal Systems in African and Commonwealth Nations* (Madison: University of Wisconsin Press, 1968), 126. Asante argues that "a close examination of the motivations of the main opposition groups . . . will reveal that the dominant factors were revulsion at the totalitarian excesses of the government, disillusionment over corruption and nepotism, exasperation with erratic policy determination, political frustration, especially among the disappointed adherents of the CPP, and most of all, genuine economic grievances."

18. See Allman, Field Notes: Interview with N. B. Abubekr (FN/16/1), dd. Akowuasaw, Kumase, 28 July 1984, 127.

19. Appiah's son has recently written of the "tensions [of] . . . these paired adherences, yoked so uneasily together" with which he grew up in the late 1950s: "I knew my father cared that he was an Ashanti man, and I knew he cared that he

was a Ghanaian nationalist. . . . It did not then occur to me—it never occurred to him—that these identities might be in conflict." Kwame A. Appiah, "Altered States," *Wilson Quarterly* 15:1 (1991), 20.

20. Lonsdale, "States and Social Processes," 195.

21. J. W. K. Appiah was also one of the founders of the Kotoko Society, a group of educated Asante men who worked for the repatriation of the Asantehene beginning in 1916. See Tordoff, *Ashanti Under the Prempehs*, 175, and Asante Kotoko Society, Editorial Committee, *Asante Kotoko Society, 60th Anniversary* (pamphlet; Kumase, 1976), passim. For further discussion of the Kotoko Society, see Owusu, "Kingship in Contemporary Asante Society," 166.

22. See PRO, CO.554/1062: Secretary of State for the Colonies to Governor, dd. London, 23 November 1954.

23. Allman, Field Notes: Interview with Nana Antwi Buasiako (FN/8/1), dd. Tophigh, Kumase, 19 July 1984, 60–1. In London, Dame Isobel Cripps, Appiah's mother-in-law, made a visit to the Colonial Office in mid-February and informed R. W. Piper that "following the publication of his [Appiah's] statement, many others had followed his lead and had joined the National Liberation Movement." See, PRO, CO.554/1062: File Minute, dd. 19 February 1955.

24. After returning to London from a February visit to Kumase, one colonial official did report that Joe Appiah was "treated with some suspicion" and that the Asantehene did not "approve completely of him or of his marriage," choosing to refer to Peggy Appiah as " 'that young English girl that Joe Appiah chose to marry.' " This appears to be an isolated account, however, uncorroborated by any other evidence, oral or written. See PRO, CO.554/1062: File Minutes, dd. 17 and 24 March 1955. If, indeed, there were suspicions on the part of the Asantehene, they were put to rest in the next weeks.

25. Allman, Field Notes: Interview with K. A. M. Gyimah (FN/9/1), dd. Manhyia, Kumase, 20 July 1984, 70. Gyimah was a member of the AYA and one of the founders of the NLM.

26. Allman, Field Notes: Interview with Kusi Ampofu (FN/24/1), dd. Asante New Town, Kumase, 15 October 1984, 200.

27. I use the term *new* here to distinguish this group from the old-guard intelligentsia of the UGCC. See Chapter 2 for a discussion of the nature of the Gold Coast's intelligentsia, old and new, in the pre-1954 political struggles. For broader discussions of nationalism and the intelligentsia, see esp. Smith, *Theories of Nationalism*, 132–50, and idem, *National Identity*, 95–9. Smith argues that "nationalism's primary function is the resolution of the crisis of the intelligentsia." (*Theories*, 133, and *Identity*, 96). While this formulation may oversimplify the complex dynamics of nationalist movements, it underscores the central role of the intelligentsia in the articulation of nationalist ideologies. For a similar discussion, see Anderson, *Imagined Communities*, 127–8. Cf. Markovitz, who argues for the use of the term *organizational bourgeoisie* in Markovitz, ed., *Studies of Power and Class in Africa* (Oxford, 1987), 209.

28. *Sentinel*, 9 February 1955.

29. The *Sentinel's* report is somewhat corroborated by one colonial official's first-hand account that "there seemed to be a struggle for power going on inside the N.L.M." See, PRO, CO.554/1062: File Minute, dd. 24 March 1955.

30. Bafuor Osei Akoto Papers, Amponsah to NLM, dd. Kumase, 4 February 1955.

31. Allman, Field Notes: Interview with Kusi Ampofu (FN/24/1), dd. Asante New Town, Kumase, 15 October 1984, 198.

32. Ibid.

33. Ibid.

34. Ibid.

35. See *Sentinel, 17 February 1955, and Pioneer,* 7 March 1955.

36. Allman, Field Notes: Interview with Kusi Ampofu (FN/24/1), dd. Asante New Town, Kumase, 15 October 1984, 199.

37. Allman, Field Notes: Interview with N. B. Abubekr (FN/16/1), dd. Akowuasaw, Kumase, 28 July 1984, 127.

38. Ibid.

39. Osei Assibey-Mensah Papers; R. R. Amponsah, "Proposals for Reorganization for Consideration by the Executive Committee," dd. Kumase, 21 February 1955.

40. Ibid.

41. Ibid.

42. Appiah, *Autobiography,* 241–2.

43. *Pioneer,* 14 February 1955.

44. *Pioneer,* 18 March 1955.

45. On March 7, Yaw Broni, the propaganda secretary of the Kwadaso branch of the NLM, left Kumase for the Ivory Coast with the intent of extending the Movement "beyond the borders of the country to those Gold Coasters who now reside in French Territory." See *Pioneer,* 5 March 1955.

46. For the full text of Nkrumah's motion, see Gold Coast, Legislative Assembly, *Debates* (5 April 1955), cols. 1864–74.

47. *Pioneer,* 5 and 6 April 1955. For the text of Dombo's statement before leading the exodus of opposition members, see Gold Coast, Legislative Assembly, *Debates* (5 April 1955), cols.. 1875–7.

48. *Pioneer,* 5 April 1955.

49. *Pioneer,* 13 April 1955.

50. PRO, CO.554/804: "Joint Statement of the Asanteman Council and the National Liberation Movement on the Select Committee on Federal System of Government and Second Chamber," dd. Kumase, 5 May 1955.

51. PRO, CO.554/1804: Secretary, Northern Territories Council to Select Committee on Federal System of Government and Second Chamber, dd. Tamale, 28 May 1955.

52. *Pioneer,* 3 May 1955.

53. *Pioneer*, 22 January 1955. Ironically, Nkrumah would proclaim five years later that "the Convention People's Party is Ghana, and Ghana is the Convention People's Party." See Kwame Nkrumah, "What the Party Stands For," *The Party* 1:1 (1960), cited in Apter, *Ghana in Transition*, 326.

54. See, for example, the editorial in the *Pioneer,* 9 October 1954.

55. *Pioneer,* 25 September 1954.

56. Smith, *State and Nation*, 95.

57. Gold Coast, Legislative Assembly, *Debates* (21 February 1955), col. 202.

58. Ibid., (21 March 1955), col. 1263.

59. Ibid.

60. For a full discussion of the Brong secessionist movement, see Kwame Arhin, ed., *A Profile of Brong Kyempim* (Accra: Afram, 1979), passim. See esp. Arhin's "Introduction," 1–21, and F. K. Drah, "The Brong Political Movement," 119–68. The Brong people, as Arhin writes, constitute a distinct Akan subgroup which inhabits the area to the north of Asante proper. By the middle of the eighteenth century, most Brong areas were incorporated into the Asante empire. While the name Brong can be traced to Bono, the first northern Akan state, "since the last quarter of the nineteenth century, it has acquired a distinctively political meaning," according to Arhin. It is primarily a "protest word adopted by those living northeast, north and northwest of Asante who deny political allegiance to the Asantehene." (Arhin, 10–11)

61. Gold Coast, Legislative Assembly, *Debates* (18 February 1955), col. 186. The states which seceded from the Asanteman Council included Dormaa, Tekyiman, Abease, Odumase, Drobo, Suma, Wiase, Sunyani, and Bekyem.

62. For the early debates over the petition of the Brong-Kyempim Federation, see Gold Coast, Legislative Assembly, *Debates* (18 February 1955), cols. 185–94; (21 February 1955), cols.. 213–9. In 1951, the CPP government appointed a committee to investigate the "differences" between the Brong chiefs and the Asanteman Council. The committee's report was finally released in March, 1955, and Nkrumah announced to the Assembly that the government would now consider recognition of the Brong-Kyempim Council and the possibility of establishing "two administrative regions for Ashanti." See *Debates*, 25 March 1955, and Gold Coast, *Report of the Committee on the Asanteman-Brong Dispute* (Chairman: A. Mate Kole) (Accra, 1955), passim. Hereafter cited as Mate Kole, *Report*. Drah argues convincingly that early in 1955, the CPP "was still reluctant to commit itself totally to a separate Brong region," but realized that the Brong question could be exploited "to its political advantage." See Drah, "Brong Political Movement," 138–41. For further discussion of the process by which the Brong-Asante dispute became inextricably linked to the political battle between the NLM and the CPP, see Chapter 5.

63. Cited in Rooney, *Sir Charles Arden-Clarke*, 165.

64. PRO, CO.554/1063: Political Secretary, MAP to Secretary of State for the Colonies, dd. Accra, 14 March 1955.

65. *Pioneer,* 2 March 1955.

66. *Pioneer,* 23 March 1955.

67. *West Africa* (26 March 1955), 279.

68. See *Pioneer,* 22 March 1955.

69. Ibid.

70. Allman, Field Notes: Interview with K. A. M. Gyimah (FN/9/1), dd. Manhyia, Kumase, 20 July 1984, 73.

71. A. C. Russell Papers, Chief Regional Officer, Asante to Governor, "Security Appreciation," dd. Kumase, 21 March 1955.

72. Hobsbawm, *Nations and Nationalism,* 79.

73. *Pioneer,* 26 March 1955.

74. NAGK, ROA/2491: "Strictly Confidential Report to the Chief Regional Officer from District Commissioner, Bekwae," dd. Bekwae, 29 March 1955.

75. Allman, Field Notes: Interview with Nana Sewaa Benkuo (FN/17/1), dd. Asante New Town, Kumase, 30 July 1984, 139.

76. Allman, Field Notes: Interview with Maame Yaa Baa (FN/20/1), dd. Asante New Town, Kumase, 4 August 1984, 159–60. Maame Yaa Baa was one of the earliest women members of the NLM. Her son, Kwaku Danso (a.k.a. "Burning Spear"), was one of the AYA founders of the NLM and a leader of the Movement's Action Groupers.

77. A. Kendrick, "Growing Up to Be a Nation," *New Republic* (23 April 1956), 15–6. Cited in Yaw Manu, "Conflict and Consensus in Ghanaian Politics: The Case of the 1950s," *Conch* 7:1/2 (1975), 103.

78. See *Pioneer,* 10 May 1955.

79. A *West Africa* reporter wrote at the end of May that "tension and clashes were worse than in the early days of the NLM." *West Africa*, 21 May 1955, 458. For a brief discussion of the Yaa Asantewa uprising, see Tordoff, *Ashanti Under the Prempehs*, 99–109.

80. *Pioneer,* 26 August 1955.

81. *Pioneer,* 16 May 1955.

82. A. C. Russell Papers, Chief Regional Officer, Asante to Governor, "Security Appreciation," dd. Kumase, 23 May 1955.

83. See *Pioneer,* 26 August 1955.

84. PRO, CO.554/804: Acting Governor to Secretary of State for the Colonies, dd. Accra, 20 June 1955. See also *Daily Graphic,* 17 May 1955, and *West Africa*, 28 May 1955, 495.

85. PRO, CO.554/1276: File Minute, dd. 17 May 1955.

86. *Daily Graphic,* 19 May 1955.

87. Ibid.

88. *Daily Graphic,* 21 May 1955.

89. *Pioneer,* 25 May 1954.

90. Allman, Field Notes: Interview with Alex Osei (FN/3/1), dd. Asante New Town, Kumase, 26 June 1984, 14.

91. A. C. Russell Papers, Chief Regional Officer, Asante to Governor, "Security Appreciation," dd. Kumase, 28 February 1955.

92. *Pioneer,* 28 March 1955.

93. A. C. Russell Papers, Chief Regional Officer, Asante to Governor, "Security Appreciation," dd. Kumase, 31 May 1955.

94. Allman, Field Notes: Interview with Alex Osei (FN/3/1), dd. Asante New Town, Kumase, 26 June 1984, 14.

95. The "Ashanti Zone Internal Security Schemes" were authored by the chief regional officer in Asante. All copies of the "Schemes" were to be destroyed by fire immediately after being read by district officers and members of the Ashanti Zone Intelligence Committee, consisting of representatives of the colonial administration in Asante, the police and the army. Fortunately, one of the "Schemes" survived–no. 4, dated February, 1957. That "Scheme" suggests that the first concerted security plans were developed in 1954 and then updated in 1955 and 1956 to deal with the threat posed by the development of Asante nationalism. The "Schemes" included detailed information on intelligence gathering and on evacuation plans, noting that in the event of "civil war or guerrilla war," the scheme would be superseded by a central

plan devised in Accra. See NAGK, ROA/2842: "Ashanti Zone Internal Security Scheme," dd. Kumase, February, 1957.

96. PRO, CO.554/805: R. J. Vile, "Constitutional Developments in the Gold Coast," dd. London, 22 March 1955.

97. PRO, CO.554/1162: Governor to Secretary of State for the Colonies, "Gold Coast: The NLM," dd. Accra, 29 July 1955.

98. PRO, CO.554/805: Colonial Office to Secretary of State for the Colonies (on tour in Hong Kong), dd. London, 29 July 1955.

99. See, for example, *Sentinel,* 16 April 1955.

100. Allman, Field Notes: Interview with K. A. M. Gyimah (FN/9/1), dd. Manhyia, Kumase, 20 July 1984, 77.

101. Ivor Wilks, who was in the Gold Coast during this time, recently recalled that "travellers from the north to the south, with no business in Kumase itself, systematically took the road through Dwaben and by-passed Kumase." Ivor Wilks to Allman, dd. 12 July 1986.

102. See *Pioneer,* 28 May 1955.

103. *Sentinel,* 24 May 1955.

104. A. C. Russell Papers, Chief Regional Officer, Asante to Governor, "Security Appreciation," dd. Kumase, 6 June 1955.

105. *Pioneer,* 1 June 1955.

106. Austin, *Politics in Ghana,* 167.

107. Allman, Field Notes: Interview with B. F. Kusi (FN/14/1), dd. Patasi, Kumase, 26 July 1984, 112.

108. *Ashanti Times,* 24 June 1955.

109. *Pioneer,* 13 July 1955.

110. *Pioneer,* 16 July 1955. Austin notes that nearly 25 percent more votes were cast in the by-election than in the previous 1954 election. In that election, Kusi, running as a GCP candidate, polled 1709 votes, and John Baidoo 3203. See Austin, *Politics in Ghana,* 275–6.

111. *Pioneer,* 18 July 1955.

112. *West Africa,* 23 July 1955, 673.

113. A. C. Russell Papers, Chief Regional Officer, Asante to Governor, "Security Appreciation," dd. Kumase, 2 August 1955.

114. PRO, CO.554/1162: Governor to Secretary of State for the Colonies, "Gold Coast: The NLM," dd. Accra, 29 July 1955.

115. MRO, Asanteman Council, *Minutes* (2 August 1955), 57.

116. *Pioneer,* 18 August 1955.

117. MRO, Asanteman Council, *Minutes* (4 August 1955), 11. Amponsah, in his meeting with R. J. Vile of the Colonial Office, let it be known that the Movement's immediate goal was to organize a conference to plan for the creation of a Constituent Assembly. See PRO, CO.554/805: "Notes on meeting between R. R. Amponsah and R. J. Vile," dd. London, 16 June 1955.

118. *West Africa,* 16 July 1955, 649, and *Pioneer,* 16 July 1955. Rooney writes that Busia's sojourn in London was directed and financed by Edward Spears, the Director of the Ashanti Goldfields Corporation. Spears, he argues, was upset by the new constitution, which removed the special mining representatives from the Assembly. "From that time onwards," he writes, Spears "was determined to do all

he could to back the NLM, to oppose the CPP and to delay independence." See Rooney, *Kwame Nkrumah*, 101.

119. See *Pioneer*, 21 July 1955 and 22 July 1955.

120. *Daily Graphic*, 18 July 1955.

121. Movements and Parties Other than the CPP, *Proposals for a Federal Constitution for an Independent Gold Coast and Togoland* (Kumase, 1955).

122. See Gold Coast, *Report of the Select Committee on the Federal System of Government and Second Chamber for the Gold Coast* (Accra, 1955), iii–xii and passim. Hereafter, Select Committee, *Report*.

123. Movements, *Proposals for a Federal Constitution*, 5–6.

124. See Austin, *Politics in Ghana*, 278.

125. *Pioneer*, 9 August 1955. The day after Nkrumah made his motion in the Legislative Assembly, the NLM sent a copy of its *Proposals* to the chief regional officer in Asante with instructions that copies be forwarded to the governor, the prime minister and the secretary of state for the colonies. MRO, AC/024/55: NLM to Chief Regional Officer, Asante, dd. Kumase, 9 August 1955.

126. *Pioneer*, 11 August 1955.

127. *Pioneer*, 31 August 1955.

128. The MAP, though it worked closely with the NLM from its inception and would continue to do so, did not merge its identity with the NLM at this time because, it argued, it was not "prepared to forgo its political identity under any circumstances." See *Pioneer*, 20 September 1955.

129. *Daily Graphic*, 3 September 1955.

130. *Pioneer*, 21 September 1955.

131. *Pioneer*, 5 September 1955.

132. PRO, CO.554/805: File Minute, dd. 2 June 1955.

133. PRO, CO.554/805: Notes of meeting with Secretary of State for the Colonies, dd. London, 22 July 1955.

134. PRO, CO.554/805: Secretary of State for the Colonies to Governor, dd. London, 27 July 1955.

135. PRO, CO.554/805: Governor to Secretary of State for the Colonies, dd. Accra, 29 July 1955.

136. Nkrumah, *Autobiography*, 242.

137. Bourne entered the Indian Civil Service in 1920. By 1945 he was the governor of the Central Province, Berar and Assam. In 1946, he was named governor to East Bengal, as well. *Daily Graphic*, 20 September 1955. See also PRO, CO.554/805: "Press Release on Sir Frederick Bourne," dd. London, 19 September 1955. The Colonial Office first considered Sir Keith Hancock for the role of constitutional advisor, but the CPP rejected Hancock because of his experience in Uganda. There was a fear on the part of the CPP, according to Arden-Clarke, that Hancock might try to solve the Asante problem as he had the Buganda problem. See PRO, CO.554/805: Governor to Secretary of State for the Colonies, dd. Accra, 20 August 1955.

138. *Pioneer*, 1 October 1955.

139. *Pioneer*, 4 October 1955.

140. *Pioneer*, 11 October 1955.

141. Andoh, "The Asante National Liberation Movement," 180.

142. The Women's Section was presented to the Kumase State Council on the March 28, 1955. It was led by Madame Akosua Nyameba, sister of Osei Assibey-Mensah. The general secretary was Nancy Tsiboe, former GCP stalwart and wife of *Pioneer* publisher John Tsiboe. See MRO, Kumase State Council, *Minutes,* 28 March 1955. According to Maame Yaa Baa, a Women's Section member, the Section was formed by the men, but the women supported it. See Allman, Field Notes: Interview with Maame Yaa Baa (FN/20/1), dd. Asante New Town, 4 August 1984, 160.

143. See MRO, Asanteman Council, *Minutes,* 18 August 1955.

144. Smith, *Ethnic Origins of Nations,* 171.

Chapter 5. Off the Streets and into Parliament

1. For the full text of the debate surrounding Edusei's motion, see Gold Coast, Legislative Assembly, *Debates* (11–12 August 1955), cols. 550–64 and cols. 578–614. The Amendment became law on 17 November 1955.

2. Drah, "Brong Political Movement," 140–41.

3. MRO, AC/SC/293/52: "Resolution of Protest by the Kumase State Council," dd. Kumase, 11 August 1955.

4. MRO, AC/SC/293/52: "Resolution of Protest by the Edweso State Council," dd. Edweso, 26 September 1955.

5. For copies of nearly forty of the resolutions that were sent to the Governor between August and late October, see MRO, AC/SC/293/52: (State Councils [Ashanti] Ordinance).

6. MRO, AC/SC/293/52: "Resolution of Protest by Edweso Youth Association," dd. Edweso, 9 October 1955.

7. For the full text of Abubekr's letter, see MRO, AC/SC/293/52: N. B. Abubekr to General Secretary, NLM (with copies to Bafuor Akoto and the Asanteman Council), dd. Obuasi, 25 October 1955.

8. A. C. Russell replaced Loveridge as Asante's chief regional officer in October, 1955. Like his predecessor, Russell betrayed a sympathy for the cause of the NLM—a sympathy which placed him into direct conflict with colonial officials in Accra.

9. MRO, Asanteman Council, *Minutes,* 27 October 1955.

10. Ibid.

11. Ibid.

12. Ibid.

13. MRO, Asanteman Council, *Minutes,* 28 October 1955.

14. For the full text of the Asanteman Council's protest resolution to the governor, see MRO, Asanteman Council, *Minutes* (27 and 28 October 1955), Appendix B: "Resolution to the Governor." Copies of the resolution were forwarded to the secretary of state for the colonies, the prime minister, Frederick Bourne, and the minister of local government.

15. Ibid.

16. A. C. Russell Papers, Chief Regional Officer, Asante to Governor, "Security Appreciation," dd. Kumase, 29 October 1955.

17. Rooney, *Sir Charles Arden-Clarke,* 179.

18. Gold Coast, Legislative Assembly, *Debates*, (16 November 1955), col. 554.

19. Ibid., 535–6.

20. Nkrumah, *Autobiography*, 220. With no small dose of irony, Nkrumah justifies the passage of the State Councils Amendment Ordinance in his autobiography with lengthy reference to Busia's *The Position of the Chief in the Modern Political System of Ashanti* (see 220–3).

21. PRO, CO.554/805: Governor to Colonial Office, dd. Accra, 12 September 1955.

22. PRO, CO.554/805: Colonial Office to Governor, dd. London, 23 September 1955.

23. PRO, CO.554/806: Prime Minister to Secretary of State for the Colonies, dd. Accra, 30 September 1955.

24. PRO, CO.554/806: Secretary of State for the Colonies to Prime Minister, dd. London, 31 October 1955.

25. PRO, CO.554/806: Secretary of State for the Colonies to Governor, dd. London, 14 November 1955.

26. PRO, CO.554/806: File Minute, dd. 13 November 1955.

27. PRO, CO.554/1162: Governor to Secretary of State for the Colonies, "Gold Coast: Political Situation," dd. Accra, 18 December 1955. Arden-Clarke's contention that Nkrumah was forced by back-benchers into publishing the bill is not corroborated by Nkrumah's own account of the introduction of the amendment. See, Nkrumah, *Autobiography*, 219–20.

28. PRO, CO.554/1162: Governor to Secretary of State for the Colonies, "Gold Coast: Political Situation," dd. Accra, 18 December 1955.

29. A. C. Russell Papers, Chief Regional Officer, Asante to Governor, "Security Appreciation," dd. Kumase, 22 November 1955.

30. A. C. Russell Papers, Chief Regional Officer, Asante to Governor, "Security Appreciation," dd. Kumase, 30 November 1955.

31. *Pioneer*, 18 November 1955.

32. *Pioneer*, 30 November 1955.

33. NAGK, ROA/5260: B. E. Dwira, Managing Editor of the *Ashanti Sentinel* to the Assistant Commissioner of Police, dd. Kumase, 19 December 1955.

34. NAGK, ROA/2720: "Quarterly Report on Sunyani-Wenchi District, 1 October 1955 to 31 December 1955."

35. *Pioneer*, 9 and 12 December 1955.

36. *Pioneer*, 27 January 1956.

37. See *Pioneer*, 12, 26, 28, and 30 November, 15 December 1955.

38. The governor informed the Colonial Office that the reason for the CPP's weak and isolated resistance to the NLM was that "there has been a lot of intimidation, and the rank and file of the CPP in Ashanti have never been visibly the inheritors of their ancestor's martial virtues." See PRO, CO.554/1162: Governor to Secretary of State for the Colonies, "Gold Coast: Political Situation," dd. Accra, 28 December 1955.

39. *Daily Graphic*, 9 December 1955.

40. PRO, DO.35/6171: Excerpt from the *News Chronicle*, 28 February 1956.

41. *Pioneer*, 6 December 1955.

42. *Pioneer*, 28 November 1955.

43. *Pioneer,* 1 December 1955.

44. NAGK, ROA/2850: Bafuor Akoto to Chief Regional Officer, dd. Kumase, 22 December 1955.

45. *Liberator,* 8 December 1955.

46. *Asika Dwa* is the Golden Stool.

47. *Liberator,* 8 December 1955.

48. Cited in the *Pioneer,* 24 November 1955.

49. *Pioneer,* 19 December 1955.

50. MRO, Asanteman Council, *Minutes* (24 November 1955), Appendix A: Chief Regional Officer, Asante to Asantehene, dd. Kumase, 19 November 1955.

51. MRO, Asanteman Council, *Minutes* (24 November 1955), Appendix B: Asantehene to Sir Frederick Bourne, dd. Kumase 28 November 1955.

52. Cited in *Daily Graphic,* 29 November 1955. If Bourne's observations were correct, some of the NLM's allies had misgivings about the refusal to meet with the Constitutional Advisor. Bourne wrote that he suspected that both Awooner-Renner of the MAP and Dombo of the NPP did not favor the decision. See PRO, CO.554/806: Bourne to Governor, dd. Kumase, 29 November 1955.

53. PRO, CO.554/806: Bourne to Governor, "Confidential Report," dd. Accra, 19 December 1955.

54. See Gold Coast, *Report of the Constitutional Advisor,* (Accra, 1955).

55. See *Pioneer,* 5 January 1956; *West Africa,* 7 January 1956, 15; *Daily Graphic,* 2 January 1956.

56. *Pioneer,* 11 January 1956.

57. *West Africa,* 14 January 1956, 26.

58. MRO, Asanteman Council, *Minutes,* (17 and 18 January 1956), Appendix C: "Council's Reply to Prime Minister's Invitation," dd. Kumase, 17 January 1956.

59. MRO, Asanteman Council, *Minutes* (13 February 1956), Appendix B2: Prime Minister to Asantehene, dd. Accra, 31 January 1956.

60. *Daily Graphic,* 7 February 1956.

61. *Pioneer,* 22 February 1956.

62. The conference concluded its proceedings on 16 March 1956. The *Report* which was later issued reflected a general acceptance by the delegates of the recommendations made by Frederick Bourne in December, 1955. It was agreed that Regional Assemblies should be established "to afford an effective link between Regions and the Central Government and thereby to remove any danger of excessive centralisation [and] to provide for the formation and ventilation of local opinion on matters of national importance." See Gold Coast, *Report of the Achimota Conference* (Accra, 1956), 10 and passim.

63. Alessandro Triulzi, "The Ashanti Confederacy Council, 1935–1957," (unpublished field interviews, Institute of African Studies, University of Ghana, 1969), 38–9.

64. Allman, Field Notes: Interview with Osei Assibey-Mensah (FN/15/1), dd. Asante New Town, Kumase, 27 July 1984, 122.

65. Allman, Field Notes: Interview with Kusi Ampofu (FN/24/1), dd. Asante New Town, Kumase, 15 October 184, 205. See also Interview with N. B. Abubekr (FN/16/2), dd. Akowuasaw, Kumase, 10 October 1984, 184; Interview with K. A. M. Gyimah (FN/9/1), dd. Manhyia, Kumase, 20 July 1984, 68.

66. Karl Marx, "The Eighteenth Brumaire of Louis Bonaparte" in K. Marx and F. Engels, *Selected Works* (New York: International, 1977), 123.

67. *Pioneer,* 7 November 1955; *Ashanti Times,* 13 December 1955.

68. *Pioneer,* 7 November 1955.

69. *Daily Graphic,* 9 December 1955.

70. Ibid.

71. *Daily Graphic,* 10 December 1955.

72. See, for example, *Daily Graphic,* 9 January 1956.

73. Lonsdale, "States and Social Processes," 162.

74. I have drawn here from the broader, theoretical discussion of anticolonial nationalisms in Anderson, *Imagined Communities,* 104–28. P. Chatterjee's recent work provides a fascinating interrogation of nationalist ideology and politics in the colonial world—one which problematizes discourse by refusing to accept anticolonial nationalism as a given. "Why is it," he asks, "that non-European colonial countries have no historical alternative but to try to approximate the given attributes of modernity when that very process of approximation means their continued subjection . . . ?" To pose this question, he argues, is to raise the possibility that "thought itself . . . can dominate and subjugate. It is to approach the field of discourse . . . as a battle ground of political power." See Partha Chatterjee, *Nationalist Thought and the Colonial World* (London: Zed Press, 1986), 10–11 and passim.

75. A. C. Russell Papers, Chief Regional Officer, Asante to Deputy Governor, dd. Kumase, 6 March 1956.

76. For an excellent example of this sentiment, see the editorial, "British Attitude," in the *Liberator,* 27 February 1956.

77. Hobsbawm, *Nations and Nationalism,* 75.

78. In February, 1956, the lay members of the Council included I. B. Asafu-Adjaye, B. D. Addai, Cobbina Kessie, J. H. Gambrah, and Victor Owusu. See MRO, Asanteman Council, *Minutes,* 13 February 1956.

79. Lonsdale, "States and Social Processes," 201.

80. While the consolidation of Asante's ruling class was not manifested in an institutional framework until 1956, it was evident from the cocoa boycotts of the 1930s through the 1948 riots. See Crook, "Decolonization in the Gold Coast," 98–9.

81. Allman, Field Notes: Anonymous Interview, October 1984. I have preserved the anonymity of the informant here because of the nature of his allegations.

82. NAGK, ROA/2850: R. R. Amponsah, "Working Committee for a Constitutional Conference," dd. Kumase, 13 March 1956. Invitations were sent to the JPC, the Trans-Volta/Togoland Council, the Northern Territories Council, the Asanteman Council, and the NPP, MAP, ARPS, TC, NLM, and CPP.

83. NAGK, ROA/2850: Assistant Information Officer, Asante to Director of Information Services, Accra, dd. Kumase, 17 March 1956.

84. *Daily Graphic,* 27 February 1956.

85. Nkrumah released a statement denying that the Gold Coast "intends to adopt unconstitutional methods in order to complete the transfer of power." He affirmed that "the Government has already demonstrated to the world its respect

for constitutional methods and it will continue to pursue the achievement of full independence within the Commonwealth by constitutional means." Cited in Austin, *Politics in Ghana*, 305fn.

86. *Pioneer*, 10 March 1956.

87. *Pioneer*, 12 March 1956.

88. *Pioneer*, 12 March 1956.

89. *Liberator*, 6 March 1956.

90. MRO, Asanteman Council, *Minutes*, 7 May 1956.

91. Ibid.

92. Ibid.

93. The 25 and 26 April 1956 issues of the *Pioneer* contain reprints of articles published in the *Telegraph, Economist, Times*, and *Observer* supporting the idea of a general election before independence.

94. PRO, CO.554/806: Secretary of State for the Colonies to Prime Minister, dd. London, 31 October 1955. The evidence suggests that as early as July, 1955, members of parliament were pressuring Lennox-Boyd to address the question of another general election in the Gold Coast. See, PRO, CO.554/804: "Notes for Debate on the Colonial Territories in the House of Lords on the 6th of July," and John Tilney, Member of Parliament to the Secretary of State for the Colonies, dd. London, 18 July 1955.

95. PRO, CO.554/806: Governor to Colonial Office, dd. Accra, 19 December 1955.

96. PRO, CO.554/806: "Brief on Prime Minister's Views Regarding the Holding of a General Election in the Near Future," dd. Accra, February, 1956. Included in the "Brief" was a timetable of events as Nkrumah foresaw them prior to the Achimota Conference. June 8 was cited as the day for the government to announce the holding of another election. The election was slated for July 16. July 24 was put up as the date for the Prime Minister to receive a mandate for independence and March 6, 1957, the anniversary of the Bond of 1844, was slated for independence day.

97. PRO, CO.554/806: Prime Minister to Acting Governor, dd. Accra, 24 February 1956. Governor Arden-Clarke was on leave.

98. PRO, CO.554/806: Secretary of State for the Colonies to Prime Minister, dd. London, 14 March 1956.

99. See PRO, CO.554/806: Secretary of State for the Colonies to Acting Governor, dd. 20 March 1956 and R. W. Piper, "The Gold Coast," London, [no date].

100. Basically, Nkrumah argued that another election could only lead to more violence in the country and that there was no guarantee that the NLM "would change their present attitude even after a general election had been held." His instructions to Botsio were "to make it clear from the onset that neither I, my Party, nor, indeed, the overwhelming majority of the people of the Gold Coast can accept the proposal to go to a general election before Independence . . . this would lead to confusion and would tend to destroy the confidence that the people have in the Government." For Nkrumah's account of the events leading up to the call for a general election and his reasons for wanting to avoid another election, see Nkrumah, *Autobiography*, 246–53.

101. PRO, CO.554/807: "Prime Minister's Brief for Botsio," dd. Accra, April, 1956.

102. PRO, CO.554/807: Secretary of State for the Colonies to Prime Minister, dd. London, 4 April 1954.

103. Nkrumah, *Autobiography,* 251–2.

104. PRO, CO.554/807: Prime Minister to Secretary of State for the Colonies, dd. Accra, 20 April 1956.

105. PRO, CO.554/1162: Governor to Secretary of State for the Colonies, "Gold Coast: Steps Toward Independence," dd. Accra, 16 August 1956.

106. House of Commons, *Debates* (11 May 1956), col. 1557–8.

107. Gold Coast, Legislative Assembly, *Debates,* (15 May 1956), col. 1–4.

108. PRO, CO.554/1162: Governor to Secretary of State for the Colonies, "Gold Coast: Steps Toward Independence," dd. Accra, 16 August 1956.

109. Governor to Lady Arden-Clarke, dd. Accra, 3 May 1956. Cited in Rooney, *Sir Charles Arden-Clarke,* 188.

110. Nkrumah, *Autobiography,* 253.

111. *Pioneer,* 25 May 1956.

112. Busia was the parliamentary leader of the Ghana Congress Party and its allies when they formed the opposition in the 1951–1954 Legislative Assembly.

113. *Pioneer,* 21 June 1956.

114. The debate began on July 6 with a two-page political advertisement in the *Daily Graphic,* in which Busia set out the opposition's grievances against the CPP, citing in particular cases of corruption within the CPC and of inefficiency in the CPP's spending policies. In laying out the opposition's platform for an independent Gold Coast of the future, Busia stressed the need to "safeguard the country against dictatorship, provide constitutional checks against centralization of power, and do justice to the legitimate and manifest desire of each region for a large measure of autonomy." Gbedemah responded on the 11th in the *Evening News,* arguing that corruption had existed in Gold Coast politics for some time and that the CPP was working diligently to end it. He then poignantly asked whether the NLM really wanted federation and asserted that what Busia and his allies really "want and have never been able to say so openly is that THEY should be in office and not the CPP." The debate continued in the July 14 issue of the *Pioneer* and the July 16 issue of the *Evening News,* with both men expressing total confidence that their respective parties would win the election and both asserting that their parties would abide by the decision of the electorate. For a thorough recounting of the debate, see Austin, *Politics in Ghana,* 324–8.

115. Quoted in *Daily Graphic,* 15 July 1956.

116. According to Austin, there was some disagreement within the Executive over this election strategy. While Busia and Bafuor Akoto were confident of the NLM's strength in Asante and believed that the key to an election victory lay in galvanizing support in the South, others, notably Amponsah, Appiah, and the Asantehene, believed that initially, anyway, the NLM should "make sure of [its] . . . Ashanti base." In the end, those who supported the move into the Colony won the day. See Austin, *Politics in Ghana,* 342.

117. Austin, *Politics in Ghana,* 333.

118. *Pioneer,* 26 June 1956.

119. Osei Assibey-Mensah, "Vote for NLM" (leaflet; Kumase, 1956). It is unclear whether "Countries" is a typographical error or represents a purposeful effort to underscore the Gold Coast's national diversity.

120. Osei Assibey-Mensah, "Flash" (leaflet; Kumase, 1956). The red cockerel was the CPP's party symbol.

121. Austin, *Politics in Ghana*, 333.

122. Ibid.

123. CPP, *Operation Independence* (pamphlet; Accra, 1956). See also Andoh, "The Asante National Liberation Movement," 182.

124. Published in the *Pioneer*, 2 July 1956. The cocoa tree was the NLM's party symbol in the 1956 election.

125. The five seats the NLM knew would be difficult were Sekyere East—Krobo Edusei's constituency and the home of the Kumawuhene—and the four Brong constituencies whose chiefs had seceded from the Asanteman Council and sought CPP support for a separate Council. These constituencies were Wenkyi East, Sunyani East, Sunyani West, and Berekum.

126. Austin, *Politics in Ghana*, 318–9. In Chapter 7, "The 1956 General Election," Austin provides his thorough overview of the election, including data on many individual constituencies and the factors influencing polling in those areas (see 316–62).

127. On the eve of the election, the opposition was able to field candidates in 99 of the 104 constituencies. Two seats in the North and 3 in the Colony saw the CPP running unopposed; 81 of the 99 contested seats were straight fights between the CPP and the opposition. Unlike the election of 1954, when 156 Independents ran, only 45 Independents ran in 1956, and of those 17 declared "independent support" for Busia as parliamentary leader. See Austin, *Politics in Ghana*, 320–1.

128. *Pioneer*, 3 July 1956 and 18 July 1956.

129. *Pioneer*, 19 July 1956.

130. *West Africa*, 21 July 1956, 507–8.

131. In Asante, of 224,569 votes cast, 96,968 went to the CPP. The NLM received 119,533 votes; the MAP, 7565; and an Independent, 503. See Austin, *Politics in Ghana*, 354.

132. Ibid., 534.

133. Allman, Field Notes: Interview with Bafuor Osei Akoto and Antwi Buasiako (FN/4/1), dd. Asokwa, Kumase, 27 June 1984, 19.

134. See *Ghana Nationalist*, 20 October 1954. For a summary of the article which appeared in the *Evening News* and an account of the Asantehene's response to the charges, see *Pioneer*, 17 March 1956.

135. *Pioneer*, 16 August 1955.

136. The original core of the rival Congress consisted of seven trade unions who elected Pobee Biney their president: the Public Works Department Employees Union, the Gold Coast Hospital Workers Union, the Gold Coast Railway Employees Union, the Maritime Workers Union, the Municipal Council Workers Union, the R. T. Briscoe Workers Union, and the UAC Employees Union. See Richard Jeffries, *Class, Power and Ideology in Ghana: The Railwaymen of Sekondi* (Cambridge: Cambridge University Press, 1978), 69–81; Paul S. Gray, *Unions and Leaders in Ghana: A Study of the Institutionalization of Ghanaian Labour* (Owerri: Conch Magazine Ltd., 1981), 27–154; Ian Davies, *African Trade Unions* (Harmondsworth: Penguin, 1966), 109.

137. *Pioneer*, 20 September 1955.

138. PRO, DO.35/6213: "Extract from Colonial Political Intelligence, April 1955."

139. A. C. Russell Papers, Outgoing Chief Regional Officer, Asante [Loveridge] to Incoming Chief Regional Officer, Asante [Russell], dd. Kumase, 30 September 1955.

140. A. C. Russell Papers, Chief Regional Officer, Asante to Governor, dd. Kumase, 5 November 1955.

141. A. C. Russell Papers, Outgoing Chief Regional Officer, Asante to Incoming Chief Regional Officer, Asante, dd. Kumase, 30 September 1955.

142. There is some controversy over the nature of the relationship between Pobee Biney's CFTU and the NLM. Marable, Gray, and Davies argue that the CFTU allied with the NLM shortly after it was organized. However, Jeffries asserts that "contrary to some accounts, the CFTU did not align itself with the major opposition party during 1954–6, the Ashanti-based National Liberation Movement." There is probably an element of truth in all four accounts. In late 1955, there were apparently attempts from both sides to forge some sort of alliance. However, by the 1956 election, it was clear that the rebel trade unionists had written off the NLM and that the leadership of the NLM, after neglecting the trade unionists' struggle for several months, had abandoned much hope of winning working class support for its election platform, particularly in the Colony. See Marable, *African and Caribbean Politics*, 118; Gray, *Unions and Leaders*, 27; Davies, *African Trade Unions*, 109; Jeffries, *Class, Power and Ideology*, 81.

143. *Liberator*, 29 May 1956.

144. Noted in Austin, *Politics in Ghana*, 352fn.

145. Ibid., 351fn.

146. Appiah, *Autobiography*, 246.

147. *West Africa*, 21 July 1956, 507–8.

148. See, for example, Andoh, "The Asante National Liberation Movement," 182; Austin, *Politics in Ghana*, 351–3; Chazan, "Ghana," 95–6; Drah, "The Brong Political Movement," 135–44 and passim; and Horowitz, *Ethnic Groups*, 270.

149. See Drah, "The Brong Political Movement," 141–3 and Austin, *Politics in Ghana*, 353. See, also, Chapter 4 above. The CPP polled 61.3 percent of the votes in the five Brong constituencies. Busia was victorious in Wenkyi West, the fifth constituency.

150. Austin, *Politics in Ghana*, 352.

151. See A. C. Russell Papers, "State Councils Ordinance," and Minister of Local Government to Chief Regional Officer, Asante, "Constitutional Appeals As Arising Out Of Amendments To State Councils Ordinance (Ashanti)," dd. Accra, March, 1956.

152. Austin, "Opposition in Ghana," 542.

153. Austin, *Politics in Ghana*, 321.

154. According to the Asanteman Council *Minutes*, Asante Chief Farmer Kofi Buor "contacted Messrs Cadbury and Fry for financial assistance. Upon strong negotiation. . . . Farmers within the Union may have been advanced (according to their cocoa supply output per farm or farms). A total of £70,000 have been advanced up to date. . . . By this, the Union have been able to liberate the farmers from the depressive and deceptive clutches of the CPC." See MRO, Asanteman

Council, *Minutes* (2–9 August 1955), Appendix E: "Asante Farmers' Union: Progress Report Of." Similarly, Rooney argues that Edward Spears of the Ashanti Goldfields Corporation financed Busia's mission in London. See Rooney, *Sir Charles Arden-Clarke*, 173, and *Kwame Nkrumah*, 101. Though he offers no specifics, Rooney also maintains that other expatriate firms threw their weight behind the NLM.

155. Allman, Field Notes: Interview with Abdul Rahim Alawa (FN/26/1), dd. Zongo, Kumase, 19 October 1984, 229.

156. Allman, Field Notes: Interview with Kusi Ampofu (FN/24/1), dd. Asante New Town, Kumase, 15 October 1984, 199, 201, 206–7.

157. Allman, Field Notes: Interview with Abdul Rahim Alawa (FN/26/1), dd. Zongo, Kumase, 19 October 1984, 225, 228–9. During the 1950s, Abdul Alawa was a Zongo (MAP) representative to the Kumase Municipal Council.

158. For the voting tabulations upon which these statistics are based, see Austin, *Politics in Ghana*, 238 and 347.

159. The gist of this argument was repeated by all of the major leaders of the opposition. This particular statement was made by Busia at a press conference on July 20. See *Pioneer*, 21 July 1956.

160. Gold Coast, Legislative Assembly, *Debates*, (1 August 1956), col. 52.

161. In the somewhat extravagant statement he issued explaining why the opposition walked out of the Assembly, Busia declared that "since it is quite apparent that the Government has decided to impose the will of the Colony region on the three other regions despite the fact that the majority of people of these three other regions have voted for a Federal Constitution, we decided to withdraw from the Legislative Assembly. . . . The attitude and practice of the CPP Government show ominous signs of intolerance and party dictatorship, and flagrant disregard of each region's right of self-determination. The opposition, after serious discussion, consider it our duty to fight these dangerous tendencies now. The lesson of Nazi Germany is too recent to be forgotten." A. C. Russell Papers, "Busia's Statement (On Why Opposition Walked Out of the Assembly)," 3 August 1954.

Chapter 6. "And a Thousand More Will Come?"

1. *Liberator*, 13 August 1956.

2. *Pioneer*, 14 August 1956.

3. *Pioneer*, 15 August 1956.

4. See Jibowu, *Report* paras. 203–16 and passim. The *Report* was made public on August 31.

5. Austin, *Politics in Ghana*, 356.

6. PRO, CO.554/1061: "Memorandum by Delegation Representing Ashanti, the Northern Territories, Southern Togoland and the Opposition in the Legislative Assembly . . . on the Subject of Their Interview on 10th September 1956." The full opposition delegation included Alhaji Yakubu Tali, President of the Northern Territories Council and Member of the Legislative Assembly; H. A. Azure, Nangodi-Naba; S. G. Antor, MLA; Victor Owusu, MLA; J. A. Braimah, MLA and vice-president of the Northern Territories Council; A. Amandi; A. Karbo, MLA; and R. R. Amponsah, MLA.

7. PRO, CO.554/1060: "Minutes of Meeting between Opposition Delegation and Minister of State."

8. PRO, CO.554/1060: "Note of a Meeting Held in the Secretary of State's Room on the 11th September, 1956."

9. Fabian Colonial Bureau Papers, "Notes of a Meeting at the House of Commons with Professor K. A. Busia, R. R. Amponsah and Mr. W. E. Ofori-Atta of the Gold Coast Opposition," dd. London, 12 September 1956. A few days after the delegation met with the secretary of state for the colonies, Busia decided to take his plea for an official visit by the secretary straight to the press. In a letter to the editor of *The Times* (subsequently published), Busia suggested that "before the date of independence is formally announced, the Secretary of State for the Colonies should himself visit the Gold Coast and make an effort to bring the parties together to settle the constitutional issues." See PRO, CO.554/1060: Busia to Editor of *The Times*, dd. London, 13 September 1956.

10. Fabian Colonial Bureau Papers, "Notes of a Meeting at the House of Commons with Professor K. A. Busia, R. R. Amponsah and Mr. W. E. Ofori-Atta of the Gold Coast Opposition," dd. London, 12 September 1956.

11. PRO, CO.554/1060: File Minute, dd. 3 September 1956.

12. PRO, CO.554/1060: Secretary of State for the Colonies to Governor, dd. London, 12 September 1956.

13. PRO, CO.554/1160: File Minute, dd. 3 September 1956.

14. PRO, CO.554/1060: Secretary of State for the Colonies to Governor, dd. London, 12 September 1956.

15. Ibid.

16. *Pioneer*, 19 September 1956; *Daily Graphic*, 19 September 1956.

17. PRO, CO.554/808: Secretary of State for the Colonies to Governor [with message to be passed on to the Prime Minister], dd. London, 17 September 1956.

18. *Pioneer*, 20 September 1956.

19. Still in London in early October, Busia made yet another plea for either the secretary or minister of state to preside over constitutional talks in the Gold Coast. He was told that "these matters should be settled in [the] Gold Coast and that it would be worse than useless if a Minister appeared to come out to support one side only and that the Opposition." See PRO, CO.554/1060: Secretary of State for the Colonies to Governor, dd. London, 11 September 1956.

20. *Pioneer*, 17 October 1956. See, also, PRO, CO.554/1060: Secretary of State for the Colonies to Governor, dd. London, 11 October 1956.

21. See, for example, the description of Joe Appiah's address to a rally in Obuasi in the *Pioneer*, 2 October 1956.

22. PRO, CO.554/825: "Record of Conclusions Reached at the Talks between Delegations Representing the Government and the Parliamentary Opposition . . . ," dd. Accra, 29 October 1956. See also, Fabian Colonial Bureau Papers, Parliamentary Opposition, "Notes and Counter-Proposals on the 'Government's Revised Constitutional Proposals for Gold Coast Independence,'" dd. Accra, 19 October 1956.

23. PRO, CO.554/808: Colonial Office to Arden-Clarke, dd. London, 11 October 1956.

24. See *Pioneer*, 12 October 1956. Rumors such as this were not entirely unsubstantiated. Evidence reveals that by mid-September, the CPP had already sent a draft of their constitutional proposals to the Colonial Office. The secretary of

state for the colonies referred to the government's White Paper in a September 17 message to Nkrumah. Busia suspected that this was the case, and enquired in early October whether the Colonial Office had seen a draft. His question was not directly answered. He was told that the Office "had some indication that Gold Coast Ministers would make a genuine effort to meet Opposition requests" at the negotiations in Accra. "This was based on [the] fact," a dispatch to the Governor continued, "that in some respect their Proposals go further towards doing so than Bourne or Achimota Reports." See PRO, CO.554/1060: Secretary of State for the Colonies to Governor, dd. London, 11 September 1956.

25. *Pioneer,* 5 November 1956.

26. *Daily Graphic,* 10 November 1956.

27. Gold Coast, *The Government's Revised Constitutional Proposals for Gold Coast Independence* (Accra, 1956), 6.

28. Ibid., 6–7.

29. Ibid., 11.

30. The main text of the White Paper details the government's proposals. Appendix I outlines the major areas of disagreement between the government and the opposition. Appendix II gives a paragraph-by-paragraph summary of agreement and disagreement between the government, the opposition delegates, and the representatives of the territorial councils. See Gold Coast, *The Government's Revised Constitutional Proposals,* passim.

31. See Gold Coast, Legislative Assembly, *Debates,* (12–14 November 1956), passim. Nkrumah contended in a private memorandum that the debate over the White Paper indicated that the opposition was seriously divided: "The Government's proposals . . . were first debated in general and were then considered paragraph by paragraph. The Opposition did not divide against any particular paragraph. It is the impression of the Government that the reason why the Opposition did not ask for a vote was that they were not united in their opposition to any particular one of the Government's proposals nor were they united in regard to any of the counter-proposals which they put forward." See PRO, CO.554/813: "Memorandum by the Prime Minister," dd. Accra, November, 1956.

32. PRO, CO.554/1060: Governor to Secretary of State for the Colonies [forwarding NLM/NPP resolution], dd. Accra, 21 November 1956. Quoted in *Pioneer,* 20 November 1956.

33. *Ashanti Times,* 29 November 1956.

34. PRO, CO.554/1060: Governor to Secretary of State for the Colonies [forwarding Asanteman Council resolution], dd. Accra, 23 November 1956.

35. See *Pioneer,* 21 and 22 November 1956.

36. PRO, CO.554/1060: Deputy Governor to Secretary of State for the Colonies [forwarding NLM resolution], dd. Accra, 29 November 1965. The resolution appeared in full in the *Pioneer,* 27 November 1956.

37. *Pioneer,* 27 November 1956.

38. PRO, CO.554/827: Coward, Chance and Company to Secretary of State for the Colonies, dd. London, 17 October 1956.

39. PRO, CO.554/827: Coward, Chance and Company to Secretary of State for the Colonies, dd. London, 30 November 1956.

40. See *Pioneer,* 27 November 1956, and *Daily Graphic,* 27 November 1956.

41. *Daily Graphic,* 11 December 1956.

42. See, for example, PRO, CO.554/821: Woodrow Wyatt to Secretary of State for the Colonies, dd. London, 18 January 1957. In his private letter to the secretary, Wyatt wrote, "I don't think they are bluffing when they say they have bought arms (probably from French territory)."

43. Allman, Field Notes: Interview with Joe Appiah (FN/11/1), dd. Mbrom, Kumase, 23 July 1984, 91.

44. A. C. Russell Papers, Chief Regional Officer, Asante to the Secretary to the Governor, dd. Kumase, 15 November 1956.

45. PRO, CO.554/808: Secretary of State for the Colonies to Acting Governor, dd. London, 23 November 1956. Some of the secretary's concerns were addressed in an internal security brief in December which revealed that less than 10 percent of the police and 5 percent of the military were drawn from Asante. See PRO, CO.554/895: "Draft Brief: Internal Security, dd. London, December 1956.

46. PRO, CO.554/808: Acting Governor to Secretary of State for the Colonies, dd. Accra, 25 November 1956.

47. PRO, CO.554/1060: Acting Governor to Secretary of State for the Colonies, dd. Accra, 4 December 1956.

48. Quoted in the *Daily Graphic*, 11 December 1956. The original draft of the secretary's statement was prepared in the governor's office in Accra. See PRO, CO.554/1060: Acting Governor to Secretary of State for the Colonies, dd. Accra, 5 December 1956.

49. Evidence suggests that the Colonial Office recognized that Busia and the Asantehene were capable of leading a retreat from the secessionist demand. Often the office relied on "inside" information from Isobel Cripps, Joe Appiah's mother-in-law. In mid-December she informed the office that Busia and the Asantehene were "moderating influences" within the Movement and that the Asantehene "hates the idea of violence." See PRO, CO.554/809: "Note of Meeting with Lady Cripps," dd. London, 11 December 1956.

50. PRO, CO.554/1060: Governor's Deputy to Secretary of State for the Colonies [forwarding NLM reply], dd. Accra, 14 December 1956. See also *Pioneer*, 12 December 1956.

51. PRO, CO.554/1060: Governor to Secretary of State for the Colonies [forwarding Asanteman Council reply], dd. Accra, 21 December 1956. See also *Ashanti Times*, 21 December 1956.

52. *Daily Graphic*, 12 December 1956.

53. *Pioneer*, 15 December 1956.

54. A. C. Russell Papers, Chief Regional Officer, Asante to Governor, "Security Appreciation," dd. Kumase, 2 January 1957.

55. A. C. Russell Papers, George to Chief Regional Officer, Asante, dd. Cyprus, 9 January 1957.

56. A. C. Russell Papers, "Notes of an Informal Meeting Held in the Governor's Office," dd. Accra, 4 January 1957.

57. Ibid.

58. *Daily Graphic*, 20 December 1956.

59. *Daily Graphic*, 23 December 1956. The London *Times* of 21 December 1956 published a letter by Busia in which he once again suggested that the secretary of state for the Colonies come to the Gold Coast.

60. *Daily Graphic*, 5 January 1957; *Pioneer*, 5 January 1957.

61. See *Pioneer*, 8 January 1957.

62. PRO, CO.554/820: File Minute, dd. 12/13 December 1956.

63. PRO, CO.554/1060: Secretary of State for the Colonies to Governor, dd. London, 24 December 1956.

64. PRO, CO.554/820: Governor to Secretary of State for the Colonies, dd. Accra, 22 December 1956. See also PRO, CO.554/820: Governor to Secretary of State for the Colonies [forwarding prime minister's message], dd. Accra, 22 December 1956.

65. PRO, CO.554/820: Governor to Secretary of State for the Colonies [forwarding prime minister's message], dd. Accra, 22 December 1956.

66. Quoted in *Evening News*, 9 January 1957.

67. *Ashanti Times*, 4 January 1957.

68. *Daily Graphic*, 9 January 1957.

69. *Pioneer*, 28 January 1957; *Daily Graphic*, 28 January 1957.

70. MRO, AC/[no file number; file is entitled, "NLM: Political, II"]: "Untitled Mimeo," no date. It is obvious from the contents and by subsequent newspaper reports of the meeting that this statement was prepared for and read at the session with Lennox-Boyd on 26 January 1957.

71. Ibid.

72. Ibid. See also *Daily Graphic*, 28 January 1957.

73. See Gold Coast, *Report of the Constitutional Advisor*, 1955; *Report of the Achimota Conference*, 1956; *The Government's Revised Constitutional Proposals for Gold Coast Independence*, 1956.

74. *Daily Graphic*, 31 January 1957.

75. *Pioneer*, 31 January 1957.

76. *Ashanti Times*, 29 January 1957.

77. PRO, CO.554/1162: Governor to Secretary of State for the Colonies, "Gold Coast: Review of Events Leading up to Independence," dd. Accra, 5 March 1957.

78. *Liberator*, 11 February 1957.

79. *Pioneer*, 11 February 1957.

80. The Colonial Office realized it faced a difficult task. During December and January they operated under the assumption that "given a few of the safeguards for which they are asking, the Opposition will be prepared, reluctantly, to acquiesce in the present constitutional proposals." At the same time, however, the office believed that "if too much is given to the Opposition . . . the Government will almost certainly tear up the Constitution after Independence and go their own way." For assorted correspondence, memoranda, and minutes lending insight into the Colonial Office's attempts to "find the balance between these two forces," see PRO, CO.554/821.

81. Great Britain, Colonial Office, *The Proposed Constitution of Ghana* (London, 1957), 7–8.

82. Ibid., 11.

83. Ibid.

84. *Pioneer*, 12 February 1957.

85. *Ashanti Times*, 12 February 1957.

86. Gold Coast, Legislative Assembly, *Debates*, 12 February 1957.

87. PRO, CO.554/1060: "Statement by the Asanteman Council," dd. Kumase, 13 February 1957.

88. A. C. Russell Papers, Chief Regional Officer, Asante to Secretary of State for the Colonies, dd. Kumase, 26 March 1957. As Drah argues, the Brong chiefs delivered "the political goods" in the 1956 election, and in 1959 the CPP would "redeem its promise to the Brong." See Drah, "The Brong Political Movement," 143–4.

89. See *Ashanti Times*, 26 February 1957.

90. *Pioneer*, 26 and 27 February 1957.

91. A. C. Russell Papers, Chief Regional Officer, Asante to Secretary to the Governor, dd. Kumase, 23 February 1957.

92. Allman, Field Notes: Interview with Kusi Ampofu (FN/24/1), dd. Asante New Town, Kumase, 15 October 1984, 206.

93. *Pioneer*, 28 February 1957. On March 6, Independence Day, some members of the Togoland Congress translated the disaffection expressed by Antor into action. In the Alavanyo district, many supporters of the Congress, according to Austin, "banded themselves together in camps, marched up and down in ragged military formation, and practised with shotguns in the hope that they might thereby hasten the day of Togoland unification." The government quickly moved troops into the area and squashed the revolt. Antor was later arrested and charged with complicity in the plot. See Austin, *Politics in Ghana*, 372.

94. See PRO, CO.554/1060: Governor to Secretary of State for the Colonies [forwarding NLM statement], dd. Accra, 2 March 1957 and Governor to Secretary of State for the Colonies [forwarding Asanteman Council statement], dd. Accra, 4 March 1957.

95. A. C. Russell Papers, Chief Regional Officer, Asante to Secretary to the Governor, dd. Kumase, 26 February 1957.

96. A. C. Russell Papers, Chief Regional Officer, Asante to Secretary of State for the Colonies, dd. 26 March 1957.

97. PRO, CO.554/1162: Governor to Secretary of State for the Colonies, "Gold Coast: Review of Events Leading up to Independence," dd. Accra, 5 March 1957.

98. Allman, Field Notes: Interview with Joe Appiah (FN/11/1), dd. Mbrom, Kumase, 23 July 1984, 91.

99. McCaskie makes a similar point when he characterizes the struggle between the NLM and the CPP as simultaneously an "historically predictable battle *between* Asante." See McCaskie, "Accumulation," II: 17.

100. Following the 1956 election, a report in *West Africa* jubilantly proclaimed, "At last the Gold Coast has a real Opposition." See *West Africa*, 21 July 1956, 505.

101. For example, Cobbina Kessie recalled that he left the United Party in 1957 or 1958 because "an amount of money was collected and Busia, who was then . . . leading, was the President and couldn't give us an account of where it was. And not only that . . . there were some of the members who were backsliding . . . they were going behind us and sending information to Nkrumah and his Party. So we became suspicious . . . [and] some of us—I was not the only one—left to become independent . . . . Dombo left, too. And some of the important chiefs in the North did too." See Allman, Field Notes: Interview with Cobbina Kessie (FN/1/2), dd. Suame, Kumase, 6 July 1984, 48.

102. In December, 1957, the government introduced the Avoidance of Dis-

crimination Act which banned all organizations, parties, and societies which were confined to particular tribal, racial, or religious groups yet were used for political purposes. In effect, this law made the NLM, the NPP and all of the other political groups who had banded together in the United Party only a month before illegal. For Nkrumah's justification for the introduction of this bill, see Kwame Nkrumah, *Africa Must Unite* (New York: International, 1970), 72–5.

103. Austin, *Politics in Ghana*, 386.

104. See, for example, Austin, *Politics in Ghana,* 363–421; Apter, *Ghana in Transition,* 336–86; Fitch and Oppenheimer, *Ghana: End of an Illusion,* passim; A. Adu Boahen, *Ghana: Evolution and Change in the Nineteenth and Twentieth Centuries* (London: Longman, 1975), 191–221; Marable, *African and Caribbean Politics,* 120–49; Mohan, "Nkrumah and Nkrumahism," 191–228; and Nkrumah, *Africa Must Unite,* 72–86.

105. The KMC was suspended on April 26, and the CPC was liquidated on May 2. See *Pioneer,* 3 May 1957. For an excellent study of the UGFC which, in the author's words, analyzes the Council "both as a vehicle for mobilizing resources for national development and as an instrument of class appropriation, serving the self-advancement of a new commercial-bureaucratic class," see Beckman, *Organizing the Farmers,* 12 and passim.

106. See Sarkodee-Addo, *Report*, passim.

107. See Ghana, *Government Statement on the Report on the Kumasi State Council and the Asanteman Council* (Accra, 1958), passim.

108. Austin, *Politics in Ghana,* 378–9. See also Ghana, Regional Constitutional Commission, *Regional Assemblies: Report to His Excellency the Governor* (Accra, 1958), passim.

109. For a brief, yet thorough, account of these constitutional changes, see Austin, *Politics in Ghana,* 379–80.

110. NAGK, ROA/2491: Government Agent, Bekwae to Regional Commissioner, "Monthly Intelligent Report," dd. Bekwae, 9 May 1957. See, also, MRO, AC/006/54/3: Regional Commissioner's Secretary to the Asanteman Council, dd. Kumase, 10 April 1958.

111. For Lardan's personal recollections of his deportation, see Allman, Field Notes: Interview with Alfa O. Lardan (FN/19/1), dd. Zongo, Kumase, 3 August 1984, 153–5, and (FN/9/2), dd. Zongo, Kumase, 25 September 1984, 169. Lardan, in fact, was born in Kumase. His father migrated to Kumase from the Okwara state in Nigeria some time during World War I. When Lardan was deported to Kano in 1957, it was the first time he had set foot on Nigerian soil.

112. Boahen, *Ghana,* 194.

113. Amponsah was then general secretary of the United Party. His detention was based on the fact, according to Austin, that he had "bought those relatively harmless pieces of military accoutrement—Sam Brown belts, canes, badges of rank and hackles—which were later to figure at the Granville Sharp inquiry into the alleged plot to assassinate Nkrumah." See Austin, *Politics in Ghana,* 380, and Boahen, *Ghana,* 194–5. For the United Party's response to Amponsah's detention, see United Party, *Unwarranted Detention* (pamphlet; Accra, 1960), passim.

114. According to the United Kingdom's High Commissioner, by April, 1960, detention orders had been issued against eighty-six people, and seventy had actually been detained. One was released in January, 1960, on the grounds of old age

and ill health. See PRO, DO.35/6190: United Kingdom High Commissioner to Commonwealth Relations Office, dd. Accra, 20 April 1960 and 15 June 1960.

115. Kwame Kesse-Adu, *The Politics of Political Detention* (Accra-Tema: Ghana Publishing Corp., 1971), 20–30.

116. MRO, AC/006/54/3: Asante Youth Association to Asanteman Council, dd. Kumase, 14 February 1958, and "Statement Issued by the Kumase State Council at a Meeting Held on 31 March 1958."

117. United Party, *In Defense of Justice and Baffuor Akoto* (pamphlet; Kumase, 1961), 1.

118. Kwame Nkrumah, "What the Party Stands For," *The Party* 1:1 (1960), cited in Apter, *Ghana in Transition*, 326.

119. Ivor Wilks informed me of the existence of this group. To date, we have only one document as evidence of its existence—the letter written by the Warriors to Nkrumah on 26 July 1962. A copy of the letter is in Wilks' possession.

120. The author had great difficulty obtaining information about the subsequent activities of the Warriors. Only one informant acknowledged the existence of the group and was willing to discuss it, provided the tape recorder was turned off and his identity protected. He reluctantly stated that the group was quite small (roughly twenty people) and was a direct descendant of the Asante Action Groupers. When asked if there were any connection between the Warriors and the coup which toppled Nkrumah in 1966, the informant replied, "No." He stated that the group was too small and isolated and, although it supported the coup, it had no involvement in it.

121. C. Van Woodward, "Comments on the Panel, *The Strange Career of Jim Crow* Revisited," (American Historical Association Annual Meeting, Chicago, IL), December, 1986.

122. For a brief discussion of conflicting definitions of "nation" in the context of nineteenth-century Europe, see Hobsbawm, *Nations and Nationalism*, 14–45. At one point, Hobsbawm differentiates between the "revolutionary democratic" definition, which rests on the concept of a sovereign people, and the "nationalist" definition, which is "derived from the prior existence of some community distinguishing itself from foreigners" (22).

123. Roger Murray, "The Ghanaian Road," *New Left Review* 32 (1963), 70. Marx made a similar argument eighty years earlier in a letter to Karl Kautsky (1882) concerning the Polish national question: "History yet proves that a great nation, as long as it lacks national independence, has no conditions even for a serious debate about any of its internal affairs. . . . Every Polish peasant and worker who awakes from his stupor and starts taking part in matters of general concern meets the fact of national subjugation as the first obstacle in his path. . . . To be able to fight one must feel the ground under one's feet, and air, light and space. Otherwise everything else remains empty talk." Cited in Lucjan Blit, *The Origins of Polish Socialism* (Cambridge: Cambridge University Press, 1971), 39.

124. Allman, Field Notes: Interview with Bafuor Akoto and Antwi Buasiako (FN/4/1), dd. Asokwa, Kumase, 27 June 1984, 22.

Bibliography

Primary Sources

Archival Deposits

All sources in this classification have been fully identified in the footnotes.

Ghana

Balme Library, University of Ghana, Legon:

Ashanti Chief Commissioner's Office. Ashanti Confederacy Council, "Memorandum on the Proposed Native Constitution of Ashanti by the Chief Commissioner, Ashanti." No date.

Institute of African Studies, University of Ghana, Legon:

Asanteman Council and Others, "Constitutional Dispute, 1954–57; Draft of Memorandum to the Secretary of State for the Colonies." Kumase, 1956.

Ashanti Farmers Association, Limited, *The Minutes of the Ashanti Farmers Association, Limited, 1934–6*. (Edited and introduced by Kwame Arhin.)

Manhyia Record Office, Kumase:

Asanteman Council (earlier known as Asante Confederacy Council) *Minutes*, 1936–1958.

Asanteman Council, Miscellaneous Files.

Kumase State Council, *Minutes*, 1954–1958.

Kumase State Council, *Record Book of Court Cases*, 1954–57.

National Archives of Ghana, Kumase:

Regional Office Files (ROA).

Miscellaneous Files (including District Officers' Quarterly Reports).

Great Britain

Public Record Office, Colonial Office Papers:

CO.96, *Original Correspondence*, 1948–51.

CO.98, *Sessional Papers*, 1948–1955.

CO.343, *Register of Original Correspondence*, 1948–51.

CO.554, *West Africa, Original Correspondence*, 1948–57.

CO.555, *West Africa, Register of Original Correspondence*, 1948–51.

Public Record Office, Dominions and Commonwealth Relations Office Papers:

DO.35, *Original Correspondence*, 1953–1958.

Collected Papers and Manuscripts

Africa Bureau Papers, Rhodes House, Oxford.
Bafuor Osei Akoto Papers, privately held by collector, Kumase.
Osei Assibey-Mensah Papers, privately held by collector, Kumase.
A. G. Beeton Papers, Rhodes House, Oxford.
Cadbury Papers, University of Birmingham Library.
Fabian Colonial Bureau Papers, Rhodes House, Oxford.
R. W. M. Hatfield Papers, Rhodes House, Oxford.
A. J. Loveridge Papers, Rhodes House, Oxford.
Methodist Mission Society Archives, School of Oriental and African Studies, University of London.
A. C. Russell Papers, Rhodes House, Oxford.
J. P. Tyrie Papers, Rhodes House, Oxford.

Published Government Sources

Ghana

Government Statement on the Report on the Kumasi State Council and the Asanteman Council. Accra, 1958.

Proceedings and Report of the Commission Appointed to Enquire into the Matters Disclosed at the Trial of Captain Benjamin Awhaitey Before a Court-Martial and the Surrounding Circumstances (Chairman: G. Granville Sharp). Accra, 1959.

Report of a Commission Appointed to Enquire into the Affairs of the Akim Abuakwa State (Chairman: J. Jackson). Accra, 1958.

Report of a Commission Appointed to Enquire into the Affairs of the Kumasi State Council and the Asanteman Council (Chairman: Justice Sarkodee Addo). Accra, 1958.

Office of the Government Statistician. "Survey of Cocoa Producing Families in Ashanti, 1956–1957." *Statistical and Economic Papers* 7. Accra, 1960.

Regional Constitution Commission. *Regional Assemblies: Report to his Excellency the Governor*. Accra, 1958.

Gold Coast

Census of the Population, 1948. London, 1950.

Gazettes. Accra, 1954–57.

The Government's Revised Constitutional Proposals for Gold Coast Independence. Accra, 1956.

Report of the Achimota Conference (Chairman: C. W. Tachie-Menson). Accra, 1956.

Report of the Commission of Enquiry into the Affairs of the Cocoa Purchasing Company, Ltd. (Chairman: O. Jibowu). Accra, 1956.

Report of the Commission of Enquiry into Mr. Braimah's Resignation and Allegations Arising Therefrom (Chairman: K. A. Korsah). Accra, 1954.

Report of the Commission of Enquiry into Representational and Electoral Reform. (Chairman: W. B. Van Lare). Accra, 1953.

Report of the Commission of Enquiry into Regional Administrations (Chairman: S. Phillipson). Accra, 1951.

Report of the Committee on the Asanteman-Brong Dispute (Chairman: A. Mate Kole). Accra, 1955.
Report of the Constitutional Advisor (Frederick Bourne). Accra, 1956.
Report of the Select Committee of the Legislative Council Appointed to Make Recommendations Concerning Local Government in Ashanti. Accra, 1951.
Report of the Select Committee on the Federal System of Government and Second Chamber for the Gold Coast. Accra, 1955.
Legislative Assembly. *Debates*, 1951–57.

Great Britain, Colonial Office

Annual Report on the Gold Coast, 1920–55.
Despatches on the Gold Coast Government's Proposals for Constitutional Reform Exchanged Between the Secretary of State for the Colonies and His Excellency the Governor, 24 August 1953–15 April 1954. London, 1954.
The Proposed Constitution of Ghana. London, 1957.
Report of the Commission of Enquiry into Disturbances in the Gold Coast (Chairman: A. Watson). London, 1948.

Political Pamphlets and Booklets

Asante Kotoko Society, Editorial Committee. *Asante Kotoko Society, 60th Anniversary*. Kumase, *1976*.
Asanteman Council, Farmers, NLM and Allies and the Opposition in the Legislative Assembly. *Why CMB–CPC Probe?* Kumase, 1955.
Busia, K. A. *Judge for Yourself*. Accra, 1956.
CPP. *Operation Independence: Manifesto for the General Election, July 1956*. Accra, 1956.
CPP. *Operation 104: Manifesto for the General Election, 1954*. Accra, 1954.
Kesse-Adu, Kwame. *The National Labour Party: A Blue-Print—Object and Policy*. Kumase, 1950.
Movements and Parties Other than the CPP. *Proposals for a Federal Constitution for an Independent Gold Coast and Togoland*. Kumase, 1955.
NLM and Its Allies. *Statement by the National Liberation Movement and Its Allies on the Gold Coast Government's Constitutional Proposals for Gold Coast Independence*. Kumase, 1956.
Parliamentary Opposition. *Statement by the Parliamentary Opposition Justifying and Giving Reasons for the Constitutional Safeguards on which No Agreement Was Reached with the Government*. Kumase, 1956 (mimeo).
United Party. *Ghana at the Crossroads: A Statement by the National Executive of the UP on the Government's Decision to Change Ghana into a Republic*. Accra, 1960.
United Party. *In Defense of Ghana: A Statement by the National Executive of the United Party on the Granville Sharp Commission's Reports and the Government's White Paper on the Reports*. Accra, 1959.
United Party. *In Defense of Justice and Bafuor Akoto*. Kumase, 1961.
United Party. *Unwarranted Detention: A Plea to the Legal Conscience*. Accra, 1960.

Newspapers and Periodicals

Ashanti Pioneer
Ashanti Sentinel
Ashanti Times
Daily Graphic
Evening News
Ghana Nationalist
Liberator
West Africa

Secondary Sources

Books

Akyeampong, H. K. ed. *The Doyen Speaks: Some of the Historic Speeches by Dr. J. B. Danquah*. Accra: George Boakie, 1976.

Akyeampong, H. K. ed. *Journey to Independence and After*, Vol. 3 (1952–1957, the letters of J. B. Danquah). Accra: George Boakie, 1972.

Amamoo, Joseph G. *The New Ghana*. London: Pan Books, 1958.

Amin, Samir. *Class and Nation: Historically and in the Current Crisis*. New York: Monthly Review Press, 1980.

Amin, Samir. *Neo-Colonialism in West Africa*. New York: Monthly Review Press, 1973.

Anderson, Benedict. *Imagined Communities: Reflections on the Origin and Spread of Nationalism*. London: Verso, 1983.

Appiah, Joseph. *Joe Appiah: The Autobiography of an African Patriot*. New York: Praeger, 1990.

Appiah, Joseph. *The Man J. B. Danquah*. Accra: Academy of Arts and Sciences, 1974.

Apter, David. *Ghana in Transition*. Princeton: Princeton University Press, 1972.

Arhin, Kwame, ed. *A Profile of Brong Kyempim*. Accra: Afram, 1979.

Armah, Kwesi. *Ghana: Nkrumah's Legacy.* London: Collings, 1974.

Austin, Dennis. *Ghana Observed: Essays on the Politics of a West African Republic*. Manchester: Manchester University Press, 1976.

Austin, Dennis. *Politics in Ghana, 1946–1960*. London: Oxford University Press, 1964.

Austin, Dennis, and Luckman, R., eds. *Politicians and Soldiers in Ghana, 1966–1972*. London: Cass, 1975.

Barker, Peter. *Operation Cold Chop: The Coup that Toppled Nkrumah*. Accra: Ghana Publishing Corp., 1969.

Barth, Fredrik, ed. *Ethnic Groups and Boundaries: The Social Organization of Culture Difference*. Boston: Little, Brown, 1969.

Beckman, Björn. *Organizing the Farmers*. Uppsala: Scandinavian Institute of African Studies, 1976.

Bhabha, Homi, ed. *Nation and Narration*. London: Routledge, 1990.

Bing, Geoffrey. *Reap the Whirlwind: An Account of Kwame Nkrumah's Ghana from 1950–1966*. London: McGibbon and Kee, 1968.

Birmingham, Walter; Neustadt, I.; and Omaboe, E. N., eds. *A Study of Contemporary Ghana*. Vol. 1. *The Economy of Ghana*. London: Allen and Unwin, 1966. Vol. 2. *Some Aspects of Social Structure*. London: Allen and Unwin, 1967.

Blit, Lucjan. *The Origins of Polish Socialism*. Cambridge: Cambridge University Press, 1971.

Boahen, A. Adu. *Ghana: Evolution and Change in the Nineteenth and Twentieth Centuries*. London: Longman, 1975.

Bourret, Florence M. *Ghana: The Road to Independence, 1919–1957*. London: Oxford University Press, 1960.

Bretton, Henry L. *The Rise and Fall of Kwame Nkrumah*. New York: Pall Mall Press, 1966.

Breuilly, John. *Nationalism and the State*. Manchester: Manchester University Press, 1982.

Busia, Kofi A. *Africa In Search of Democracy*. London: Routledge and Kegan Paul, 1967.

Busia, Kofi A. *The Position of the Chief in the Modern Political System of Ashanti*. London: Oxford University Press, 1951.

Cabral, Amilcar. *Revolution in Guinea*. London: Stage 1, 1969.

Cabral, Amilcar. *Unity and Struggle: Speeches and Writings of Amilcar Cabral*. Introduced by Basil Davidson. London: Heinemann Educational Books, 1979.

Chatterjee, Partha. *Nationalist Thought and the Colonial World: A Derivative Discourse?* London: Zed Press, 1986.

Chazan, Naomi. *Anatomy of Ghanaian Politics: Managing Political Recession, 1969–1982*. Boulder, Colo: Westview, 1982.

Christaller, J. G. *Dictionary of the Asante and Fante Language*, 2d ed. Basel: Basel Evangelical Missionary Society, 1933.

Coleman, James S., and Rosberg, C. G., eds. *Political Parties and National Integration in Tropical Africa*. Berkeley: University of California Press, 1966.

Crowder, Michael. *Pagans and Politicians*. London: Hutchinson, 1959.

Davidson, Basil. *Black Star*. London: Allen Lane, 1973.

Davies, Ian. *African Trade Unions*. Harmondsworth: Penguin, 1966.

Davis, Horace. *Toward a Marxist Theory of Nationalism*. London: Monthly Review Press, 1978.

Dunn, John, and Robertson A. F. *Dependence and Opportunity: Political Change in Ahafo*. Cambridge: Cambridge University Press, 1973.

First, Ruth. *Barrel of a Gun: Political Power in Africa and the Coup d'Etat*. Harmondsworth: Penguin, 1972.

Fitch, Bob, and Oppenheimer, M. *Ghana: End of an Illusion*. New York: Monthly Review Press, 1968.

Geertz, Clifford. *Old Societies and New States: The Quest for Modernity in Asia and Africa*. New York: Collier-Macmillan, 1963.

Gellner, Ernest. *Nations and Nationalism*. Oxford: Blackwell, 1983.

Genoud, Roger. *Nationalism and Economic Development in Ghana*. New York: Praeger, 1969.

Gifford, Prosser, and Louis, W. R., eds. *The Transfer of Power in Africa*. New Haven: Yale University Press, 1982.

Gray, Paul S. *Unions and Leaders in Ghana: A Study of the Institutionalization of Ghanaian Labour*. Owerri: Conch Magazine Ltd., 1981.

Hailey, Malcolm. *Native Administration in the British African Territories, Part III*. London: HMSO, 1951.

Hansard Society. *What Are the Problems of Parliamentary Government in West Africa?* London: Hansard Society, 1958.

Hill, Polly. *Migrant Cocoa Farmers of Southern Ghana*. Cambridge: Cambridge University Press, 1963.

Hill, Polly. *Studies in Rural Capitalism in West Africa*. Cambridge: Cambridge University Press, 1970.

Hobsbawm, Eric. *Nations and Nationalism Since 1780: Programme, Myth, Reality*. Cambridge: Cambridge University Press, 1990.

Hobsbawm, Eric, and Ranger, T., eds. *The Invention of Tradition*. Cambridge: Cambridge University Press, 1983.

Hodgkin, Thomas. *African Political Parties*. Harmondsworth: Penguin, 1961.

Hodgkin, Thomas. *Nationalism in Colonial Africa*. London: Muller, 1956.

Horowitz, Donald. *Ethnic Groups in Conflict*. Berkeley: University of California Press, 1985.

Howard, Rhoda. *Colonialism and Underdevelopment in Ghana*. London: Croom Helm, 1978.

Ismagilova, R. N. *Ethnic Problems of Tropical Africa: Can They be Solved?*. Moscow: Progress Publishers, 1978.

James, C. L. R. *Nkrumah and the Ghana Revolution*. London: Allison and Busby, 1977.

Jeffries, Richard. *Class, Power and Ideology in Ghana: The Railwaymen of Sekondi*. Cambridge: Cambridge University Press, 1978.

Kay, Geoffrey B. *The Political Economy of Colonialism in Ghana*. Cambridge: Cambridge University Press, 1972.

Kesse-Adu, Kwame. *The Politics of Political Detention*. Accra-Tema: Ghana Publishing Corp., 1971.

Kimble, David. *A Political History of Ghana: The Rise of Gold Coast Nationalism, 1850–1928*. Oxford: Clarendon Press, 1963.

Kyerematen, A. A. Y. *Daasebre Osei Tutu Agyeman Prempeh II Asantehene: A Distinguished Traditional Ruler of Contemporary Ghana*. Kumase: University Press, 1970.

Ladouceur, Paul A. *Chiefs and Politicians: The Politics of Regionalism in Northern Ghana*. London: Longman, 1979.

LaPalombara, Joseph, and Weiner, M., eds. *Political Parties and Political Development*. Princeton: Princeton University Press, 1966.

LeVine, Victor. *Political Corruption: The Ghana Case*. Stanford: Hoover Institution Press, 1975.

Lewin, Thomas. *Asante Before the British*. Lawrence, Kansas: Regents Press of Kansas, 1978.

Marable, Manning. *African and Caribbean Politics: From Kwame Nkrumah to Maurice Bishop*. London: Verso, 1987.

Markovitz, Irving L., ed. *Studies in Power and Class in Africa*. New York: Oxford University Press, 1987.

Marx, K., and Engels, F. *Selected Works*. New York: International, 1977.

Milne, June, ed. *Kwame Nkrumah: The Conakry Years*. London: Panaf, 1990.

Nkrumah, Kwame. *Africa Must Unite*. New York: International, 1970.

Nkrumah, Kwame. *Ghana: The Autobiography of Kwame Nkrumah*. London: Nelson, 1957.

Nkrumah, Kwame. *Osagyefo in Kumasi: Four Speeches by Kwame Nkrumah*. Accra: Ghana Publishing Corp., 1962.

Ofosu-Appiah, L. H. *Encyclopedia Africana Dictionary of African Biography*, Vol. 1. New York: Reference Publications, 1977.

Osei-Kwame, Peter. *A New Conceptual Model for the Study of Political Integration in Africa*. Washington, D.C.: University Press of America. 1980.

Owusu, Maxwell. *Uses and Abuses of Power: A Case Study of Continuity and Change in the Politics of Ghana*. Chicago: University of Chicago Press, 1970.

Padmore, George. *The Gold Coast Revolution*. London: Dennis Dobson, 1953.

Powell, Erica. *Private Secretary (Female) Gold Coast, 1952–1966*. London: C. Hurst, 1984.

Rattray, Robert S. *Ashanti Law and Constitution*. Oxford: Clarendon Press, 1929.

Rooney, David. *Kwame Nkrumah: The Political Kingdom of the Third World*. London: Tauris, 1988.

Rooney, David. *Sir Charles Arden-Clarke*. London: Collings, 1982.

Schildkrout, Enid, ed. *The Golden Stool: Studies of the Asante Center and Periphery. Anthropological Papers of the American Museum of Natural History* 65:1. New York, 1987.

Schildkrout, Enid. *People of the Zongo*. Cambridge: Cambridge University Press, 1978.

Smith, Anthony D. *The Ethnic Origins of Nations*. Oxford: Blackwell, 1986.

Smith, Anthony D. *National Identity*. London: Penguin, 1991.

Smith, Anthony D. *State and Nation in the Third World: The Western State and African Nationalism*. New York: St. Martin's Press, 1983.

Smith, Anthony D. *Theories of Nationalism*. London: Duckworth, 1971.

Smock, David R., and Bensti-Enchill, K. *The Search for National Integration*. New York: Free Press, 1976.

Smock, David R., and Smock, A. C. *The Politics of Pluralism: A Comparative Study of Lebanon and Ghana*. New York: Elsevier, 1975.

Tordoff, William. *Ashanti Under the Prempehs, 1888–1935*. London: Oxford University Press, 1965.

Vail, Leroy. *The Creation of Tribalism in Southern Africa*. London: James Currey, 1989.

Wilks, Ivor. *Asante in the Nineteenth Century: The Structure and Evolution of a Political Order*. Cambridge: Cambridge University Press, 1975.

Wright, Richard. *Black Power*. New York: Harper and Brothers, 1954.

Wudu, F. *The Man Pobee Biney: A Fallen Labour Hero of Ghana*. Accra: Ghana Publishing Corp., 1968.

Yarak, Larry. *Asante and the Dutch, 1744–1873*. Oxford: Clarendon Press, 1990.

Zolberg, Aristide. *Creating Political Order: The Party-States of West Africa*. Chicago: University of Chicago Press, 1966.

Articles

Allman, Jean M. "The Youngmen and the Porcupine: Class, Nationalism and Asante's Struggle for Self-Determination, 1954–1957." *Journal of African History* 31:2 (1990), 263–79.

Allman, Jean M. "Discussion (with Richard Rathbone): 'The Youngmen and the Porcupine.' " *Journal of African History* 32:2 (1991), 333–38.

Allman, Jean M. " 'Hewers of Wood, Carriers of Water': Islam, Class and Politics on the Eve of Ghana's Independence." *African Studies Review* 34:2 (1991) 1–26.

Andoh, A. S. Y. "The Asante National Liberation Movement of the 1950s in Retrospect." In E. Schildkrout, ed., *The Golden Stool,* 173–83.

Anonymous. "Asantehene in Eclipse." *Economist* 188 (1958), 922.

Appiah, Kwame A. "Altered States." *The Wilson Quarterly* 15:1 (1991), 20–32.

Apter, David. "Ghana." In J. S. Coleman and C. G. Rosberg, eds., *Political Parties and National Integration in Tropical Africa.* Berkeley: University of California Press, 1966, 259–315.

Apter, David. "The Role of Traditionalism in the Political Modernization of Ghana and Uganda." *World Politics* 13 (1960), 45–68.

Apter, David. "Some Reflections on the Role of a Political Opposition in New Nations." *Comparative Studies in Society and History* 4 (1962), 154–68.

Arhin, Kwame. "A Note on an Aspect of Indirect Rule in Ashanti: The Appam." *Universitas* 2:2 (1972), 107–114.

Arhin, Kwame. "Peasants in Nineteenth-Century Asante." *Current Anthropology* 24:4 (1983), 471–80.

Arhin, Kwame. "Rank and Class Among the Asante and Fante in the Nineteenth Century." *Africa* 53:1 (1983), 2–22.

Asante, S. K. B. "Bankole Awooner-Renner." In L. H. Ofosu-Appiah, *Encyclopedia Africana Dictionary of African Biography,* Vol. 1. New York: Reference Publications, 1977, 208–9.

Asante, S. K. B. "Law and Society in Ghana." In T. Hutchinson, et al., eds., *Africa and Law: Developing Legal Systems in African and Commonwealth Nations.* Madison: University of Wisconsin Press, 1968, 121–32.

Austin, Dennis. "The British Point of No Return." In P. Gifford, and W. R. Louis, eds., *The Transfer of Power in Africa.* New Haven: Yale University Press, 1982, 225–48.

Austin, Dennis. "Opposition in Ghana: 1947–1967." *Government and Opposition* 2:4 (1967), 539–55.

Austin, Gareth. "The Emergence of Capitalist Relations in South Asante Cocoa-Farming, c. 1916–33." *Journal of African History* 28:2 (1987), 259–79.

Bascom, William. "Tribalism, Nationalism and Pan Africanism." *Annals of the American Academy of Political and Social Science* 343 (1962), 21–9.

Beckman, Björn. "Government Policy and the Distribution of Cocoa Income in Ghana, 1951–60: A Synopsis." *Proceedings of the Cocoa Economics Research Conference,* Legon, 1973.

Bening, R. B., "Internal Colonial Boundary Problems of the Gold Coast, 1907–1951." *International Journal of African Historical Studies* 17:1 (1984), 81–99.

Benneh, George. "The Impact of Cocoa Cultivation on the Traditional Land Tenure System of the Akan of Ghana." *Ghana Journal of Sociology* 6:1 (1970), 43–61.

Bennett, G. "The Gold Coast General Election." *Parliamentary Affairs* 8:2 (1954), 430–9.

Bernstein, Henry. "Modernization Theory and the Sociological Study of Development." *Journal of Development Studies* 7:2 (1971), 141–60.

Blaut, James M. "Nationalism as an Autonomous Force." *Science and Society* 46:1 (1982), 1–23.

Boahen, A. Adu. "A Nation in Exile: The Asante on the Seychelles Islands, 1900–1924." In E. Schildkrout, ed., *The Golden Stool,* 146–60.

Boaten, K. "Asante and Colonial Rule, 1902–1935." *Universitas* 3:1 (1973), 57–63.

Bretton, Henry. "Current Political Thought and Practice in Ghana." *American Political Science Review* 52:1 (1958), 46–64.

Busia, Kofi A. "The Present Situation and Aspiration of Elites in the Gold Coast." *International Social Science Bulletin* 98:3 (1956), 424–30.

Busia, Kofi A. "The Prospects for Parliamentary Democracy in the Gold Coast." *Parliamentary Affairs* 5:2 (1952), 538–44.

Chazan, Naomi, "Ghana: Problems of Governance and the Emergence of Civil Society." In L. Diamond, J. J. Linz, and S. M. Lipset, eds., *Democracy in Developing Countries: Africa.* Boulder, Colo.: Westview Press, 1988.

Cohen, Robin. "Class in Africa." *Socialist Register* (1972), 321–55.

Crook, Richard. "Colonial Rule and Political Culture in Modern Ashanti." *Journal of Commonwealth Political Studies* 11:1 (1973), 2–27.

Crook, Richard. "Decolonization, the Colonial State, and Chieftaincy in the Gold Coast." *African Affairs* 85:338 (1987), 7–24.

Crowder, Michael. "Whose Dream Was It Anyway?: Twenty-Five Years of African Independence." *African Affairs* 86:342 (1987), 7–24.

Davidson, Basil. "On Revolutionary Nationalism: The Legacy of Cabral." *Race and Class* 27:3 (1986), 21–45.

Diamond, Larry. "Ethnicity and Ethnic Conflict," *Journal of Modern African Studies* 25:1 (1987), 117–128.

Drah, F. K. "The Brong Political Movement." In K. Arhin, ed., *A Profile of Brong Kyempim.* Accra, 1979, 119–68.

Fortes, Meyer. "The Ashanti Social Survey: A Preliminary Report." *Rhodes-Livingstone Journal* 6 (1948), 1–36.

Geertz, Clifford. "The Integrative Revolution: Primordial Sentiments and Civil Politics in the New States." In Geertz, ed., *Old Societies and New States: The Quest for Modernity in Africa and Asia.* New York: Collier-Macmillan, 1963, 109–30.

Hargreaves, John D. "Toward the Transfer of Power in British West Africa." In P. Gifford, and W. R. Louis, eds., *The Transfer of Power in Africa.* New Haven: Yale University Press, 1932, 117–40.

Ibingira, Grace. "The Impact of Ethnic Demands on British Decolonization in Africa: The Example of Uganda." In Gifford and Louis, eds., *The Transfer of Power,* 283–304.

Isaacman, Allen. "Peasants and Rural Social Protest." *African Studies Review* 33:2 (1990), 1–120.

Jackson, R. H., and Rosberg, C. G. "Popular Legitimacy and African Multi-Ethnic States." *Journal of Modern African Studies* 22:2 (1984), 177–98.

Jahoda, Gustav "Nationality Preferences and National Stereotypes in Ghana Before Independence." *Journal of Social Psychology* (1959), 165–74.

Jones-Quartey, K. A. B. "Press and Nationalism in Ghana." *United Asia* 9 (1957), 55–60.

Kennedy, Paul. "Indigenous Capitalism in Ghana." *Review of African Political Economy* 8 (1977), 21–38.

Killick, Tony. "The Economics of Cocoa." In W. Birmingham, I. Neustadt and E. N. Amaboe, eds., *A Study of Contemporary Ghana: The Economy of Ghana*. Vol. 1. London: Allen and Unwin, 1966, 365–90.

Killingray, David. "The Maintenance of Law and Order in British Colonial Africa." *African Affairs* 85:340 (1986), 411–439.

Killingray, David. "Repercussions of World War I in the Gold Coast. *Journal of African History* 19:1 (1978), 39–59.

Kilson, Martin. "Nationalism and Social Classes in British West Africa," *Journal of Politics* 4:1 (1957), 368–87.

Kirk-Greene, A. H. M. "A Historiographical Perspective on the Transfer of Power in British Colonial Africa: A Bibliographical Essay." In Gifford and Louis, eds., *The Transfer of Power*, 567–602.

Leys, Colin. "The 'Overdeveloped' Post-Colonial State: A Reevaluation." *Review of African Political Economy* 6 (1976), 39–48.

Lonsdale, John, "African Pasts in Africa's Future." *Canadian Journal of African Studies* 23:1 (1989), 126–46.

Lonsdale, John, "The Emergence of African Nations: A Historiographical Analysis." *African Affairs* 67:266 (1968), 11–28.

Lonsdale, John, "States and Social Processes in Africa: A Historiographical Survey." *African Studies Review* 24:2/3 (1981), 139–225.

Mafeje, Archie. "The Ideology of Tribalism." *Journal of Modern African Studies* 9:2 (1971), 253–62.

Magubane, Bernard. "Toward a Sociology of National Liberation from Colonialism: Cabral's Legacy." *Contemporary Marxism* 7 (1983), 5–27.

Manu, Yaw. "Conflict and Consensus in Ghanaian Politics: The Case of the 1950s." *Conch* [New Paltz, New York] 7:1/2 (1975), 93–112.,

McCaskie, Thomas C. "Accumulation, Wealth and Belief in Asante History. I: To the Close of the Nineteenth Century." *Africa* 53:1 (1983), 23–43.

McCaskie, Thomas C. "Accumulation, Wealth and Belief in Asante History. II: The Twentieth Century." *Africa* 56:1 (1986), 3–22.

McCaskie, Thomas C. "*Ahyiamu*—'A Place of Meeting': An Essay on Process and Event in the History of the Asante State." *Journal of African History* 25.2 (1984), 169–89.

McCaskie, Thomas C. "Asantesem: Reflections on Discourse and Text in Africa." In K. Barber and P. F. de Moroes Farias, eds., *Discourse and Its Disguises: The Interpretation of African Oral Texts*. Birmingham: Centre for West African Studies, 1989, 70–86.

McCaskie, Thomas C. "Komfo Anokye of Asante: Meaning, History and Philosophy in an African Society." *Journal of African History* 27: 2/3 (1986), 315–39.

Mohan, Jitendra. "Nkrumah and Nkrumahism." *The Socialist Register* (1967), 191–228.

Murray, Roger. "The Ghanaian Road." *New Left Review* 32 (1963), 63–71.

Murray, Roger. "Second Thoughts on Ghana." *New Left Review* 42 (1967), 25–39.

Owusu, Maxwell. "Kingship in Contemporary Asante Society." In E. Schildkrout, ed., *The Golden Stool*, 161–72.

Price, J. H. "Analysis of Legislators' Backgrounds." *West Africa* 2041 (21 May 1956), 324–5.

Price, J. H. "The Future of Democracy in Ghana." *Universitas* 4:5 (1961), 136–8.

Price, J. H. "The Muslim Vote in the Accra Constituencies, 1954." *Proceedings* of the 4th Annual Conference of the West African Institute of Social and Economic Research. Legon, 1956, 160–7.

Price, J. H. "The Role of Islam in Gold Coast Politics." *Proceedings* of the 3rd Annual Conference of the West African Institute of Social and Economic Research. Legon, 1954, 104–11.

Rathbone, Richard. "Businessmen in Politics: Party Struggle in Ghana, 1949–1957." *Journal of Development Studies* 9:3 (1973), 390–401.

Rathbone, Richard. "The Government of the Gold Coast After the Second World War." *African Affairs* 67:268 (1968), 209–18.

Rathbone, Richard. "Opposition in Ghana: The National Liberation Movement." In *Political Opposition in the New African States*. University of London, Institute of Commonwealth Studies Collected Seminar Papers Series, no. 4, 29–53.

Rathbone, Richard. "Politics and Factionalism in Ghana." *Current History* 60:355 (1971), 164–7.

Rhodie, S. "The Gold Coast Cocoa Hold-Up of 1930–1931." *Transactions of the Historical Society of Ghana* 9 (1968), 105–18.

Robertson, A. F. "Ousting the Chief: Deposition in Ashanti." *Man* 11:3 (1976), 410–27.

Saul, John. "The State in Post-Colonial Society: Tanzania." *Socialist Register* (1974), 349–68.

Schildkrout, Enid, "Islam and Politics in Kumasi." *Anthropological Papers of the American Museum of National History* 52:2 (1974), 113–37.

Schildkrout, Enid. "Strangers and Local Government in Kumasi." *Journal of Modern African Studies* 8:2 (1970), 251–69.

Sklar, Richard. "Political Science and National Integration." *Journal of Modern African Studies* 5:1 (1967), 1–11.

Smithers, Peter. "Westminster at the Gold Coast Elections." *Corona* 8:12 (1956), 457–9.

Triulzi, Alessandro. "The Asantehene-in-Council: Ashanti Politics Under Colonial Rule, 1935–1950." *Africa* 42:2 (1972), 98–111.

Uphoff, N. "An Element of Repetition in Ghanaian Elections: 1956 and 1969." *Legon Observer* 5:1 (1970), 19.

Wallerstein, Immanuel. "Ethnicity and National Integration in West Africa." *Cahiers d'Etudes Africaines* 3 (1960), 129–59.

Wasserstein, B. "Whose History Is It, Anyway?" *Times Literary Supplement*, 25 July 1986, 814.

Weiner, Myron. "Political Integration and Political Development." *Annals of the American Academy of Political and Social Science* 358 (1965), 52–64.

Wilks, Ivor. "Dissidence in Asante Politics: Two Tracts from the Late Nineteenth Century." In Ibrahim Abu-Lughod, ed., *African Themes: Northwestern University Studies in Honor of Gwendolyn Carter*. Evanston: Northwestern University Press, 1975, 47–63.

Wilks, Ivor. "The Golden Stool and the Elephant Tail: An Essay on Wealth in

Asante." In George Dalton, ed., *Research in Economic Anthropology* Vol. 2. Greenwich, Conn.: JAI Press, 1979, 1–36.

Wilks, Ivor. "What Manner of Persons Were These? Some Reflections on Asante Officialdom." In E. Schildkrout, ed. *The Golden Stool*, 109–30.

Wilks, Ivor. and McCaskie, Thomas, eds. *Asantesem*. Bulletin of the Asante Collective Biography Project 1–11 (1975–9).

Young, M. Crawford. "Nationalism, Ethnicity and Class in Africa: A Retrospective." *Cahiers d'Etudes Africaines* 103:26:3 (1986), 421–95.

Zolberg, Aristide. "Patterns of National Integration." *Journal of Modern African Studies* 5:4 (1967), 449–68.

Zolberg, Aristide. "The Structure of Political Conflict in the New States of Tropical Africa." *American Political Science Review* 62:1 (1968), 70–87.

Unpublished Manuscripts, Theses, and Dissertations

Arhin, Kwame. "Chieftancy Under Kwame Nkrumah." Paper delivered at the Symposium on the Life and Work of Kwame Nkrumah, Institute of African Studies, University of Ghana, Legon, 27 May–1 June 1985.

Austin, Dennis, and Rathbone, R. "Trade Unions and Politics: Ghana." Seminar Paper, Institute of Commonwealth Studies, University of London, 1966.

Austin, Gareth. "Rural Capitalism and the Growth of Cocoa Farming in South Ashanti, to 1914." Ph.D. thesis, University of Birmingham, 1984.

Crisp, Jeffrey F. "Labour Protest and Labour Control in the Ghanaian Goldmining Industry, 1890–1978." Ph.D. thesis, University of Birmingham, 1980.

Crook, Richard. "The Decolonization Period in Ghana: Political and Economic Factors Underlying NLM Opposition to the CPP, 1950–1957." Seminar Paper, Centre for West African Studies, University of Birmingham, 1972.

Crook, Richard. "Ghanaian Political Structures and Leadership Patterns: The Careers of Nana Wiafe Akenten II and E. K. Duncan Williams of Offinso, 1946–1972." Seminar Paper, Institute of Commonwealth Studies, University of London, 1972–3.

Crook, Richard. "Local Elites and National Politics in Ghana: A Case Study of Political Centralization and Local Politics in Offinso (Ashanti), 1945–1966." Ph.D. thesis, University of London, 1978.

Effah-Appenteng, Victor. "Gold Coast Politics: The Federalist Agitation." Master's thesis, Institute of African Studies, University of Ghana, 1970.

Fitch, Bob. "Opposition Movements in Ghana, 1954–1958." Master's thesis, University of California—Berkeley, 1966.

Grier, Beverly C. "Cocoa, Class Formation and the State in Ghana." Ph.D. thesis, Yale University, 1979.

Howell, David. "The Opposition and Ghanaian Politics." Senior thesis, Kalamazoo College, 1972.

Jeffries, Richard. "Trade Unions and Politics in Ghana." Ph.D. thesis, University of London, 1974.

Kirk-Greene, A. H. M. "Interview with A. J. Loveridge and W. T. Beeton." Oxford, Rhodes House, 18 December 1968 (typescript).

Kraus, Jon. "Cleavages, Crises, Parties and State Power in Ghana." Ph.D. thesis, Johns Hopkins University, 1970.

McLaren, C. A. "Report on the Kumase Municipal Council." Kumase, 1957 (typescript).

Morrison, K. C. "Ethnicity and Political Integration: Ashanti, Ghana." Ph.D. thesis, University of Wisconsin—Madison, 1977.

Ninsin, Kwame, "The Nkrumah Government and the Opposition on the Nation State: Unity Versus Fragmentation." Paper presented at the Symposium on the Life and Work of Kwame Nkrumah, Institute of African Studies, University of Ghana, Legon, 27 May–1 June, 1985.

Price, J. H. *The Gold Coast*. "Chapter 3." Unpublished manuscript, 1956.

Rathbone, Richard. "Some Links Between the CPP and the NLM." Seminar Paper, Institute of Commonwealth Studies, University of London, 1971.

Rathbone, Richard. "The Transfer of Power in Ghana, 1954–1957." Ph.D. thesis, University of London, 1968.

Sclafani, J. A. "Trade Unionism in an African State: The Railway and Ports Workers' Union of the TUC (Ghana)." Ph.D. thesis, Brown University, 1977.

Silver, James B. "Class Structure and Class Consciousness: An Historical Analysis of Mineworkers in Ghana." Ph.D. thesis, University of Sussex, 1981.

Triulzi, Alessandro. "The Ashanti Confederacy Council, 1935–1957." Unpublished field interviews, Institute of African Studies, University of Ghana, Legon, 1969.

Van Hear, N. "Northern Labour and the Development of Capitalist Agriculture in Ghana." Ph.D. Thesis, University of Birmingham, 1982.

Walker, H. K. "The Constitution Debate Between Opposition and Government in the Gold Coast on the Eve of Independence." Ph.D. thesis, Boston University, 1968.

Field Materials

The author's field notes are on deposit in the Melville J. Herskovits Memorial Library at Northwestern University Library. Because of the politically sensitive nature of some of the issues raised, the transcripts of the interviews are under restricted access until 2004. They can be consulted with the author's permission.

Schedule of Interviews

Date	Name	Number
21 June 1984	Cobbina Kessie	FN/1/1
21 June 1984	I. K. Agyeman	FN/2/1
26 June 1984	Alex Osei	FN/3/1
27 June 1984	Bafuor Akoto/ Antwi Buasiako	FN/4/1
28 June 1984	I. K. Agyeman	FN/2/2
2 July 1984	Alex Osei	FN/3/2
2 July 1984	Akosua Nyameba	FN/5/1
3 July 1984	Sam Boateng	FN/6/1
6 July 1984	Cobbina Kessie	FN/1/2
10 July 1984	B. D. Addai	FN/7/1
19 July 1984	Antwi Buasiako	FN/8/1

20 July 1984	K. A. M. Gyimah	FN/9/1
21 July 1984	Alhaji Abdullai Mamprussi	FN/10/1
23 July 1984	Joe Appiah	FN/11/1
23 July 1984	B. K. Owusu	FN/12/1
24 July 1984	Sam Boateng	FN/6/2
25 July 1984	A. S. Y. Andoh	FN/13/1
26 July 1984	B. F. Kusi	FN/14/1
27 July 1984	Osei Assibey-Mensah	FN/15/1
28 July 1984	N. B. Abubekr	FN/16/1
30 July 1984	Sewaa Benkuo	FN/17/1
1 August 1984	Isaac B. Asafu-Adjaye	FN/18/1
3 August 1984	Alhaji Abdullai Mamprussi	FN/10/2
3 August 1984	Alfa O. Lardan	FN/19/1
4 August 1984	Maame Yaa Baa	FN/20/1
6 August 1984	Amma Paa	FN/21/1
25 September 1984	Alfa O. Lardan	FN/19/2
27 September 1984	Alhaji Moru (Omorufillo)	FN/22/1
9 October 1984	Cobbina Kessie	FN/1/3
10 October 1984	Alhaji Ibrahima Futa	FN/23/1
10 October 1984	N. B. Abubekr	FN/16/2
15 October 1984	N. B. Abubekr	FN/16/3
15 October 1984	Kusi Ampofu	FN/24/1
16 October 1984	Kwame Kyem Panin	FN/25/1
18 October 1984	Kusi Ampofu	FN/24/2
19 October 1984	Abdul Rahim Alawa	FN/26/1

Political Leaflets and Handbills

Copies of the following were given to the author by Osei Assibey-Mensah.

"Arise! Arise!! Arise!!!" Osei Assibey-Mensah. Kumase, 1954.

"Awake All Yea Sons and Daughters of the Great Ashanti Nation . . . " Osei Assibey-Mensah. Kumase, 1954.

"AYA Calling!" Osei Assibey-Mensah. Kumase, 1954.

"Atwima-Nwabiagya Constituency of NLM Calling!" J. E. Antwi. Kumase, 1956.

"Baffuor Osei Akoto Will Officially Introduce Dr. E. K. K. Kurankyi-Taylor . . . " Jeffrey Osei Tutu. Kumase, 1956.

"Baffuor Ossei Akoto Will Officially Introduce Mr. J. B. Siriboe, B. L. . . . " Kumase, 1956.

"Cocoa Price Agitation and the Position of Ashanti in Our Struggle for Self-Government." E. Y Baffoe. Kumase, 1954.

"Down with Unitary Government. On With Federation!" Kusi Ampofu. Kumase, 1954.

"Flash! All Ashanti Youth Organization (Mother of NLM) Calling a Historic General Meeting . . . " Osei Assibey-Mensah and Frank Tawiah. Kumase, 1955.

"Flash! The General Elections Are at Your Doors . . . " Osei Assibey-Mensah. Kumase, 1956.

"Flash! Kumasi Ratepayers Association Meeting . . . " Osei Assibey-Mensah. Kumase, 1957.

"Invitation In the Name of the Great Ashanti Nation of King Osei Tutu and Okomfo Anokye . . . " J. K. Prempeh. Kumase, no date.

"Kumasi Is Burning . . . " Osei Assibey-Mensah. Kumase, 1956.

"Kumase South Constituency Calling at Gyinyase." F. O. Agyeman and A. K. Edusei. Kumase, 1956.

"The National Liberation Movement and Allies' Victory." Osei Assibey-Mensah. Kumase, 1956.

"People of Kumasi South! Vote for K. K. Vote for Cocoa! Vote for NLM . . . " Kumase, 1956.

"Royal Commission." Thomas A. Codjoe. Kumase, no date.

"Royal Commission." Osei Assibey-Mensah. Kumase, 1954.

"Save Your Nation All Ye Sons and Daughters . . . " Osei Assibey-Mensah. Kumase, 1954.

"Save Your Nation. Oman Asante Kotoko." Osei Assibey-Mensah. Kumase, 1954.

"Vote for NLM and Its Allies." Osei Assibey-Mensah. Kumase, 1956.

"What Is Unitary Government and What Are Its Vices and Virtues?" Osei Assibey-Mensah. Kumase, 1955.

Index